GLOBAL RISK

BUSINESS SUCCESS IN TURBULENT TIMES

Seán Cleary and Thierry Malleret

palgrave
macmillan

First published 2007 by
PALGRAVE MACMILLAN
Houndmills, Basingstoke, Hampshire RG21 6XS and
175 Fifth Avenue, New York, N.Y. 10010
Companies and representatives throughout the world

PALGRAVE MACMILLAN is the global academic imprint of the Palgrave
Macmillan division of St. Martin's Press, LLC and of Palgrave Macmillan Ltd.
Macmillan® is a registered trademark in the United States, United Kingdom
and other countries. Palgrave is a registered trademark in the European
Union and other countries.

ISBN-13: 978–0–230–52531–3
ISBN-10: 0–230–52531–8

This book is printed on paper suitable for recycling and made from fully
managed and sustained forest sources. Logging, pulping and manufacturing
processes are expected to conform to the environmental regulations of the
country of origin.

A catalogue record for this book is available from the British Library.

A catalog record for this book is available from the Library of Congress.

10   9   8   7   6   5   4   3   2   1
16   15   14   13   12   11   10   09   08   07

Printed and bound in Great Britain by
Creative Print & Design (Wales), Ebbw Vale

Contents

List of figures

List of tables

Foreword

Global Risk – Business Success in Turbulent Times grew out of collaboration between two colleagues of mine: Seán Cleary, who is one of my strategic advisers; and Thierry Malleret, who was with the World Economic Forum for several years and left his position as Senior Director responsible for the Global Risk Network in March 2007. This book reflects their long-standing interest in the theory and practice of risk analysis and mitigation.

Risk, and the opportunities associated with it, is omnipresent in today's globalized world. Increasing complexity, the magnifying effect of information flows and media attention, the links connecting apparently different risks in surprising ways and the proliferation of unintended consequences – all make risk pervasive and ubiquitous. In my exchanges with global CEOs, public policymakers and those who lead nongovernmental organizations, I have become convinced that understanding risk – and how best to manage and mitigate it – lies at the heart of the challenges we face in business, government and civil society. We shall be taking this insight further in the Forum, placing our Global Risk Network at the heart of out activities.

In such an environment, a book on risk that is both accessible and erudite seems overdue. Many publications already address the topic of risk: it is enormously broad, rich in intellectual history, literature and debate. *Global Risk* brings something innovative: it succeeds in shedding an encompassing light on the many different facets of risk and the challenges we face in understanding these, while displaying sharp insight into the context within which these risks will manifest themselves in the future. The future cannot be predicted, but surely we can – and must – think about the forces that will shape it.

Seán and Thierry's book exemplifies what we strive for at the Forum in pursuit of our mission of *improving the state of the world*: intellectual rigor in understanding the issues and connecting the dots, bringing foresight to bear to identify the challenges beyond the immediate horizon, and emphasizing that today's problems cannot be solved in isolation. My long-held view, since founding the World Economic Forum in 1971, has been that only sustained and well-focused dialog between all the different global stakeholders will enable us to address the challenges we face. Strategic insight into all key elements of our global reality is necessary to focus these discussions and improve the chances that they will bring solutions.

Global Risk makes this plain and does so with gusto. I recommend it not only to all those who deal with risk in their daily activities, but also to those keen to understand how the world of tomorrow is taking shape.

Klaus Schwab
Founder and Executive Chairman, World Economic Forum

Acknowledgments

This book had its origins in an earlier text entitled *Resilience to Risk* which we wrote for the South African market, over the European summer in 2005, and which saw a French edition by Maxima and a Russian one by Voprosy Ekonomiki follow the original by Human & Rousseau. Palgrave Macmillan was kind enough to suggest that we might focus on the challenges posed by global risks in an international edition. We hope that we have succeeded in putting some important contemporary events into a useful historical, geographical and functional context. Thierry's experience in heading the Global Risk Network at the World Economic Forum from 2004 to 2007 and Seán's association with the program as its 'mentor' have added particular insights.

This book is written for the proverbial 'man (or woman) in the street,' the business person who has to deal with risk in a business context, the government minister or official who grapples with the challenges of a turbulent environment in making or implementing policy, the teacher or lecturer in disciplines from international relations to business administration who has to put events and human reactions into context, to help students make sense of them. Although we refer frequently to examples from the world of business – and hope that this book will have special value for business people – we do not believe that risks can be neatly divided into different classes that affect firms, governments, consumers and citizens separately. *Global Risk – Business Success in Turbulent Times* is the story of the world we live in and the way we grapple with the challenges and the chances that events throw our way.

It is easy to be critical of the way others have dealt with some of the challenges they have faced, and we have not pulled punches in this regard. To learn from experience, one has to admit what went wrong. But there is no room for *schadenfreude* at the mistakes of others; the ancient Greeks knew that *nemesis* follows *hubris* and the folkloric insight '*There but for the grace of God go I*'[1] underscores our universal vulnerability. Chapter 1 and especially chapter 2 explain why.

Our gratitude is due to Palgrave Macmillan for suggesting the project, to Stephen Rutt, Alexandra Dawe and the staff of Macmillan India Ltd., for so ably shepherding us and the book to completion and for their insightful editing, and to the World Economic Forum for providing the canvas against which several shadowy forms took more meaningful shape. Seán owes a debt to his colleagues in the Parmenides Foundation for deepening his insight into the relationship between the workings of the brain and complex systems; and to members of the Arab Business Council, Rabbi David Rosen of the Caux Round Table, Iman Feisal Abdul Rauf and Professor Bassam Tibi of the University of Gottingen for encouraging reflection on the evolution of Islam over a millennium. Howard Kunreuther of the Risk Management and Decision Processes Center at the Wharton School of the University of Pennsylvania gave generously of his time in reviewing the original text and made many most helpful suggestions.

Our colleagues in the global risk team at the World Economic Forum, the wide network of experts associated with the production of the Global Risk Reports and the Forum's partners in this endeavor at MMC (Marsh & McLennan Companies, Inc.), Merrill Lynch, Swiss Re and Citi all enriched our insights.

No errors or misinterpretations can, of course, be attributed to any of them. We take full responsibility for any shortcomings.

Our greatest thanks are due to our wives, Natalie Cleary and Mary Anne Malleret, and our children, who have shared all the risks we have faced, enabled us to triumph over a few and offered much needed balm when we have stumbled.

Introduction

Risk is a word we all use, but which each of us interprets differently.

This is in part because, as we shall see, it is a paradoxical notion. The concept of *risk,* as we know it today, is a relatively modern one, yet risk has always permeated human experience. Death, after all, is universal, and gambling in some form or other a common human experience, dating back at least 6000 years to the use of primitive dice, or *astragali,* the ankle bones of deer, goats or sheep, found in archaeological digs in many parts of the world and depicted in Egyptian tomb paintings from predynastic times and, much later, on ancient Greek vases.

Surprisingly for a circumstance so common, the origins of the word 'risk' are uncertain. It derives from the early Italian *risicare,* meaning 'to dare,' and appears in late Latin as *risigus.* Skeat's etymological dictionary[1] relates it to the Spanish *risco* – '*a steep, abrupt rock, from whence the sense of "danger" may easily have arisen among sailors.*' Skeat cites the Spanish *arriesgar* – '*to venture into danger, literally to go against a rock.*' In the 16th century, this variation also appears in Portuguese to describe the voyages of navigators venturing into unchartered waters to discover the world.

The *Shorter Oxford English Dictionary* dates the word's origin in English to 1661 and defines it as '*hazard, danger; exposure to mischance or peril.*' *Hazard* has its origins in the Arabic *al zahr,* meaning dice. The modern concept of *risk* arose only about 300 years ago. The *OED* notes that by 1719 the word denoted the '*chance or hazard of commercial loss,* specifically *in the case of insured property or goods.*' Its synonym, *chance,* derives from the late Latin *cadentia* (from *cadere,* to fall) – '*that which falls out, especially that which falls out favourably, as used in dice-playing.*'[2]

Time is the central concept in risk. We can, within reason, assess the present with some confidence. The past holds few fears, even if not all its mysteries are easily accessible. But the future is unknown, a source of fascination, its uncertainty tinged with hope and fear alike. It is easy to understand the trepidation of early sea-travelers; their primitive charts marked with drawings of fantastic monsters, their heads filled with the tales of those bold yet superstitious folk who had ventured into similarly unknown waters before them.

In his splendid book on the nature and history of risk, Peter Bernstein calls the mastery of risk:

> [the] revolutionary idea that defines the boundary between modern times and the past: the notion that the future is more than a whim of the gods and that men and women are not passive before nature. Until human beings discovered a way across that boundary, the future was a mirror of the past, or the murky domain of oracles and soothsayers who held a monopoly over knowledge of anticipated events.[3]

For most of us, risk equates with danger, but that is not always the case. The Chinese ideogram for risk,[4] for example, is composed by two symbols, one for *threat,* the other for *opportunity.* The idea that a risk represents both a threat *and* an opportunity does not occur to many people: Risk is mainly associated in most Western minds with exposure to danger or hazard,[5] with the fear of loss.

In the jargon associated with risk management, risk relates to the *uncertainty associated with possible future outcomes.* The proverbial man in the street feels uncomfortable when facing risk because he senses threat. For the economist, risk equates to variation of mathematical outcomes. For a business person, on the other hand, it represents a potential financial loss, or loss of reputation. A surgeon sees it as the possibility that something will go wrong in an operation, leading to the death or disablement of a patient. For a rock climber, risk is personal; a fall can result in death.

One could go on citing examples, but irrespective of the context, the risks we confront must always be assessed, and then assumed, mitigated and managed. Risk, being characterized in its original state by uncertainty,[6] must be clarified. We need to assess its scale, the probability of its occurring and the potential impacts if it does. Rational people do not assume risks without reflection. Indeed, it may even seem surprising that they do at all. Would a prudent person, the Roman *bonus paterfamilias,*[7] for example, not seek to avoid all risks that might place the security and honor of his family in jeopardy?

Perhaps not, if we reflect on the Chinese ideogram and its symbiotic balance between threat and opportunity. What unites all people with an appetite for risk is the opportunity associated with assuming it. The potential upside of risk is reward. Assuming a calculated risk often translates into a substantial reward for the person who accurately assesses the scale of the risk and sees how to shape the future outcome to advantage. What many see only as risks often mask exceptional opportunities for the advancement of wealth, reputation and human welfare.

Risk: The business of business

Risks are all around us, and success is rarely achieved without risk-taking. How else would any firm secure the advantage that leads to profit? Risk-taking is the essence of what business people and investors do. One might argue that entrepreneurs have a particular propensity for risk, singling them out as natural optimists. Successful entrepreneurs demonstrate an unusual aptitude for assessing and managing risk as well. They see opportunity where others see only threats.

Just as most people do not expect to divorce when they decide to marry, entrepreneurs rarely start a business thinking it might collapse, even though only 10 percent of new businesses survive and some 10 percent of economically active firms in the United States go out of business each year.[8] The difference between an entrepreneur and someone in a secure job may tally with Winston Churchill's definition of an optimist and a pessimist: 'An optimist sees an opportunity in every danger, while a pessimist sees a danger in every opportunity.' This is one of the reasons why business schools have turned to teaching entrepreneurial skills and progressive governments encourage more of their citizens to follow this path.[9]

In a nutshell, risk is the business of business, and the fundamental job of executives is to anticipate change and manage it on the basis of *an opinion about the future*. This, in the end, is what risk management is all about. As the great Austrian economist, Ludwig von Mises, put it more than 50 years ago, 'what distinguishes the successful entrepreneur and promoter from other people is precisely the fact that he does not let himself be guided by what was and is, but arranges his affairs on the ground of his opinion about the future ... In his actions, he is directed by an opinion about the future which deviates from those held by the crowd.'[10]

Risk and return

In the world of business and investment, risk is first and foremost the possibility that the actual return on an investment will differ from that which is expected. When an entrepreneur launches a new business, he knows there is a possibility of losing some or even all of his investment. He naturally seeks a return that will compensate for that risk. One could thus assume that the greater the risk, the greater the return one expects – the higher the chance of losing, the higher the compensation required to take on the risk.

This relationship between risk and return is a fundamental feature of our lives. Every time we make a decision, we measure – usually unconsciously[11] – the benefit we will derive against the cost we will incur. In business, where decisions are expected to lead to the maximization of benefit, it is necessary to calculate the relationship between the expected (future) return and the cost required to ensure it, as well as the risk of failure and underperformance. The requirement that expected return should be commensurate with risk is known as the *risk/return trade-off*, a concept very similar to the familiar *cost/benefit analysis*. The risk/return trade-off does not suggest that higher risks will necessarily bring greater returns; it tells us only that higher risks can be justified by the prospect of higher returns. As many business people know only too well, higher risks can also mean higher losses. Of course, the innovative business person may be able to identify opportunities for exceptional returns in an environment that his or her competitors see as too risky and decide to avoid.

Risk and innovation

The notion of risk is intimately linked to *innovation* (the place 'where invention meets the market'). As the engine of the market economy – the only human institution that sustains a 'permanent revolution'[12] – the need to assume risk is the main driver of innovation. Business risk did not exist in centrally planned or command economies, where enterprise managers did what their political masters instructed. From this perspective, centrally planned economies were risk-free. Conversely, in a market economy, it is the hope of a gain and the fear of a loss (the positive and negative sides of risk) that drive inventors and innovators to produce new products and develop new ways of doing things.

The economist William Baumol has shown in an excellent book[13] that innovation (inventions that reach the market), more than competition or the hope of profit, is the most important feature of a market economy. It is competition, of course, that forces businessmen to invest in innovation, and most innovation emerges within companies, not institutes or universities. Assessing, assuming, mitigating and managing risk is at the core of business behavior, and those who do not take and manage risks properly, lose ground and are eventually driven out. Innovation, which itself poses risks, is the only sustainable way of managing business risk in a fast-changing competitive marketplace.[14]

Risk and uncertainty

Risk can be defined more accurately as *measurable uncertainty*, character-ized by (a measure of) randomness, with knowable – and thus calculable – probabilities. *Uncertainty* (as opposed to *risk*)is immeasurable – randomness with unknowable probabilities. How can businesses or investors decide how much risk they are willing to incur if they cannot ascribe some order of magnitude to the risk they are contemplating?

Raw entrepreneurs on their first venture often take significant risks because they do not (or cannot) ascribe probabilities to alternative out-comes. They thus confront not risk, but true uncertainty, though rather like people in the first flush of love, they usually do not reflect on it. Analysis of the probabilities of success would discourage action. On the positive side, this is part of the reason why successful small firms and entrepreneurs often produce fundamental innovations while large firms usually focus on incremental improvements. Start-ups and small businesses often take risks (or gambles) that large firms, with more rigorous assessment procedures, would reject out of hand.

But the choice should not be between taking a chance and rejecting an opportunity. Bernstein[15] defines the *essence* of risk management (and indeed, risk assessment) as 'maximiz(ing) the area where we have some control over the outcome, while minimiz(ing) the areas where we have absolutely no control ... and [where] the linkage between effect and cause is hidden from us.' Put slightly differently, this involves minimizing the uncertainty inherent in the human condition, and using the instruments we have developed to understand, calculate and manage, as accurately as possible, the risks we face and choose to assume.

Global risks

In this book, we focus mainly on 'global risks,' risks of a global character with far-reaching consequences for our global society and global economy. As we will see in chapter 4, there are many different ways to categorize risks. One way is to consider their scale and scope of impact, from those that impact an individual or a firm to those which have potentially profound impacts on our global system. We can define global risks as events that have the potential to affect many different industries in several countries or regions and which may inflict major economic and social damage in some or all of these. Their scope extends well beyond the universe of the firm although their impacts are felt by many firms and people. Because of their reach, no single entity can address them in isolation: co-operative responses are needed to avert them or mitigate their impacts.

From a company's standpoint, these global risks are 'nonbusiness' risks with the potential to impact the firm's business decisively. Many global risks have been in the headlines repeatedly since the turn of the millennium: terrorism, pandemics like SARS and avian 'flu, natural disasters like earthquakes, tsunamis and tropical cyclones, failed and failing states, oil-price spikes and the deleterious effects of, climate change all currently dominate our sense of the risk landscape. Others have not yet penetrated public consciousness worldwide, but are impacting on particular regions or industries. Violations of intellectual property rights and, counterfeiting have passed beyond the boundaries of the entertainment and luxury goods industries where their effects were first felt, while the risk of identity theft has as yet unplumbed implications for financial services, the sanctity of contract and inter-personal trust. All these can be related back to the spread of global crime. A hard-landing of the Chinese economy would affect national economies and firms well beyond the frontiers of Asia. If electro-magnetic fields (EMF) were found to have harmful effects on human health; this could have a serious impact on certain ICT sectors and energy utilities and entail widespread societal consequences. The loss of biodiversity – an issue just below the radar screen of public consciousness and driven by mass production of food and textiles – may prove to have a profoundly negative effect on environmental sustainability and sharply reduce the potential for new pharmaceutical remedies. One could go on-and-on.[16]

Perhaps just as disturbingly, many people living in the developed economies are becoming shy of assuming the risks they know, or more often hear about. The spread of liability (or foreign tort) regimes from the United States into European jurisdictions is a powerful signal of increasing risk aversion. Excessive reliance on punitive damages awarded by the courts in cases of medical mishaps risks raising costs and inhibiting both research-based development and treatment, without improving service standards.

The willingness to assume risk has always driven human progress, but the ability to assess and manage risks properly has been a focus for us for only the past 300 years. Those readers who are interested in understanding why that is, and how our insights into what is possible, have evolved over time are referred to the short history of risk in appendix 1. It's a fascinating story of human progress, characterized by meticulous research, overconfident extrapolation, excessive caution, ebullient *hubris* and the inevitable *nemesis*. Throughout it all, our insights have improved and our judgment has matured. But as we shall see in other parts of this book, certainty is not within our grasp, nor will it ever be.

This book has three main purposes: firstly, it is a reference for business executives who must comply with all kinds of new requirements in identifying, assessing, managing and communicating the risks their companies face. This material is in chapters 3, 4, 5 and 6.

Secondly, it explains why developing the insight and the skills to do this is not a trivial task, by discussing, in chapters 1 and 2 the nature of global risks and our inability to make purely rational judgments about many aspects of risk. Hopefully, by making these explicit, we can help executives in the public and private sectors to understand what biases we must try to correct for when making such judgments. Chapter 8 and Conclusion conclude by seeking to pull the most important lessons together.

Finally, for those with a deeper interest on the subject of risk, the book puts these matters into both an historical and a contemporary context, by considering a number of the biggest global risks we face today, as well as those that have shaped the development of risk instruments over the centuries. In chapter 7 we discuss some of the biggest challenges of our time, while key aspects of the history of risk are reviewed in appendix 1; the origins of some of our contemporary challenges are explored in appendix 2. We hope that each reader will be able to assemble the mix of information that is most relevant for his or her personal needs.

CHAPTER 1

Today's risks are different: The impact of global risks

1.1. An expanding range

Today, business leaders face many different kinds of risks, ranging from those that are traditionally within the canvas of the firm (project risks, competitive risks, industry risks, currency risks and the like) to a set of new, more dangerous, global risks, briefly described in the Introduction, and which are now increasingly on the radar screen of senior executives.

Firms now have instruments and procedures to deal successfully with most of the traditional business risks. Take inventory risk as an example. Fifty years ago, this was one of the greatest risks businesses faced. Today, after the introduction of *just-in-time* manufacturing, supply management processes and UPC bar codes on almost every product, inventory risk is largely irrelevant, unless supply chains are disrupted by some of the global risks we shall discuss below. Interest-rate risks that were, until 20 years ago, beyond the control of the most seasoned chief executive and could bring a well-run company to its knees, have almost disappeared in the advanced economies. Currency exchange-rate risks are still a major factor, especially in emerging market economies, but treasury departments can hedge exchange rates (or interest rates) successfully by skillful use of hedging instruments, including interest-rate swaps, options and futures.[1] We shall look at some of these instruments more closely in chapter 3.

Businesses in the 21st century, however, face an array of risks that are *systemic*[2] in nature and global in scope. All global risks mentioned in the Introduction are, in essence, 'nonbusiness risks' that now exercise an increasingly large impact on the activities of individual firms.

Different institutions and experts classify and rank global risks in different ways. As the three lists of the 'top ten' global risks below indicate, there is no standard set. The significance of any particular risk for an investment

Top ten risks[3] – They depend on who you are

Top ten risks for the Western Intelligence Community
1. Persistent and challenged differences between high and low opportunity geographical areas, resulting in uncontrollable migratory flows and humanitarian crises
2. The intelligence community's inability to overcome cognitive straitjackets and adopt new approaches
3. Competition for resources (primarily oil and water)
4. The synergies between terror, crime and drug networks
5. Pandemics, including avian flu and HIV/AIDS
6. The ability of extremist factions to shape the face of Islam
7. Weapons of mass destruction in the hands of terrorist organizations and rogue states
8. The inability of societies to deal with cultural diversity or minorities
9. The inability to come to grips with the roots of radicalization and extremism
10. Irreversible disruption of global environmental equilibriums (including global warming)

Top ten risks for Goldman Sachs
1. Hedge funds and derivatives
2. World oil supply
3. Wealth disparities in emerging economies
4. Opportunities and challenges for growth in China
5. Trade liberalization
6. The dollar and the twin deficits
7. Environmental accords
8. Geopolitical conflicts
9. Global terrorism
10. World health conditions

Top ten risks identified by experts for the World Economic Forum
1. Instability in Iraq
2. Terrorism
3. Emerging fiscal crises
4. Disruption of oil supplies
5. Islamic radicalism
6. A sudden decline in China's growth
7. Pandemics – infectious diseases
8. Climate change
9. Weapons of mass destruction
10. Unrestrained migration and related tensions

Sources: The 'top ten' lists were generated in 2005: those for the World Economic Forum were defined in January, while the lists for Goldman Sachs and the Western Intelligence Community were developed in November 2005.

bank may, moreover, differ substantially from that for a national security agency or a global foundation.

Most of these risks have been around for a long time. Wars, civil strife, public disorder and pandemics like the Black Death, the Great Plague and the Spanish flu were familiar to our ancestors. Events like these have been part of human experience throughout history. But what is new is that while the risks flowing from civil unrest, the rise of religious extremism or fiscal crises in one country used to have only a local effect, the interconnectedness of our world today means that their effects are much wider and often more unpredictable.

Today's global economy owes its features to the emergence of multinational corporations over the past 40 years; the ready availability of information on global demographics and market conditions around the world; the opening up of markets in Eurasia and China after the collapse of the Soviet Union; the commercialization of the information technologies and systems developed in the defense industries in the 1980s, which accelerated the confluence of communications, computing and entertainment; and the adoption of digital technologies by financial institutions in the 1990s to create integrated global markets.

Its definitive characteristics are the universal availability of information through the Internet; the internationalization of production, shifting the balance of power between corporations and governments; the scale and speed of global financial flows (at least $1.5 trillion per day); and the dissemination of products and services by global broadcasting, branding and advertising. The principles of market economics are its *leitmotif,* though protectionism has prevailed in trade. The commitment to markets has exacted costs: Liberalization of capital account transactions caused exceptional currency volatility after the Asian financial crisis in 1997–8 and again after 9/11 at the end of 2001.

Two dates illustrate different aspects of this new era: the Battle of Seattle in November 1999, when demonstrators protesting against the effects of globalization disrupted the proceedings of the World Trade Organization; and the attacks on the World Trade Center in Manhattan on September 11, 2001. On both of these occasions, a group of people, disturbed by their different experiences of the effects of the new globalized era, acted in protest against those effects and set in motion a train of events that shaped the next several years. In this respect, global risks are very much a creature of the new millennium. We shall explore this further a little later.

There is plenty of evidence to suggest that in our flattening and shrinking world,[4] exogenous risks[5] now affect business more than ever before. A study by the consulting firm A.T. Kearney in September 2004 revealed that many Fortune 100 CEOs blame a variety of exogenous risks for their companies' failure to meet earning expectations. A.T. Kearney estimates that over a period of 15 years, 46 percent of the companies that disappeared from the Fortune 500 list did so as a result of exogenous factors.[6] In May 2005, a survey of 9300 business leaders around the world by the McKinsey partnership concluded that growing geopolitical instability, increasing risks to the supply of natural resources and mounting environmental hazards posed the biggest risks to profitability in the period ahead.[7] Figure 1.1 below, based on a study by A.T. Kearney in 2006, shows that 'second tier risks' – issues that range from the disruption of suppliers and information systems, through theft of intellectual property and natural disasters, to attacks by activists on corporate brands – are increasingly the risks that demand the attention of CEOs.

The need for business leaders to focus their attention on 'nonbusiness' risks has been compellingly made from another perspective by Professor Nitin Nohria of the Harvard Business School. A member of the leadership initiative at Harvard, Nohria and his team have analyzed the leading US business figures of the past 100 years, trying to identify the leadership

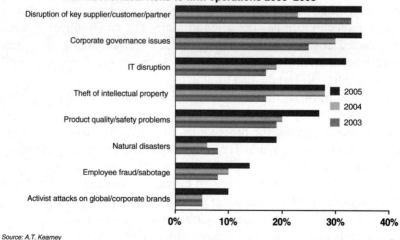

Figure 1.1 The increasing importance of 'nonbusiness' risks
Source: The Global Business Policy Council of A.T. Kearney.

qualities of the executives who led the companies that generated outstanding shareholder value over 15 years. Professor Nohria concluded that only one trait, that of *contextual intelligence,* linked effective leaders across the generations.

According to the study, all successful leaders:

> were shrewd in calculating the impact of factors such as technology, globalization, government regulation and social mores ... What makes a leading business figure is the ability to understand and capitalize on the sweeping trends influencing the marketplace of their time.

In the business community, one iconic example of an individual able to 'connect the dots' of many different trends is Jack Welch, the former CEO of General Electric (GE), who saw in the 1980s what very few other executives of that era recognized: the decline of the basic industries that had long driven the US economy. At about the same time IBM, which dominated the corporate mainframe market, almost went out of business because its top management misread the trend toward personal and small business desktop computing.

In an uncertain world, the ability to anticipate, or create, trends by 'connecting the dots' is a prerequisite for success, and perhaps for survival. Those who perceive and exploit emerging trends before their competitors often benefit disproportionately. One example is the Toyota Prius. Toyota seems to have found a way to turn a global threat – climate change – into a profitable opportunity. The Prius (a hybrid gas-electric vehicle) is now recognized as the *green* vehicle in the United States, with almost 200,000 vehicles being produced in 2005, primarily for the domestic market.

In December 2006, Nissan, whose highly successful chief executive, Carlos Ghosn, had dismissed hybrid vehicles 15 months earlier as a niche play with an uncertain market demand, announced that it too would develop a hybrid vehicle. This was eerily reminiscent of the early 1990s when Toyota's success in bringing its luxury offering, the Lexus, to the market six months ahead of Nissan's Infiniti, led to exceptional profits for Toyota and a serious setback for Nissan, contributing to the decline from which Mr Ghosn had to rescue the second Japanese automaker a decade later.

On a different scale and in an unrelated market segment, many companies, both young and mature, have developed profitable businesses responding to the threat of terrorism, which has generated high-tech opportunities for screening and detection devices as well as data mining and analysis. The US market for information security, which was already worth $8.7 billion in 2004, is expected to grow by about 20 percent a year until the end of the decade.

1.2. Is today's world riskier than before?

By their nature, risks come and go. Some risks diminish or disappear while new risks emerge or come to the fore. Smallpox, for example, has been virtually eradicated, while the risk of a major nuclear conflict has diminished greatly since the end of the Cold War. The risk of dying from scurvy on an ocean voyage is negligible, although drowning or death from thirst is still possible if one is an African migrant escaping to the Canary Islands from Senegal, or a Cuban seeking a new life in Miami. On the other hand, new risks continually emerge: global warming as a result of carbon emissions, the loss of biodiversity because of crop standardization and species transplantation, and systemic financial risks as a result of opaque hedge fund transactions were not risks with which our forebears had to contend in the 18th century.

We also often discover that we have been exposed to risks that we were not aware of. Apart from the outstanding example of tobacco smoking, where growing awareness of life-threatening risks led to prolonged congressional hearings in the United States, enormous liability awards by the courts, legislative intervention, profound changes in social behavior and at least two Hollywood films, two other cases come to mind. First, asbestos, where the risk of ingesting fibers was poorly understood or ignored during and after World War II, when shipyard and construction workers in the developed world, as well as miners and primary fabrication workers in producing countries suffered substantial exposure. When the effects of inhalation of asbestos fibers were recognized 20 years later lawsuits were launched against companies that mined and fabricated asbestos products and public agencies that permitted its use. Some continue until today. Enron is a second example: when employees who lost their pension savings and shareholders who saw stock values collapse discovered that senior executives had harmed them through reckless and illegal behavior, they initiated lawsuits.

Every risk, properly understood, has two facets: the potential threat and the opportunity associated with it. Genetic research offers an extreme example of the interplay between tremendous new health benefits and the risk of catastrophic consequences. Among the tens of thousands of scientists conducting genetic research today in the hope of coming up with a treatment that will put an end to hereditary diseases, there may be a few whose activities are focused on reproducing viruses to create a biological warfare arsenal for terrorist groups. Less dramatically moreover, science is a journey toward knowledge; unintended consequences are its natural corollary. We are not that far from the period when bleeding and the application of leeches were thought to be the best remedies for inexplicable fevers or torpors; and psychotic disorders were routinely treated with electro-shock 'therapy' just one generation ago. Thalidomide seemed an excellent way to combat morning sickness and to help women get rest during pregnancy, but led to serious birth defects, blighting many lives. Our new ventures into the unknown will produce some unhappy results.

Conversely, just as pandemics pose exceptional threats, they offer opportunities for important learning. SARS – the bird flu pandemic whose spread from China almost fractured the global tourism industry a few years ago – offers an example of both. Research into the workings of SARS in the past few years has led to the identification of the protein in the SARS virus that causes the collapse of lung function and death. Researchers in Vienna discovered, as a result, that the purpose of this protein, of whose existence bioscientists had long been aware without knowing what its role was, is to protect us against chronic lung failure. This allows for the development of new pharmaceutical treatments.

So is the world today riskier than it used to be? That is an extremely difficult question to answer, because risk is ubiquitous. In OECD countries and robust emerging economies, life is much more pleasant than it was 100 years ago, or indeed ever, for the great majority of people. Nobody in those countries faces famine, war or pestilence the way previous generations did, or the inhabitants of Darfur, Colombia, Iraq or Afghanistan still do.

Certainly the world has experienced war, disruptions in oil prices or supply and pandemics that killed millions of people, many times before. The bubonic plague (dubbed the Black Death because of the way it disfigured its victims' corpses), which killed 25 million Europeans in the 13th century, and the influenza pandemic in the period just after the World War, I are still reference points for scientists. If we review many of the indicators that measure the threats to which we are exposed (maternal or child mortality, deaths caused by war, civil conflict, terrorism or epidemics), the world is less threatening today than it has ever been. Throughout the 20th century, as real income levels and literacy increased, so too did the demand for safety. Longevity increased, our microenvironments[8] became cleaner and our products became safer.

On the other hand, if one assumes that risk distributions are constant, the concentration of people and assets in densely populated areas – in particular megacities of more than 10 million people – raises the aggregate level of risk to which these inhabitants are exposed. The same applies to the risk of viruses in densely configured bird and animal populations being transmitted to humans. The HIV that gives rise to AIDS, and SARS, had their origin in animal and bird populations, respectively. Furthermore, the far greater mobility of people, commodities and money in today's world threatens to act as an effective transmission mechanism for local hazards or threats to other parts of the planet. Apart from pandemics like SARS, there have been several examples of financial contagion in the past decade, notably the collapse of emerging markets in 1998, following the Asian market crash a few months earlier, and the shockwaves that followed 9/11 and fractured the Argentinean economy. The collapse of a major national stock market or a local electricity grid can create domino effects that spread at an amazing speed.

Several recent studies suggest that the perception of risk in many markets is higher today than it has been for quite some time. Why is this so? There may be two reasons:

- First, our increased sensitivity to risks formerly considered acceptable has led to a drop in the level of risk tolerance. Risk intolerance normally rises in proportion to greater wealth and education. While people in earlier times were more fatalistic about risk, now they want 'bad things' to be prevented. As societies grow richer, people assign a higher value to their existence and to their futures. Those who value the future more highly take fewer risks than those who discount its value. This is why rich people stopped smoking earlier than poor people, or why children are more widely encouraged to put on their seatbelts in Germany, than in Russia.
- Second, our national and global institutions cannot cope with these risks and this leaves the impression of a 'governance' gap. Our governments and international bodies like Interpol, the United Nations and the World Bank have not succeeded in eliminating global risks like terrorism, or resolving serious challenges like climate change and extreme poverty. The prevalence of any individual risk today is no higher – and its aggregate potential impact is probably lower than in the past – but risk often seems less manageable, not least because we know more.

What makes the world objectively riskier today than it may have been before is the extent of the interconnectedness of our systems, the speed at which a threat emerging in one environment can spread to disrupt remote systems and markets and become apparent immediately to millions almost instantaneously via the Internet and broadcast media. Executives need to continuously watch what is happening on the margins of the business to guard against the possibility that events there may cause disruptions that will threaten core success. Outsourcing – extending the supply chain across continents to get access to the cheapest inputs – has great advantages, but can broaden the spectrum of risk. Nike, the sportswear retailer, faced a consumer revolt in the 1990s when it emerged that working conditions in some of its subcontractors' factories in East Asia were well below acceptable standards. As Nike's brand is central to its business model,[9] anything that weakens that brand – whether or not the event giving rise to this effect is under Nike's control – poses a very real threat.

British Airways's setback in August 2005, which saw a caterers' strike cause millions of pounds of lost revenue, is a good example of the *bullwhip effect*, a tiny movement at one end of the supply chain causing large shocks or volatility at the other. This is a variation of the *butterfly* metaphor familiar from chaos theory – the notion that the fluttering of a butterfly's wings in Beijing can cause storm systems a month later in New York. In 1997, British Airways sold its noncore catering business, Gate Gourmet, to Swissair, which, when it collapsed four years later, sold it to the Texas Pacific Group, a private-equity firm. In August 2005, labor disputes over restructuring and pay led to 600 employees being dismissed. The resulting strike disrupted not only Gate Gourmet's ability to supply, but also BA's passenger operations. The airline had no other source of meals and decided to fly without its meal service. This would have damaged its brand in any event, but it was also hit by a solidarity strike by its ground staff, some of whom came from the same tightly knit Sikh community as the striking catering workers. The ground staff strike paralyzed the BA fleet for almost two days at a direct cost of some £40 million and knock-on impacts on customer loyalty and the share price.

These effects are not, in and of themselves, new: Clausewitz, the famous 19th-century German strategist, spoke of *frictions* that can cause the most sophisticated strategy to fail because of one unforeseen risk: 'Countless minor incidents – the kind you can never foresee – combine to lower the general level of performance, so that one always falls short of the intended goal.'[10] In today's turbulent world, however, as we shall see, even one minor incident can often cause disproportionate big results.

1.3. The changing nature of risks – An increasingly turbulent world

The risk environment is evolving in ways that make it more difficult to comprehend and analyze its different facets. Our world is characterized by increasing complexity and accelerating change. On the global scale, it is now senseless to describe and assess one systemic risk in isolation from others as these risks potentially reinforce one another through complex interactions and 'ricochet' effects. Stresses and uncertainties thus threaten

the integrity of closely connected political, economic, societal and technological systems.

Systemic risks are risks that originate in an identifiable event that threatens predictable harm to one part of a system and which, because of links
between different parts, are (or may be) amplified in either strength or
direction, leading to substantial damage to the whole. The term is widely
used in financial markets and is defined there as '... the risk that an event
will trigger a loss of economic value or confidence in, and attendant
increases in uncertainty about, a substantial portion of the financial system
that is serious enough to quite probably have significant adverse effects on
the real economy.'[11]

It is the linkages within a system and the possibility that certain events
will have grave (and possibly unforeseen) consequences for the system as
a whole, or parts of it not directly connected to the original event, that makes
certain risks systemic. Because these links and the indirect impacts of particular events are often not properly understood, we do not have instruments available to manage and mitigate these risks. Let's see why this is.

Interconnectivity exponentially increases uncertainty. The formulae are
simple but the results are frightening. An arithmetic increase in the number
of elements in a system leads to a geometric increase in the number of
potential links and an exponential increase in the number of potential patterns that may emerge.

Number of possible links: $L = N \times (N-1)/2$

4 elements	6 links
10 elements	45 links

Number of possible patterns: $P = 2^L$

4 elements	6 links	64 patterns
10 elements	45 links	3500 billion patterns

The world in which we need to assess and manage risk is thus inherently
volatile and occasionally turbulent due to the level of interconnectivity and
interdependence of its different elements. This leads to various asymmetries,
the compression of time and difficulties in distinguishing real signals from
background clutter or noise. Figure 1.2 shows these relationships.

Let's now consider the different elements in more detail.

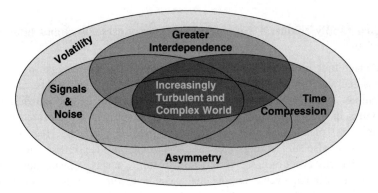

Figure 1.2   An increasingly complex and turbulent world

1.3.1. Greater interconnectivity and interdependence

Among several factors that contribute to making today's world more complex and turbulent, the increasing level of interconnectivity and interdependence (the dynamic of reciprocal responsiveness and dependence) is the most important. Remarkable advances in communications technology; the much larger scale of markets in Eastern Europe, the former Soviet Union and China to which companies had access after the end of the Cold War; and the liberalization of trade and financial services have combined to trigger an unprecedented increase in global trade and, especially, financial flows. This has led to more intense cooperation and competition, an emphasis on 'speed to market' that stresses supply chain efficiency, far higher rates of invention and markedly shorter product and industry lifecycles. As the connections among firms, markets and states have increased so markedly, the effects – and unintended consequences – of an event are felt more widely and rapidly than before. Our risk-management options are determined by the behavior of markets in the context of contractual agreements, while perceptions of risk are shaped by the often-dramatic reports of global broadcasters.

An interdependent world, moreover, means that 'the risks faced by any individual, firm, region, or country depend not only on its own choices but also on those of others,'[12] thus making such risks more difficult to manage. As we will see in the chapters dealing with specific global risks, some of the greatest challenges lie in the decision to invest in risk-reducing measures. Should some global companies and decision makers act independently even when others do not take similar action? What should they do when others refuse, or are unable, to invest appropriately? In the context of

Global supply chains: A case study on interconnectedness and interdependence

The magnitude of the challenge in dealing with complexity has dramatically intensified with the advent of global supply chains, spurred by the 'just-in-time revolution' of the 1980s and the phenomenon of offshoring and outsourcing activities in the 1990s. Today's newer, longer supply chains, nurtured by a complex set of interdependencies are much more cost-effective than in the past, but are also subject to greater risks and vulnerabilities. Interconnectivity means that any event or piece of new information can spread instantaneously, triggering cascading events. Supply chains can be disrupted in an instant by an event in any part of the chain. That was the case in 1999, when an earthquake in Taiwan sent shockwaves through the global semiconductor market and in August 2003, when a blackout in North America disrupted global supply chains.

terrorism, for example, the risks faced by any airport or airline are tied to the security standards of other carriers and airports. In the case of a pandemic, an outbreak of disease in one country that is poorly prepared raises the risks faced by other countries – and businesses in those countries – even if they are well prepared.

1.3.2. Asymmetry

Interconnectivity and interdependence create asymmetry, enabling small players and seemingly insignificant events to produce disproportionate impacts or hold disproportionate power. The example that epitomizes asymmetry is the role of nonstate terrorist actors – the September 11 attacks showed that a group of a dozen people armed with box cutters could succeed in destroying the global geopolitical equilibrium. But asymmetric effects are also apparent everywhere in niche players' challenges to the supremacy of well-established companies or institutions. As Moises Naim points out, 'the proliferation of new microplayers capable of constraining their mega-sized rivals is a rising trend everywhere. The United States is constrained by Islamist terrorists. Central banks are threatened by hedge funds. Control of large swaths of territory, critical government agencies, or the nation's most lucrative business activities rest in the hands of criminal organisations that are part of sprawling global networks. Gigantic media companies are besieged, exposed, and sometimes crippled by the daily postings of 40 million bloggers whose ranks double every five months.

Latin American governments have been overthrown by indigenous groups that only a few years earlier were politically insignificant.'[13]

A more diffuse form of asymmetry is to be found in apparently insignificant issues whose impact will be felt a few years from now. The surplus of male members in the population of India or China belongs to this category. In China, for example, the one-child policy combined with a clear preference for boys has created an asymmetric population which will have a differential 'surplus' of 30 million men over women by 2020. The full significance of this phenomenon will be apparent only when this generation has reached adulthood.[14]

Asymmetry is growing in importance and affecting business in unprecedented ways. These impacts are likely to grow. The rising importance of civil society activists and NGOs;[15] the increasing influence of blogs; far higher percentages of older, retired people in the developed countries; and unemployed (and perhaps unemployable) youth in slower growing parts of the developing world – all pose new challenges to companies and governments and make growing demands on the time of their executives. In the United States, in particular, large global businesses are feeling the impact of some of these asymmetric factors. In April 2005, a small group of activists called Children of God for Life called for a boycott of GE after the company had decided to pursue embryonic stem-cell research. In the same month, Microsoft was pressured by religious groups to stop supporting gay-rights legislation in Washington State. However, employee outrage forced Microsoft to reverse course two weeks later. The CEOs of both GE and Microsoft were forced to intervene to limit the impact of these risks.[16]

1.3.3. Volatility

Financial volatility refers to the extent and time frame within which an asset's value rises and falls. It is typically associated with risk, with volatility acting as a proxy for risk in certain models. When applied to global risks, volatility denotes very rapid changes in conditions, without certainty that there will be a return to an earlier equilibrium. Volatility is a feature of unstable systems, and requires exceptionally flexible business responses. Volatility has been exacerbated by globalization. In today's world, fierce competition (for talent, capital, resources, ideas, …) means that any firm can lose ground to rivals, anywhere, at any time. Employees have to be prepared to lose jobs, and companies to close down product lines or plants or indeed to open them elsewhere. At the macro level, volatility translates into a *kaleidoscopic comparative advantage* where only those who are flexible and able to adjust rapidly to changing conditions can seize opportunity and sustain growth.[17]

The pervasive volatility of globally connected financial systems mutates into *turbulence* on occasion. The use of the word is borrowed from chaos theory. In a phase transition from a liquid to a gaseous state, for example, the behavior of the atoms becomes incomprehensible, apparently chaotic. Only when the transition has passed and the liquid has fully gasified, is the atomic behavior understandable again. We observed this sort of behavior in the financial markets during and after the Asian markets' crash in 1997–8.

Another analogy might be that the apparently rational, linear certainty of Newtonian physics has been overtaken by the nonlinear uncertainty described by Heisenberg. We have entered a *quantum era* in which small things and hidden connections can create very large consequences. The metaphor of the butterfly's wings causing the storm is again applicable. Things can happen very quickly and unexpectedly, creating higher uncertainty. Complex situations such as global business environments or sociopolitical settings involving very large numbers of people defy prediction or control from time to time. Change becomes discontinuous.

This is particularly evident in business. Recent studies show that volatility is now the norm. Just under half of the Fortune 100 companies in the United States dropped off the list between 1998 and 2005. The risk of losing one's status as an 'industry leader' more than doubled between 1980 and 1998. Of the world's 2,500 largest companies, 383 lost their CEOs in 2005, and of these, almost half were fired. According to the consultancy Booz Allen Hamilton, CEO turnover in 2005 was the highest since the firm began to track this in 1995.[18]

1.3.4. Time compression

The acceleration of change (or the compression of time) is a distinctive feature of what we have come to call *globalization*. Over the past 20 years or so, rapid and accelerating changes have transformed political, economic and social environments as new advances in information and communications technology have changed the scale, scope and immediacy of our experiences and our ability to manipulate our environments. The acceleration of change can be seen everywhere: in remarkable scientific discoveries and technological changes affecting production systems and labor markets and in the media revolution. The human genome project, for example, the most complex study of human reality ever undertaken, comprised research by several thousands of researchers from hundreds of institutions, funded by more than 15 governments and scores of private companies over 13 years. During the first Gulf War, millions of viewers watched live broadcast coverage from Baghdad as the network's cameras focused on incoming missiles. Still more remarkably, officers in the Pentagon's operations center were watching this broadcast and receiving real-time battlefield information from the images. As a result, many older people feel they are living in a world they can no longer comprehend.

In the world of business, Moore's law ('a doubling in capacity every 18 months'[19]) epitomizes the way in which technological progress has driven the acceleration of change. For a company competing in the cut-throat CPU or hard-drive markets, this has meant that a new product which may take three years to develop and reaches the market only weeks after an equivalent offering by a direct competitor, is simply unsaleable. Moore's law will not be valid forever – nor did Gordon Moore expect that it would be – but technological change continues to accelerate and sustain the pressure on companies in almost all highly competitive technology segments. In 2003, Andy Grove, the CEO of Intel, observed that gate leakage current was about to become a major obstacle in the further miniaturization of gallium arsenide semiconductors, suggesting that limits were in sight. At about the same time, researchers discovered that hafnium arsenide exhibits a thousand times less current leakage than gallium arsenide. In a related field, scientists at Toshiba discovered in 2005 that with nanostructure absorbent lattices, they could charge a lithium ion battery 60 times faster than previous batteries. These new batteries went into production in 2006.[20]

The result is that both product and industry life cycles are contracting sharply and unpredictably, and businesses as well as governments and consumers are being subjected to sustained, but discontinuous, change.

1.3.5. Weak signals

The creation of the World Wide Web and the development of browsers and search engines have turned information, which only a decade ago still had a relatively high market value, into a pure commodity like sugar or sand. Both sugar and sand are in global oversupply; both serve economic purposes; neither commands a premium price in its natural state; and both cause irritation in one's shoe. Many CEOs are like Michael Dell, the chief executive of Dell Computer, who spends several hours a day dealing with the 200 e-mails he receives.[21] Indeed, in today's information era, we are bombarded with an unprecedented amount of data and often useless and irrelevant information. Bill Gates probably spoke for many when he said that the ever-growing flood of information is threatening to become a drain on productivity: 'It's overwhelming. Nobody's paid to search or just find information. At the end of the day you're paid for designing a new product, having a satisfied customer and doing that with the minimum amount of time, the minimum amount of people.'[22]

Retrieving relevant information for any purpose is like 'drinking water from a fire hydrant'; any Google search returns thousands of pages, but almost no one reads beyond the third or fourth. In this era of information overload, everyone knows what's happening, but almost nobody knows what it means. As a result, the information available for decision making is far from perfect. Sorting out useful signals from useless noise is often very difficult and failure to do so inevitably clouds one's judgment.[23] Information overload can even stall the decision process, or bring it to a halt. The result? Companies – and governments – either opt to 'do nothing,' or, crippled by their inability to make sense of the available data, choose to 'fly blind.'

1.4. Hurricane Katrina – A distressingly effective example

Let's take the example of the devastating hurricane Katrina that caused havoc, misery and loss of life in the area between Louisiana and Mississippi on the US Gulf Coast in late August and September 2005. Katrina touched land as a Category 1 hurricane north of Miami, Florida, on August 25, 2005, and then struck New Orleans, Louisiana, as a Category 4 storm on August 29. The flooding of New Orleans and the damage the storm wrought to the coastal strip of Louisiana, Mississippi and Alabama, resulting in the displacement of over a million people, made Katrina the costliest natural disaster in the history of the United States.

Commentators around the world speculated about the reasons for the catastrophe, not those for the hurricane itself – coastal storms of this sort are common, both in the Gulf of Mexico[24] and in the Pacific – but for the exceptional damage it caused in overwhelming the levees that protect New Orleans from the ocean, and for the government's shocking delays in respond-ing effectively to the tragedy. Only on the fourth day after the sea flooded the city to the eaves of houses well back from the waterfront, and devas-tated hundreds of kilometers of coast across two states, was the federal government able to get troops and a convoy of amphibious vehicles into New Orleans. Until then CNN[25] viewers around the world were bombarded with images of sheets of water, misery, psychological trauma and rising anger, not least from local government officials overwhelmed by their own inability to respond, including the Mayor of New Orleans, who famously told the government to stop giving press conferences and making promises, and 'get off its butt and deal with the greatest tragedy the country had experienced.'

Incompetence vied with ignorance and incapacity in addressing the challenges; no plans were in place to strengthen the barricades or evacuate the poor, the sick or the elderly who survived from the tenements and houses in which they were trapped; the Superdome, into which 25,000 people who could get out were moved, soon filled to overcapacity, stranding others who were transported there in busloads and requiring their relocation to other states. The chief of the Federal Emergency Management Agency (FEMA) excused his agency for its failure to respond effectively, pleading ignorance of circumstances in Louisiana. He was later relieved of responsibility. The whole scene played out over five days like a tragic farce. Even estimates of the dead seemed opportunistic, delivered for political purposes, rather than to inform better planning.

Everyone was seen to be at fault by the US public: an ABC News-Washington Post Survey published on September 5 indicated that two-thirds of those polled thought the federal government should have been better prepared, and three-quarters felt that state and local authorities were remiss in their responses. President Bush, fresh from largely unsuccessful attempts to bolster his standing at home in the face of continuing difficulties in Iraq, was caught flat-footed, responding publicly – in effectively scripted photo-opportunities – only after troops were under way to begin rescue operations. By then, one third of the New Orleans police had deserted their posts and looting and gunfire had echoed across the benighted city. Foreigners watched in amazement. While Washington's failure in Iraq could be attributed to inexperience, naiveté or, at worst, arrogance; few had doubted America's power. But the failure to prepare adequately for or respond effectively to Katrina changed those perceptions.

One of us was in Europe throughout the period; the other was traveling in Europe, the Middle East and Southeast Asia. Everywhere we found amazement, occasionally tinged with *schadenfreude*, and leavened with sympathy and embarrassment. Indian and Iranian commentators, familiar with the impact of natural disasters, mused on the differences in social responses between their countries and the United States. Looting and exploiting the misery of others in times of collective crisis were incomprehensible to them. Throughout Asia, contrasts were drawn with the responses of communities devastated by the tsunami that had struck only nine months earlier in the northern Indian Ocean. Sharp social inequality in the United States and the all-too-evident racial divide exposed by images broadcast around the world were uncomfortably apparent. 'I think we are morally superior,' said one Indian businessman, educated in the United States and deeply engaged there. 'Despite caste, our society is better integrated.'

This instructive, but distressing, vignette serves chiefly to allow us to reflect on the complex conflation of circumstances that led to the failure to manage a simple and specific risk – that of coastal storms, 12 others of which are predicted, as we write, for the Northern Hemisphere in 2005 – in the sophisticated, experienced and economically powerful United States.

Reports published after the self-criticism began indicated that FEMA had indicated in 1993 that the largest potential threat to the United States was a Force 5 hurricane in the Gulf of Mexico. Katrina was only a Force 4 storm, though the winds hit the city at 232 km per hour on August 29 before veering to the east and demolishing two of Mississippi's coastal cities, Gulfport and Biloxi. Subsequent interviews with the Colorado State Hurricane Forecasting Team on September 2 recorded that the world was 10 years into what the team calls a 'busy' hurricane cycle of between 25 and 40 years, higher water temperatures predispose coastal regions to more violent and damaging storms. Despite this, New Orleans was inadequately protected, with its levees poorly maintained. Poor planning and preparation, on its own, would have resulted in a badly flooded city. But other factors exacerbated the deplorable lack of response, illustrating how many factors can conflate to cause a result far worse than that which the original threat suggested.

In this case, large numbers of National Guard personnel, the state government's first line of response to local catastrophe, were out of the United States, serving in Iraq; others had recently retuned from tours of active duty and were on well-merited leave. Looting was a function of desperation encouraged by the absence of police – who deserted – and National Guardsman, who were not deployed, or indeed of any civil defense or social services personnel. In the context of conflict in Iraq, tensions around Venezuela and disturbances in the delta region in Nigeria, the damage done to oil rigs, pipelines and refineries[26] in the Gulf of Mexico caused the oil price to spike disproportionately, rising over \$70 on August 30 in an exceptionally tight market, before falling back as the president of the United States released fuel from the Strategic Petroleum Reserve. Racial tensions rose as it became clear that the vast majority of those trapped by the waters or relocated to sports stadiums to lie in squalor for several days were black, while most whites seemed to have escaped the rising waters in private transport. Imagine what would have happened if a terrorist group had been able to take advantage of the disturbance to launch an attack on a major landmark or transportation system in Chicago or Los Angeles.

The financial damage far exceeds that of the Force 5 Hurricane Andrew that lashed the Florida coast in 1992. The global insurance industry faces claims of about $40 billion.[27] The US consultancy Risk Management Solutions estimates the total damage at almost $100 billion. A large number of the 1.92 million Louisianans who were employed before the storm struck have likely lost not only their homes and possessions, but their jobs, at least until the city is pumped dry and rehabilitated. Although reconstruction will create huge opportunities for the civil engineering and construction industry, the short-term impact on the local, state and even national economies will be considerable. The New Orleans port is among the top five in the United States in tons of goods handled and provides more than 107,000 jobs.[28] The Economic Forecasting Center of Georgia State University has estimated that closure of the port and the city will lead to 0.7 percent less growth in the third quarter of 2005, a further 0.9 percent loss in the fourth and another 0.5 percent in the first quarter of 2006. The impact on new construction will only make itself felt from the second quarter.[29]

When this begins, the cost will be extraordinary. Diverting the course of the Mississippi River to aid shipping and control floods led to the drainage of 400,000 hectares of coastal marchlands around New Orleans in the 1950s and 1960s and the construction of tens of thousands of homes on land prone to flooding. Restoring the wetlands by feeding water 100 km from the Mississippi to the coastal marshes, building two new deltas, shutting canals and locks to keep out salt water and creating artificial islands as barriers – a plan devised some time ago to address the US Geological Survey's concern that another 1,800 square kilometers of coastal marshland would be lost by 2050 and to protect the city from flooding – will cost $14 billion if executed in 2006.[30] And that takes no account of the cleanup and the reconstruction of waterlogged and damaged buildings! It is no wonder that some are asking if New Orleans will ever be rebuilt.

Katrina's death toll – officially at 1302 at the end of October 2005 – is only a small fraction of the Asian tsunami's in December 2004, which left over 200,000 people dead in its wake, but its impact on the Bush presidency, already weakened by difficulties in Iraq; on race relations in the United States; on global oil prices; and on the assessment of US power and capacity in many parts of the world will be considerable. None of these are what one would normally describe as the *probable effects* of a hurricane. The government's failure to respond to what seemed to be weak *signals* once attention shifted sharply to the 'war on terror' after 9/11, the high degree of *interdependence* between the different components – particularly those impacting the oil price – the immediacy and *compression of time* brought about by continuously broadcast television images of squalor and official incapacity and the striking reality of black suffering in the United States all combined to produce results that far exceeded those that could have been foreseen from a coastal storm.

The unforeseeable permutations of these elements in different circumstances make it difficult to compute risk with precision. But that is not the end of the challenge. As we shall see in the next chapter, we do not even perceive risk accurately.

CHAPTER 2

The idiosyncrasies of risk perception: Why your risk is different from mine

The risk associated with any occurrence is equal to the probability of its occurring multiplied by its impact. According to traditional economic theory, people make *rational* decisions, and the only thing that affects their behavior is relevant information. The theory of *rational choice* suggests that people, when confronted with uncertain outcomes, assess the probability of each alternative and select the one that is likely to maximize the return, irrespective of their emotions and prejudices. But we all know that the real world is different, and that each person's assessment of both probability and impact are highly subjective. Our personal beliefs, feelings, intellectual constructs and emotions affect the way we perceive and calculate risks.

The rational agent assumption should be treated with caution. Three people in particular, Daniel Kahneman, Vernon Smith and Amos Tversky, created the discipline of experimental economics, testing how people actually behave instead of constructing models based on assumptions that we always behave rationally. Their conclusions were, as Paul Ormerod has remarked, 'a devastating blow to the postulates of the rational decision-maker. In general, people gather limited information, reason poorly and act intuitively rather than rationally.'[1] Sendil Mullainathan summarizes human behavior well: 'We tend to think people are driven by purposeful choices: we think big things drive big behaviours (...) Instead, most behaviours are driven by the moment. They aren't purposeful, thought-out choices. That's an illusion we have about others (...) We can talk abstractions of risk and return, but when the person is physically checking off the box on that investment form, all the things going on at that moment will disproportionately influence the decision they make. That's the temptation element – in real time, the moment can be very tempting. The main thing is to define what is in your mind at the moment of choice.'[2]

The 'Ultimatum Games' and the rejection of the *homo economicus* model

The ultimatum game was first developed by three experimental economists (Güth Werner, Rolf Schmittberger and Bernd Schwarte) in 1982 and reported in "An Experimental Analysis of Ultimate Bargaining", in the Journal of Economic Behavior and Organization. In this game, two players are given a sum of money (let's say $100). The first player (the proposer) offers a portion of his $100 to a second person, who can either accept or reject the offer. If the second person (the responder) accepts, he gets whatever amount the proposer has offered while the proposer keeps the balance. If he rejects it, the experimenter takes the money back and neither the first player nor the responder get anything. An economist of the "rational school" would argue that it is in the interest of the responder to accept whatever sum is offered since any amount is better then nothing. One would therefore expect the proposer to know this and make only the smallest possible, non-zero, offer ($1 for example). Both suppositions turn out to be incorrect. In different iterations of the game, the proposer typically offers sums between 40 and 50 percent of the total available to him; and the responder most often reject offers lower than 20 percent. Why? Because notions of fairness and equality, as well as anger and revenge, seem to play a much bigger role than utility maximization.

We, likewise, assess any risk in the context of our past experience, and our feelings at that moment. When we evaluate the probability and the impact associated with a risk, our perceptions are at best an approximation of reality. In particular, our perceptions of the significance of risks are seemingly shaped by biases influenced by our sense of what we can control. As a general rule, the psychological discomfort we feel in situations of uncertainty leads us to be overly concerned about risks over which we feel we have little control, and to experience little concern for risks in respect of which we believe we have significant control.

What does this mean in practice? Simply that people very often exaggerate low probability but dramatic risks such as natural disasters, terrorist attacks or a child being kidnapped by a stranger. Likewise, they underestimate common risks like having an accident on the road (almost everyone believes that he or she is a 'good driver'), or at home. The 'sniper attack' that paralyzed the Washington area in the United States, in October 2002, illustrates these seemingly paradoxical reactions.

Over the course of two weeks, nine murders brought five counties of 3.1 million people to a near-standstill, with all kinds of travel and activities being canceled by parents and hundreds of schools in the area. Yet the chance of being killed by the sniper was one in 344,000, equating to a murder rate of 7.5 for 100,000 people on an annualized basis, just over twice the 'normal' murder rate of 3.4 per 100,000 in these counties in 2000.[3] One feels intuitively that, although it was understandable to be alarmed, these reactions to the heightened risk were disproportionate.

2.1. The asymmetry of human choices: Why winning $1,000 is not the same as losing it

In 1979, Kahneman and Tversky published a remarkable paper on 'prospect theory' in *Econometrica*, which revolutionized the scientific approach to decision-making and led to the award of the Nobel Prize in economics to Kahneman (with Smith), in 2002. Amos Tversky had died in 1996, and as the Nobel committee does not make posthumous awards, he did not receive the recognition he deserved.

Kahneman and Tversky investigated apparent anomalies in human behavior which led them to recognize the asymmetry of the choices we make. When a choice is formulated in one way, subjects may evidence a *risk-averse* reaction, but when they are offered the same choice formulated differently, they may display *risk-seeking* behavior. Kahneman observed that the same person may drive across town to save $5 on a $15 calculator, but not to save $5 on a $125 coat.

The pair's best-known experiment saw them assemble a group of students to whom they gave the choice of either receiving $1,000, or having a 50 percent chance of getting $2,500. Most chose to take the $1,000 although the arithmetic expectation of the uncertain option is $1,250 (2,500 × 0.5). This is typical *risk-averse* behavior. But when the same students were offered a symmetrical choice – accepting either a certain loss of $1,000, or a 50 percent chance of either losing nothing or $2,500 – most selected the risky alternative, displaying apparent *risk-seeking* behavior.

Why would one person willingly assume a higher arithmetic risk when the choice is formulated in one way, and shy away from a symmetrical risk formulated differently? This looks like an anomaly, but it has to do with a fundamental aspect of our attitude to risk: Most of us fear losses more than we value gains. Put simply, we experience the potential pain of losing $1,000 more deeply than we prize the pleasure of a gain of $1,000. This is called *loss aversion*: People are much more willing to take risks to avoid losses than they are to obtain gains.[4] Kahneman pointed out, however, that *loss aversion* often disappears when people know the odds. They then may no longer shy away from risk and may even become overoptimistic. This is due to the phenomenon we discussed earlier: We have less concern for risks over which we believe we have control. This experiment (and others) shows that the way in which alternatives are framed influences the decisions we make.

Market players know these asymmetrical propensities well and have to deal with them every trading day. Losses predispose traders (and even fund managers) to take unnecessary risks – many traders gamble (display risk-seeking behavior) in a losing situation, holding on to a position too long in the hope that prices may recover, and even throwing good money after bad. Traders and investors who do well, meanwhile, often display an aversion to risk by taking their profits quickly, instead of letting their stakes run. *Prospect theory* rightly predicts that people tend to be risk-seeking in situations where a loss might occur and risk-averse in situations where gains are possible. In market terms, we tend to sell our winners and keep our losers.

What distinguishes entrepreneurs from the human herd is the fact that they are risk-seeking individuals. By definition, when one innovates, one cannot calculate the odds. Bankers on the other hand, are usually highly risk-averse. They endeavor to find out as much as possible about the odds and to limit the bank's risk to an irreducible minimum. An unwillingness to fund aspirant borrowers without collateral is thus understandable. There is also a problem of *asymmetric information*, as the person seeking the loan knows much more about his financial situation and prospects than the banker does.

2.2. Cognitive illusions: Why our ability to assess risk gets distorted

The world is simply too large and too complex for anyone to be able to understand everything and to make well-informed, rational decisions in the face of uncertainty. In evolutionary terms, moreover, human brains seem to have specialized in rapid decision-making at the expense of processing complexity. Survival under threat required (and often still does) rapid appreciation and effective response. The adrenal reaction, predisposing us to fight, flight or playing dead, is a simple example.

We are able to make decisions fast by resorting to *learned behaviors* – principles and practices ('rules-of-thumb') known technically as *heuristics* (from the Greek word *heuriskein: to find*). Most *heuristics* are, however, *cognitive illusions*, simplified models that enable us to make sense of complex reality.

We use many mental devices to assist us in making decisions in situations where there is great uncertainty, often due to complexity and volatility. Many make our decisions easier, but they also reduce our chances of making

Table 2.1 Heuristics as cognitive distortions

Availability	We tend to interpret any story through the lens of a superficially similar account
Confirmation bias	We glibly underpin an assumption by focusing on instances that confirm it, while ignoring those which don't
Overconfidence	We see ourselves as always being right – or at least more often than other people
Anchoring	We tend to cling mentally to any number we hear in a particular context, even if it is factually far off the mark
Representativeness	We judge the substantial similarity of things based on their superficial resemblances

good decisions. Every business person knows about the *sunk-cost effect* – the reluctance we often display to pull out of a bad deal because of the effort and money already invested in it.

There are many other *heuristics* that distort our abilities to assess risk effectively.[5] Many are not independent of one another, but rather exacerbate the effects of others. Before examining more closely, some we will explore later when discussing risk mitigation, let's make their effects clear by focusing on five important ones listed in Table 2.1.

Let us now consider each of these in turn.

2.2.1. Availability

We often make decisions on the frequency or likelihood of events occurring, based on what we can readily remember, rather than on analysis of extensive data. We assess an event as either frequent or probable if it is easy to imagine, or recall. Strongly held opinions on the relationship of this year's weather to long-standing weather patterns are good examples.

One effect of the availability heuristic is the tendency to view the future only in terms of the immediate past – the *like-the-past* fallacy that permeates financial markets. If events are sensationalized or repeatedly covered by the media, moreover, we perceive a higher frequency and assume a greater probability. After extensive news coverage of accounting and reporting scandals in the Enron, Andersen, WorldCom and Tyco cases, both media and shareholders were more disposed to assume that accounting or remuneration issues that arose in other companies were evidence of corrupt practice.

2.2.2. Confirmation bias

Once we have either made a decision or developed assumptions about the probability of an event occurring, we look for confirmation of the correctness of our decision or assumptions. When people have a set view, they tend to look for evidence that confirms it and disregard, or at least downplay, evidence that contradicts it.

Much of the heated debate about the presence or absence of weapons of mass destruction in Iraq, the utility of the invasion by coalition forces in the war on terrorism, and the costs and benefits experienced by Iraqi civilians since the fall of Saddam Hussein, is characterized by *confirmation bias* on all sides.

Many investors who lost large sums of money in the dot-com bust that followed the boom (and the bankers who took them into these issues), had focused only on the short-term evidence of rocketing share prices, and ignored the absence of plausible business plans, or any reasonable argument that justified price-earnings ratios way above 100!

CEOs who continued with acquisition sprees in pursuit of higher market valuations, ignored the difficulty of integrating ever more companies into a coherent group strategy, and widespread evidence in well-documented studies that suggest that effective change management requires a dedicated focus by CEOs.

2.2.3. Overconfidence

CEOs and other senior executives are inherently confident of their abilities. Beyond the solid evidence of their success in advancing to the top, their tendency to *confirmation bias* can lead to *overconfidence*. This propensity is reinforced by performance-related incentives and compensation packages that are disproportionately larger than those of other employees. Highly successful investment bankers, fund managers, stockbrokers and others who earn exceptional packages are all exposed to the risk of this cognitive illusion, as, of course, are prominent politicians.

Overconfidence is characterized by the belief that 'bad things won't happen.' This *heuristic* leads one to see things in black and white, rather than shades of gray, heightening the risk of overreaction in either direction.

Acquisitions also provide a fertile field for overconfidence. Study after study shows that most acquisitions destroy value in the short term. Expected synergies and cost savings do not materialize, integration fails for institutional or cultural reasons. Acquisitions, all studies indicate, are inherently risky.[6] But CEOs set on an acquisition often disregard the evident risks and pay too much, bringing upon the company the 'winner's curse,' because they overestimate the returns they can extract.

Hersh Shefrin, Professor of Finance at Santa Clara University's Leavey School of Business, says CEOs are afflicted with 'the Lake Wobegon syndrome,' named after Garrison Keillor's mythical community where 'all the children are above average.'[7] Shefrin observes that every CEO who undertakes an acquisition thinks he is different and will be able to pull it off. The proposition that most takeovers fail because of the *hubris* of CEOs, has become one of the strongest tenets of behavioral finance.

2.2.4. Anchoring

We tend to base decisions and estimates on positions we are familiar with; this serves as the *anchor* for all that follows. We often make estimates by starting with the *anchor* – the value we know – and adjusting from that point. These initial mental frameworks through which we view the world, color, inhibit and may seriously distort our ability to process or accept new data or information.

Prejudice is often a convenient anchor with dangerous consequences. Cultural stereotypes, historical experiences and versions of history that may be no more than myths, often shape political and military strategies. Events in the Balkans, the Middle East and the Great Lakes region of Africa in the past decade are recent illustrations of a perennial pattern.

Anchors are often very resilient. Many investors still retain (and prefer) valuation models learned many years ago, in a different context. Even if such a model is based on information that has been overtaken by events, many devotees simply add the new information and distort the original model. Another well-known variation of anchoring is the theory of price negotiation. One party suggests a price, which the other party then uses as an anchor on which to base his counteroffer. This is why in M&A negotiations, the first bid is rarely close to the final price.

2.2.5. Representativeness

We create personal meaning by classifying things, events and phenomena on the basis of our experiences. A review of botanical, zoological or ornithological names, or those of chemical compounds, illustrates how we proceed in the scientific realm.

When something does not fit properly within a known category, we approximate it with the nearest *representative* class: We assess unfamiliar entities and events by judging how much they resemble others with which we are familiar. Thus we attribute human emotions and behavior to our pets, and most great religions are anthropomorphic in defining their God(s). As we have some capacity and knowledge, and God is infinitely greater than we are, we hold him to be *omnipotent* and *omniscient*.

We assess the probability of an event in the same way, by identifying a 'comparable known' event and assuming that the probability will be similar, if not identical. In so doing, however, we often ignore relevant facts that should be included in our assessment. The cognitive illusion of representativeness can also lead to fallacious application of the *law of small numbers*, as when a decision-maker assumes that a small sample is representative of a much larger population. Political leaders, in particular, have been prone to assume that their advisers reflect the views of the whole electorate, or even all right-thinking people in the world.

2.2.6. Cultural specificity

There is one other element that affects our perception of risk on an aggregate, rather than personal, basis; and that is *cultural context*. To a substantial extent, the risk perception (and hence risk management) of certain classes of people are determined by the *risk culture* they inhabit, and especially the extent to which they are informed about, and have developed a degree of tolerance of specific risks. When we live with a risk for some time, we naturally acquire some resilience to it. If the risk is unfamiliar, no such process has occurred. The risk of terrorism, for example, means something completely different to a business leader in Tel-Aviv in Israel, another in Ramallah in the Palestinian territories and a third in Sacramento, California.

Public reactions may therefore vary considerably from one market to another. The public view of the cost–benefit ratio associated with GMOs – genetically modified organisms – for example, is very different in the United States and in Western Europe.

An interesting twist in cultural specificity lies in the propensity of people in all communities to 'compensate' for lowered risk. This is sometimes called *risk homeostasis* in the scientific literature. We saw in the previous chapter that those who value the future more highly tend to indulge in less risk-taking behavior than those who discount its value. One might therefore conclude that if one were to raise people's expectations about future prospects, risk-taking behavior might be dampened, and safety increased. But the evidence suggests that this is not necessarily true. Campaigns to heighten people's perceptions of risk tend to 'move risk taking behavior around' rather than reduce it. We tend to behave less cautiously when we feel better protected, because each of us has an inbuilt level of acceptable risk – largely socioculturally determined – which is resistant to change. Studies in the 1980s and 1990s on the use of seat belts and anti-locking brakes provide an interesting example. In a representative sample of Munich taxi drivers, half of the taxis were equipped with ABS (anti-lock braking systems), while the other half was left with standard systems. The rate of accidents for both groups was roughly the same because drivers of cars equipped with ABS took more risks by driving faster, following closer and braking later. Drivers wearing seatbelts also tended to drive faster and less carefully. Similar results have been observed in studies of scuba divers and children wearing cycle helmets.[8]

Despite this, there is one common element in all developed societies and mature markets today – a much lower general level of risk tolerance, and the belief that it ought to be possible to eliminate risk altogether. This is unfortunately impossible, because risks permeate our lives.

2.3. The neuroeconomics of risk – Emotions overpower reason!

Just as *behavioral* (*or experimental*) *economics* derived from important psychological insights into influences distorting what were earlier presumed to be rational choices and assessments, neuroeconomics is emerging from neuroscience, brain imaging[9] and the study of the behavior of patients with brain damage, chronic mental illnesses, developmental disorders and degenerative diseases. Neuroeconomics, though still in its infancy, is making great contributions to our understanding of decision making under conditions of uncertainty.[10] It has put to rest the notion entrenched in classical economic theory that people systematically apply rational calculations to economic decisions to enable us to optimize the utility of choices in the context of constraints.[11] In the words of the two pioneers of the discipline, 'the Platonic metaphor of the mind as a charioteer driving twin horses of *reason* and *emotion*, is on the right track – except that *cognition* is a smart pony, and *emotion* a big elephant.'[12]

We now know (because we can observe the neural activity) that each time we make a decision about risk, instincts, habits and emotions such as fear, anger or greed, interfere with any attempt at making a rational choice. Human activity is, in fact, a set of interactions between *controlled* and *automatic* processes – the latter, having evolved to address evolutionary challenges, are faster than conscious thought and occur with no sense of effort; and between *cognitive* and *affective* systems – the latter being common to humans and many animals. Much human decision-making, is shaped by the interactions between the limbic system (which rules the intuitive and affective parts of our psyches) and the analytic system (which enables most of our structured thought processes).

These interactions are necessary for us to function properly and when the *affective* (emotive) system is damaged by brain injury or stress for example, the *cognitive* (logical-deliberative) system cannot regulate behavior appropriately. As *automatic* processes occur in the (*occipital, parietal* and *temporal* parts of the) brain all the time, one can say that *controlled* (or rational) activity (observable in the *orbital* and *prefrontal* parts of the cortex), is the 'override' mode in economic decisions.

Neuroeconomics has shed new light on three economic phenomena related to risk: (1) the way we discount future rewards, (2) our fear of the unknown and (3) the way we build trust. To understand these, we must distinguish between *cognitive processes*, which answer true–false questions, and *affective processes*, which are associated with positive or negative motivations and tendencies to action. Examples of the latter would be fear, which prompts flight or freezing; anger which releases aggression; and pain, which encourages action to relieve it. All these experiences leave memories, induce preferences and influence future perceptions on an *affective*, rather than *cognitive*, level. It also seems likely that cognition itself does not lead to action, and that its active effects occur through the affective system.

2.3.1. Future rewards and time inconsistency

One of the most intriguing findings is that we are all affected by *time inconsistency* when faced with uncertainty. According to classical economic theory, we apply a rational, declining *discount factor*, rather like discounted cash-flow analysis in search of net present value (NPV), when measuring present rewards against future ones.

Neuroeconomics suggests this is not the case. The role of the analytic system remains constant while the influence of limbic system (which radically discounts the future) assumes overriding importance in the present, but declines markedly as rewards are moved into the future. This combination of *automatic* and *controlled*, and *cognitive* and *affective* behaviors leads to inconsistent discounting patterns. Decisions involving different time horizons typically require us to identify a pattern, categorize it and match it against other already familiar conditions. Self-control – the core of delayed gratification – involves *affective* appreciation of a future desired state (wealth, health or a slim body, for example) and *cognitive* insight into the relationship between abstinence and future rewards.

When making decisions about the distant future, therefore, we often exhibit controlled behavior, just as traditional economic textbooks predict we should, and act rationally and consistently, though even here – as we have shown with reference to self-control – a combination of *cognitive* and *affective* processes are involved.

But we often behave differently when deciding about the immediate future. In situations which require immediate decisions, the *limbic* system may override the *prefrontal cortex* and demand gratification without delay. This is an *automatic* behavior, related to satisfaction of physiological needs, and displaces conscious control. Most of us have experienced the urge to procrastinate when faced with a difficult task or a risky decision.

2.3.2. Fear of the unknown

Different studies suggest that there is a neural basis for the *fear of the unknown* – indeed all fear – and that this greatly influences personal decisions under conditions of uncertainty. In certain circumstances, we do all we can to assess the risk associated with different scenarios and select the risk-reward pattern that we find most acceptable. In many others, however, proximate or very large risk induces fear, and we tend to respond emotionally.

Fear (an *automatic, affective* response) is triggered by activity in the *amygdala*, an almond-shaped region below the *cortex* common to most mammals. The *amygdala* registers sensations of fear from both *automatic* and *controlled* processes in the brain, and enables both learning and unlearning of what to fear.

Both human and animal studies have shown that damage to the *amygdala* interferes with, or even eliminates, fear responses, and in humans, disrupts the ability to recognize facial expressions of fear in others.

Impaired ability to register fear can lead to irrational behavior in the face of high risk, just as intense fear can produce responses that are counterproductive to its rational appreciation. We are all familiar with the dry mouth, the 'knot-in-the-stomach' and even the vague (or not so vague) sense of panic that fear can trigger. Interestingly, fear can also induce myopic kinds of risk-averse behavior like those displayed by workaholics who risk family life, health and social balance, and by compulsive savers who deprive their families while amassing fortunes.

2.3.3. Interpersonal trust

We know that trust is a key component of economic activity, and that national or regional economic success seems to be highly correlated with institutionalized trust, whether in the form of contract law, or social institutions like *guangxi*. Many economists believe that trust is the holy grail, the ingredient that explains why some societies grow consistently richer than others. One can understand why this may well be so. If you do not have to interrogate the behavior of people you deal with in business, if you trust them, in other words, your *transaction cost* is much lower and you are likely to undertake more transactions.

The neuroscientific foundation for trust is not well understood, but the hormone *oxytocin*, whose levels are known to rise during social bonding in other contexts, seems to play a role. Higher levels of *oxytocin* are associated with trust, and the presence of such levels, whatever their origin – a relaxing massage, friendly conversation at sunset on a beautiful day, casual reciprocal touching, breast-feeding in women – reflects, and may encourage, higher trust. Likewise we know that seeing people that we consider attractive, leads to the release of *dopamine* and a positive psychological response. The physical appearance of the party with whom we are considering doing business may thus also affect our willingness to transact. It is also possible that we may 'neurally encode' trust: experiments in which the faces of people who had earlier cooperated with subjects in negotiations, were shown to them, led to activity in the *ventral striatum*, a general reward area.

Behavior that induces mistrust, such as offers that are seen as unfair or insulting, is associated – in subjects receiving them – with increased activity in the *insula cortex* of the temporal lobe, which also encodes pain and offensive smells. The *anterior cingulate cortex* (*ACC*), the part of the brain which processes both abstract thinking and emotions and resolves conflicts between them, is also activated in such cases, as is the the *dorsolateral prefrontal cortex*, which is associated with planning. The ACC seems to balance the disgust experienced at the unfair offer in the *insula*, with the prospect of financial reward recorded by the *dorsolateral prefrontal cortex*.[13]

To measure interpersonal trust, neuroeconomists have also used an investment game whose results exhibit surprising gender differences. An area of the brain called the *medial cingulate sulcus* is particularly active when men do the math to decide how much they should trust or repay, and is then deactivated after the decision has been made. The female brains studied, however, behaved differently. After the decision involving the *medial cingulate sulcus*, a different area of the brain, the *caudate nucleus*, that specializes in regulating concerns and detecting errors, became active. Unlike the men in the study, the women apparently wondered whether they had done the right thing and tried to understand how the other subject would react to their decision.

2.4. Conclusions

The way humans perceive, assess or evaluate a risk varies because different people have different preferences, experiences and values. Think, for example, about the probable approaches of a highly impulsive person and a 'control freak' to the same investment opportunity. The experiment with the investment game indicates, moreover, that some responses may also be gender-specific, perhaps deriving from the different consequences of sexual behavior and roles in child-rearing experienced by men and women. The dynamic interplay between reason and emotion and between controlled and automatic processes is, moreover, complex and continuous and varies under different conditions of stress.

Because the automatic affective processes that enable us to protect ourselves against risk are the product of our evolutionary history; and because these spontaneously dominate our intuitive responses to risk,[14] we all exhibit certain patterns of risk perception that seem to cut across cultures, genders or age groups. Among these, it appears, are the tendencies to:

- overestimate unknown risks;
- underestimate risks that we voluntarily assume;
- overestimate small risks and underestimate larger ones; and
- overreact to highly publicized risks.

Neuroscientific insights might suggest that the reason why these are nearly universal is, at least in part, because automatic brain processes that produce such biases are not cognitively accessible and cannot therefore be corrected.

These conclusions are important in considering what we can and should do in dealing with the risks we confront in managing our companies, directing our governments, making investment decisions and engaging with our families and communities in efforts to shape a better world. Figure 2.1 illustrates the relationship between the effects of the heuristics we employ to address situations involving risk, the affective processes that shape our responses, and the cognitive errors that result.[15] In simple terms, we can say that our experiences, affective state and emotive-cognitive interactions

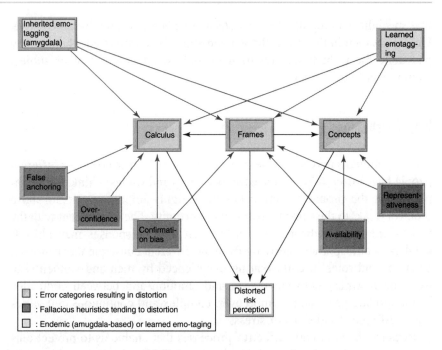

Figure 2.1 Sources of fallacious assessment of risk

lead to three categories of common errors – those involved in *framing*[16] (or *contextualizing*) the risk, defining its *content* and *calculating* its probability and impact.

As we shall see in the following chapters, addressing the challenges posed by our human propensity to commit these errors is not just a matter of being conscious of our own tendency to behave in this way; it also requires us to be aware of the same propensities in others. The core activities of risk management – identifying, assessing, mitigating, managing and communicating risk – all require integrated behavior between people who do not behave consistently in the way that the *rational actor* theories of modern finance would suggest.[17]

All members of groups experience the individual challenges to rational appreciation of risk that we have already discussed, but there are additional aspects of group behavior that one must consider. A whole series of these have been documented[18] and are familiar to many. Most are caused by a desire for acceptance by one's peers and are reinforced first by intra-group pressure to achieve consensus, and second by a tendency to herd behavior in following dominant figures. Self-censorship by individuals fearful of challenging a group consensus, mutual delusional reinforcement about capacity and competency, group cognitive resonance that reinforces established behavior, and distorted perceptions of the external environment that are influenced by *availability*, *representativeness* and *false anchoring* biases, supported by managers who act as group vigilantes in maintaining order, often lead to poor performance in identifying and assessing risks. As we shall see when discussing risk communication, other agents, including social activists and sections of the media, likewise engender certain types of herd behavior outside the firm.

None of this excludes the utility of the mathematical models developed by Markowitz, Sharpe, Merton, and Black and Scholes that we review in appendix 1, but it does suggest that we should approach with great care any unqualified assumptions about rational economic actors, and efficient markets – which are, after all, made up of people; as well as beliefs in inevitable regressions to the mean – which only occur with very large numbers over long periods of time. The challenge of managing risk is even more demanding than the mathematics of the models.

CHAPTER 3

The management of risk

We seek to manage risk in order to address our concerns about what might happen in the future. Risk management is a comprehensive task, involving the management of the full spectrum of risks with which an enterprise is confronted. But this statement makes the dilemma clear: risk management involves substantial elements of uncertainty precisely because it requires us to anticipate the future and look forward in time beyond what we know about the past and the present.

Obviously, not all risks can be anticipated with any degree of certainty; this is particularly true for global risks. The question is whether those not foreseen can nonetheless be managed. This question poses another conundrum because successful risk management depends on the readiness of managers to address unsettling questions characterized by uncertainty, precisely those questions that we often do not deal with, either by overlooking their existence or by choosing to deny their relevance.

Still more disconcertingly, we have seen that a range of generic as well as individual characteristics prevents our being able to assess and calculate risk *objectively* and *rationally*. Our consistent inability to *frame issues* correctly, to *conceptualize* them adequately and to *calculate* the *probability* and *potential impact* of their emergence, leaves us poorly equipped to manage the future with confidence.

But this, however true it may be, is unsatisfactory! Those of us who manage companies – those remarkable corporate entities with limited liability, that employ the capital of scores, thousands or millions of investors who have no active role in managing their investments – cannot afford to take a passive view of future uncertainties that affect corporate performance. There was always a risk of litigation by shareholders when companies failed, but in recent years, as the scale of uncertainty was seen to grow and more companies were liquidated or suffered enormous losses in shareholder value, stock exchanges and national legislators have intervened to oblige corporate managers to assess and manage risk more effectively.

There are regulatory requirements today in most jurisdictions – COSO[1] and Sarbanes-Oxley[2] in the United States, the Cadbury report,[3] the Combined Code[4] and the Turnbull report[5] in the United Kingdom, KonTraG[6] in Germany and CoCo[7] in Canada, among them – which require corporate boards to put in place effective risk assessment and management programs that disclose to shareholders the risks to the company and the measures taken to manage those risks.

So how should we think about the challenge of risk management?

First, risk management is an integral part of strategic management. Indeed, properly conceived, it lies at its core. The art and science of management is the *cost-effective application of scarce resources* in pursuit of the company's goals. Strategic management, therefore, is the use of *a well-conceived plan* – taking account of the opportunities and challenges of the marketplace and the broader political, economic, social and technological environments enveloping the markets – to ensure that the resources available to the firm are employed as cost-effectively and efficiently as possible. These resources are either owned by shareholders, and put at risk (at the firm's disposal) by them or loaned to the firm by financial institutions under conditions of some security. All these investors and lenders, as well as employees of the firm, whose retirement prospects are often tied to the company's performance, expect calculated, prudent management of these assets.

Business executives spend their lives pondering complex decisions related to risk. Should an airline accept the risk of volatile oil prices or pass it to an insurer? Should a retail chain risk building a supermarket in a prime area, close to thousands of target customers, that has been flooded twice in 30 years? Should a European manufacturer with major export sales in the United States take on the currency risk of the Euro/US$ exchange rate, or hedge its exposure in the markets? Should a mining company explore a concession in a failing state or in an area prone to conflicts and disturbances? Absolute responses – a yes or a no – are possible, of course, but they usually display a lack of sophistication. Experienced managers structure their exposure by capping the risk at the point that could endanger profitability or liquidity, rather than hedging the whole amount at risk. One cannot exclude uncertainty without paying for the privilege, but one must not overpay for the benefit.

Carefully considered, well-structured *risk management*, as opposed to *risk avoidance*, is central to successful corporate leadership. There is a saying in the financial markets that the first rule is to *identify* one's risk and the second to *diversify* it. This is true, but rather limited. Risk management is seen today less as a means of avoiding risk or reducing its discomfort than as a key element of strategic decision-making. The reason is obvious: the acceptance of risk allows us to create value; risk management is the way we try to optimize the balance between the opportunities we unlock by taking risks, and the cost of the protection needed if we are to survive the occasional mishap. As Peter Bernstein notes: '... the essence of risk management lies in maximizing the areas where we have some control over the outcome, while minimizing the areas where we have absolutely no control ... and the linkage between effect and cause is hidden from us.'[8]

To illustrate the point, consider the risk of terrorism, which has been so widely discussed since September 11, 2001. Few companies can do anything to curtail terrorism, but they can do something to reduce their vulnerability to terrorist acts. What each company should do, of course, depends on the nature of the risks it faces. There is no generic response to terrorism. Appropriate countermeasures in any particular case might range from investing in better intelligence, to installing surveillance cameras, effective fencing and blast-proofing at plants, through identifying potential choke points in supply chains, to developing evacuation plans for personnel in high-risk zones. The lesson is that accurate *identification* and careful *assessment* of the risks to which one is exposed, must precede development of sound risk *management* strategies.

Figure 3.1a illustrates in the simplest possible way, the three key components of an effective risk-management process: *defining* the risks, *managing* the risks and *monitoring* the effect of the management measures one has put in place. This is a continuous process; risks are dynamic, especially in the closely interconnected and volatile environments we must deal with today.

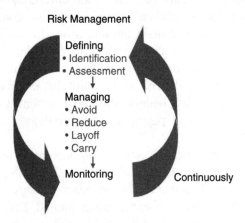

Figure 3.1a　Risk management

3.1. Enterprise risk management – What does a good system look like?

If we elaborate slightly on the simple diagram we have just considered, we can see what is required to manage risk at an enterprise level. Figure 3.1b is a more complex illustration.

This model makes the process clear. Proceeding from the top in the center, the board defines the *risk appetite, culture* and *policy* of the company, acts to heighten the risk awareness of all employees, and reviews the risk-management procedures developed by management, possibly with outside support.

The next step is to determine as accurately as possible, the company's *risk profile* – its exposure to different types of risks, including a rigorous assessment of the potential impact if these events materialize.

The third step is what we usually think of as risk management – determining how to deal with the risks to which we are actually exposed. Sometimes, rigorous assessment will disclose risks that the board, or company management, will find unacceptable, and steps will be taken to *eliminate* these risks (or *prevent* their materializing), perhaps by withdrawing from a contract, a project or a country. In other cases, careful assessment will disclose ways to *reduce* the level of risk, perhaps by reconfiguring a

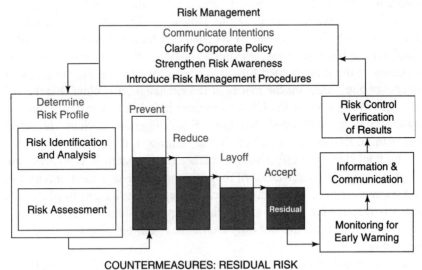

Figure 3.1b Risk management

contract or a project or altering a financial position. Having taken these sensible steps, we are left with the risks that are central to the business. Here the choice is either to *layoff* the risk, to pay a third party – a financial intermediary – to accept a risk that we are unwilling to bear, or to *accept* the risk on the company's books and manage it in the ordinary course of business, perhaps with help from consultants with particular expertise in certain areas.

With these decisions behind them, management must ensure that it has effective procedures in place to *monitor* the events giving rise to the risks it has accepted, so that it has early warning of changes that suggest that the risk is increasing, and that these observations are *communicated* rapidly to the officials who can make proper decisions about how to deal with the changes. This is often the area where risk management programs are weakest, in both companies and governments. As counterterrorism chief Richard Clarke has made clear,[9] the US government was well aware of the threat posed by *al-Qaeda* to US institutions before September 11, 2001. The bipartisan commission[10] that investigated the failure of intelligence and security which led to the aircraft hijackings, the destruction of the Twin Towers and the attack on the Pentagon, concluded that many different pieces of intelligence that could have led to pre-emptive insights were available to US intelligence agencies before the fateful day. But there was no effective procedure in place to 'connect the dots' and disclose the threatening pattern!

Clarke accused the Bush White House of diverting attention from the threat posed by *al-Qaeda* by its focus on Iraq; US Secretary of State Condoleezza Rice, who was serving as National Security Assistant to the president at the time, denied this in her testimony before the commission. Whatever one's view on the merits of the exchange, it is clear that the risk management system of the US government failed in this instance, and the commission recommended that the US intelligence services should be restructured to reduce the risk of similar failures in future.

The final step in an effective risk-management system is assessment and *verification of the effectiveness* of the assessment, management, monitoring and communication procedures which management has put in place. The board is responsible at law, and to the company's shareholders, to ensure that these procedures are not only well conceived, but also that they work in practice.

This approach is similar to that developed as a *best practice* by the British Office of Government Commerce (OGC). The OGC identifies nine steps:

- Define a framework
- Identify the risks
- Identify probable risk owners

- Evaluate the risks
- Set acceptable levels of risk
- Identify suitable responses to risk
- Implement responses
- Gain assurances about effectiveness
- Embed and review.[11]

We describe this approach as a risk management system to emphasize its iterative, systemic character. Everything we have discussed thus far – the inherently uncertain character of the future, the difficulty of contemplating the myriad complex, inter-relationships between events, and the intrinsic weaknesses of our cognitive apparatus – makes clear that we shall never be able to design perfect fail-safe systems. The only prudent response to the challenge of managing risk is to invest the necessary effort and expertise in seeking to understand it, to manage it as effectively as our insights allow, and to test the efficacy of our instruments continually in practice. It is no different to the way we run an automotive plant or a power station.

The OGC offers several constructive suggestions – it describes them as *critical success factors* – for effective risk management. These underline the iterative nature of the system and the need to continuously improve it by learning and doing.

It is imperative that CEOs and boards:

- identify the senior managers who own, lead and support the process of risk management
- ensure that
    - risk management is understood to be part of an organisational culture that supports *prudent risk-taking* and *innovation*;
    - corporate risk management *policies* and the advantages of effective risk management are known to all staff;
    - a transparent and replicable risk management *process* has been established and is effectively implemented;
    - risk management is specifically linked to the *achievement of objectives* and fully embedded in all management processes, including those associated with collaboration with other companies and consultants;
    - risks are *actively monitored* and *reviewed* regularly, on a '*no fault*' basis.[12]

To various degrees, all national commissions' reports on corporate governance locate the obligation to manage risk within the context of good corporate governance. They all point out that the *board has overall responsibility for risk management*, including assessing the efficacy of the risk management process implemented in the company. Management must design, implement and monitor the risk management process and integrate it into the firm's management systems.

3.2. Responsibilities of the board

The board determines the firm's *risk tolerance*, sets the *risk strategy* and *policy* in consultation with executive and senior management, and ensures that proper processes that take account of the competence of employees are in place to identify risk, measure its potential impact and manage it proactively.

The board must identify *key risk areas* and *key performance indicators* and monitor these to ensure that internal control systems are effective. It must employ recognized risk management and internal control models to provide shareholders and others with an interest in the firm's success, with reasonable assurance that the company's business goals will be achieved under both normal and adverse conditions; that its assets will be safe-guarded; all relevant laws are complied with; reporting is accurate and reliable, and the company is behaving responsibly toward all stakeholders.

The board must receive and review regular reports on the risk manage-ment process addressing the firm's exposure to physical and operational risks, human resource risks, technology risks, credit and market risks, com-pliance risks and provisions for business continuity and disaster recovery. Board committees should be appointed to review significant risks facing the company, and the adequacy of the risk management system. The board should specifically consider whether there is a need for a confidential report-ing process ('whistle-blowing') for fraud and other risks.

The board must ensure that a systematic and documented assessment of processes and outcomes surrounding key risks is undertaken at least annually and that the results are included in a public statement on risk management. In this, the board must disclose its accountability for the risk management system, identify the risk review and internal control processes (in place also in respect of joint ventures and associated companies) to manage risk and maximize opportunities for the firm; as well as the sys-tems developed to allow it to continue its critical business processes in the event of a disaster. Effective risk management can be a source of competi-tive advantage, and boards can state this in their reports.

Risk management processes, the commission notes, are intended to provide reasonable, not absolute, assurances that risk is being effectively managed. If the board is unable to provide any of this information however, it must disclose this and explain the reasons.

3.3. Management's tasks

Management must communicate the firm's ethical values and philosophy, as determined by the board, to all employees, incorporate a comprehensive system-risk mitigation into the language and culture of the firm, and ensure that these processes are embedded in the daily activities of all employees. Risk must be assessed continuously and control activities appropriate to the risks assumed, must be identified and applied in ways that enable employees to act appropriately at all times. These controls must be reviewed by line management and the firm's insurers.

Risk management must build more robust business processes, ensuring that key risks are managed in a way that enhances the interests of shareholders and key stakeholders. Management must therefore deliver a system that ensures: the dynamic identification of risks; the creation of a register of key risks that could affect shareholder and stakeholder interests; an effective system of risk mitigation, appropriate to the firm's risk profile; a properly documented system of internal controls and management, including a risk communication process; and documentation of the costs of non-compliance.

Management's regular reports to the board on risk must give a balanced assessment of all significant risks, include any significant control failings or weaknesses, identify the impact of these and disclose the measures taken to correct the deficiencies.

So how should we behave?

In chapter 4 we shall discuss a number of techniques that enable companies to *identify, assess* and *manage* the risks (global or not) to which they are exposed.

CHAPTER 4

Defining and assessing risk

4.1. Risk identification

Companies categorize risks in several different ways, depending in part on the nature of their activities. As we saw in the first chapter, risks both manifest and are perceived in different ways, which means that the first question to ask when identifying a risk is: 'risk to whom?' While an investment bank certainly faces risks that differ from those that confront a retail chain; and a global oil and gas company has a different risk profile to that of an audit firm, a simple taxonomy or classification of risk is a useful point of departure if one's aim is to identify comprehensively and assess the risks to which a company is exposed. Risk management entails managing the firm's exposure in all areas of its activities; shareholders suffer equally whether financial collapse follows from a failure to protect against a threat in one class or another, whether it originates from the competitive environment of business or the conflationary effects of a number of global risks. Best practice requires companies to provide for business continuity and disaster recovery in respect of all risks that they identify.

There are a number of different ways of classifying risks, and most overlap. One recent UK list includes financial, strategic, program and project, operational, environmental, technological, brand, reputation, talent and personal risks.[1] For the sake of simplicity, we suggest that all risks faced by every business can be aggregated into four distinguishable but overlapping categories:

- **Strategic risks** threaten the firm's survival or its ability to sustain profitable business activity and shareholder-value creation; and may arise from changes in the market environment, or natural or man-made external hazards.
- **Financial risks** comprise threats to solvency, profitability and liquidity, and may arise from market price movements (e.g. in currencies, interest

rates, insurance premiums, share prices, hedges, options or other derivatives), counterparty failure, settlement delays or other similar events.

- **Operational risks** arise from failures in operational effectiveness or service delivery in the ordinary course of the firm's operations and trading; and are due primarily to inadequate internal processes and systems, or ineffective responses to external challenges.
- **Project risks** arise within the scope of distinct programs or projects and typically comprise risks involving technology, human behavior, unfamiliar processes and external threats.

One can visualize these four categories as different layers Figure 4.1. A good risk-management system will address the risks in all layers in a comprehensive, systemic manner.

Every company faces risks in each of these four groups and will need to develop a more comprehensive classification system that builds on the basics. The following figure, Figure 4.2, while in no sense complete, may help in understanding how to proceed. It reflects the core categories, gives examples of some risks in each, and lists examples of risk mitigation and management measures for each class. Each company must develop an extensive risk register detailing the risks to which it is exposed in these areas.

Global risks can impact on a firm in any of these four categories. Most often, those risks that we identify at a global level[3] trigger outcomes that are specific to the firm and which may pose strategic, financial, operational or project risks to it. A few examples will suffice to make the point. Market risks and country risks for a firm may be engendered by macro-events,

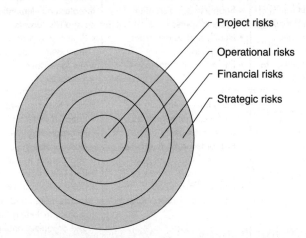

Project risks
Operational risks
Financial risks
Strategic risks

Figure 4.1 The risk universe of the firm – Four layers of risks

Main risk categories	Examples	Main Mitigation Measures
Strategic risk – threatening the firm's ability to sustain profitable business activity and shareholder value creation	• Political shocks, e.g. nationalization • Strategy or business intelligence failures, e.g. poor acquisitions, marketing failures, discontinuities in technology, customer preferences or competitive landscape • External shocks, e.g. pandemics, terrorism	Hard to predict and quantify; more sophisticated companies address strategic risk through: • Environmental scanning, scenario development; and simulations • Effective strategic management integrating key stakeholders • Development of strategic responses to each alternative scenario
Financial risk – risks pertaining to solvency, profitability and liquidity	• Market risk o Currencies o Interest rates o Commodity prices o Equity prices • Liquidity risk • Counterparty credit risk • Country risk o Sovereign risk o Political risk o Economic risk o Transfer risk o Exchange risk • Neighborhood risk	• Use of derivative instruments to hedge;[2] securitization • Standby arrangements • Rating agencies; credit terms • Published materials; rating agencies; specialized consultants; insurance; escrow accounts
Operational risk – failures of operational effectiveness or service delivery in the firm's operations and trading; due to inadequate internal processes or ineffective responses to external challenges.	• Product recall • Customer dissatisfaction • IT or plant failure • Supply chain disruption • Labor disputes • Health and safety issues • Talent loss • Environmental damage	Hard to predict and quantify and often neglected, but poor management of operational risks threatens all elements of a company's success • Project and process management approaches • Human resource development • Insurance
Project risk – risks within specific projects, involving technology, human behavior, unfamiliar processes and external threats	• Cost/time overruns – and dysfunctional responses under pressure • Risk of technology failure • Human behavioral risks • Risk of failure of new or modified processes • External environmental risks	Project Management • Effective strategic planning, incorporating internal and external stakeholders, and appropriate use of scenarios and simulations • Close monitoring of all key factors within and around the project, including behavioral and organizational dimensions

Figure 4.2 The risk universe of the firm – The four layers unpacked

whether economic (financial volatility due to market reaction to the twin deficits in the United States, or commodity price falls in the event of a hard landing of the Chinese economy) or political (the rise of populist policies in one or more countries, which can entail sovereign, political, economic, transfer or exchange risks for firms doing business in such countries or even with suppliers, partners or customers who are located there). Supply-chain disruption, a critical operational risk in the light of complex, ultra-long supply chains, can be triggered by many events outside the immediate market environment of the firm, including terrorist acts, pandemics and weather related or other natural catastrophes. Likewise, no firm can afford to underestimate the external dimensions of project risk. One of the greatest projects of the decade, the Sakhalin-2 project to be undertaken by Shell with Mitsubishi and Mitsui at a cost of more than $20 billion, is at risk as we write. The threat to revoke the environmental permit because of alleged violations, flows from the Kremlin's decision to force Shell to cede control to the Russian energy champion, Gazprom. Mr Putin's desire to use Russia's powerful leverage as a major source of oil and gas, both in global terms, and for Western Europe in particular, to restore Moscow's status as a global superpower is the source of the threat to the foreign investors. Global oil and gas companies have to grapple today with rising protectionism in tight energy markets, where the balance of power has shifted to national champions and barriers to cross-border takeovers are bring erected.

While some companies rely on their own staff, particularly those in the division that deals with each issue, to identify the risks to which they are exposed, smarter firms develop wider horizons without losing focus. One must never forget the cognitive limitations and heuristic and neuro-emotional distortions discussed in chapter 2 to which we are all subject. Relying exclusively on corporate insiders, especially an executive management team with similar mindsets and a propensity to defer to a strong CEO, is not a smart way to cover all bases. Seeking out information from alternative sources, involving experts and selected stakeholders in key discussions, and using techniques like scenario-building, can contribute to a more enlightened view.

We shall return to the examples of different ways to mitigate and manage risk in the next chapter. First we must find a way of quantifying those we have identified.

4.2. Quantifying the risk: Risk assessment

All risks are not equal. An effective risk management system is thus based on an understanding of the *extent* of the risk to which the firm is exposed in each case, the *circumstances* in which it may emerge and the *consequences* if it does. Only then can managers develop effective mitigation, management and containment strategies to deal with the hazards.

There is a good, old-fashioned saying that *we can only manage what we can measure*. This implies that we need a *risk assessment* methodology that we can use across all risk areas; that is easily understood; and that provides some guidance as to how the risks should be managed. As boards bear responsibility for reviewing and approving the risk-management strategies that corporate officers put in place, the need for transparency and relative simplicity is evident.

To develop an effective risk assessment, management needs to agree:

- The time horizon over which the firm should consider its exposure
- The means it will employ to reflect on how events will unfold
- An easily understandable *risk metric* – the unit(s) used to gauge exposure to risk
- A benchmark – the point of comparison against which the firm can measure its performance.

The metric and the other components of the assessment should be understood by all decision makers in the firm. While this may seem obvious, a survey of leading companies by McKinsey in 2002, reported that 36 percent of the directors surveyed, acknowledged that they did not understand the major risks their businesses faced. A further 24 percent said their board processes for overseeing risk management were ineffective and 19 percent confessed that their boards had no processes at all.[4] There is plenty of anecdotal evidence to suggest that not all that much has changed in many companies.

Some industries, notably the financial sector, are ahead of the curve in developing robust risk-management processes. Others, like companies in the energy sector, are particularly skilled in dealing with geopolitical and health and safety hazards. Some other companies in industries like engineering and construction are less advanced, with some only having appointed risk officers five years ago, or even less.

In risk assessment, different forms of quantitative and qualitative techniques are used. More often than not, *quantitative* modeling is complemented by *qualitative* analysis for risks that are less suited to formal modeling. As shown in Figure 4.2, strategic, operational and certain classes of project risks are particularly difficult to assess with quantitative techniques. Scenarios and simulations can be helpful adjuncts to normal business planning when we seek to explore the many different ways in which the future may unfold. These techniques do not offer precision; they are explicitly *not* forecasts, but they help to open the minds of boards and managers and allow them to plan more effectively for uncertain futures. We shall look further at scenario techniques later in this chapter.

The core benefit of quantitative risk-assessment tools is *pricing risk* properly, but, as we know, numbers can never define risk exactly. Measuring risk accurately is one of the toughest challenges that managers face. Four simple diagrams will make this clear.

Risk is usually quantified by considering two elements: the *probability* of a threatening event occurring, and the *impact* – usually expressed in terms of the financial impact[5] and the opportunity cost – if it does. The following matrix, Table 4.1, used by a mining company created to undertake a new project, illustrates the general approach. Here both probability and impact are considered in relation to a ten-point scale, with the meaning of each set of numbers described for each. So, if the project team rates the probability of an event as 4, the members are saying that it is moderately probable that the event will occur, while a rating of 9 indicates that it is almost certain that it will. Likewise, an impact of 3 suggests an event, whatever the probability of its occurrence, that poses no substantial threat to the project or to the company, as its impact can be absorbed without high cost and addressed through normal management practices. On the other hand, an event assessed as having an impact of 9 will place the company at risk of closure, forcing it to fight for survival.

Figure 4.3 illustrates the base case when probability and impact are considered together to assess risk exposure. The area marked in dark – defined by high probability and high impact – is the *high risk* area; that in brown is

Table 4.1 Quantifying probability and impact – An indicative approach

Probability	Index	Impact
Extremely low to low	1 2 3	Capable of being absorbed without high cost – (through normal management practice)
Moderate to high	4 5 6 7	High cost – (certain events may lead to withdrawal of limited numbers of expatriate staff)
Very high to certain	8 9 10	Extremely high cost – (causes company to fight for survival; at risk of closure)

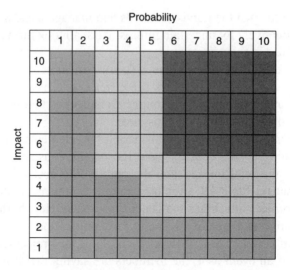

Figure 4.3 Assessing risk – A first cut

the area of *medium risk*; and the area marked in green, that of *low risk*. One should note that in this base case, high-impact risks with relatively low probabilities, and low-impact risks with high probabilities are both said to translate into *medium risks*.

This may be true in principle, but life is not that simple. First, assessing the probability of events occurring in the future is not an exact science. Second, this aggregated approach does not tell us much about what to manage or mitigate, nor how to do so most effectively. The base case is no more than a point of departure for a more systematic analysis.

The difficulty of assessing both *probability* and *impact* – but especially the former – is, at least in principle, associated with the *volatility* of the threatening event, or the environment that bears a causal relationship to that event. We can illustrate the impact on the risk profile in Figure 4.4.

This suggests that we need to temper our initial assessment of the level of risk – here defined as *inherent risk*, and assessed on the basis of *probability x impact* – with an assessment of the *volatility* of the environment that can influence either the probability of the event occurring, or the impact it will have if it does. The metaphor, in chaos theory, of the beating of the butterfly's wings in one ocean, causing a storm half a world away, is a case in point. We are also all familiar with the notion of the *perfect storm*, the conjunction of a number of events, none of which would be unmanageable if they occurred alone, but which, in combination, unleash devastation.

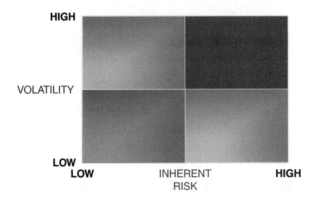

Figure 4.4 The impact of volatility

In simple terms, high inherent risk associated with high volatility poses exceptional danger; while risk that has been assessed as inherently moderate can pose threats in conditions of high volatility, that are as great as high inherent risk in less volatile environments. This is in effect what Long Term Capital Management discovered in the autumn of 1998, despite the sophistication of the firm's models.

Formulaic approaches to risk assessment can only take us so far. Risk can only be assessed in context, and the context will always be multidimensional. One way of expanding our thinking about how to assess risk is to factor in the dimension of time. As we have seen from our brief discussion of volatility, both the probability of a risk materializing and its impact when it does will vary over time. This is true even in comparatively stable environments: The impact of an event forcing the abandonment of a large capital project will be far greater at the point at which 90 percent of the loan facility has been drawn down and all the equity invested than it will be before construction has begun. Figure 4.5 illustrates how managers need to think about assessing their risk exposure over time. For the sake of simplicity, we have used only a four-point scale, instead of a ten-point one in the figure.

If the project team estimates and records the probability of each risk emerging at different periods across the duration of the project, we might see a landscape like the one at Figure 4.5a. Similarly, an estimation of the severity of the impact if the risk materializes, might produce a landscape like that at Figure 4.5b.

The team assessing the risks associated with the project not only has to assess its risk profile when the project is initiated, but also to ensure that

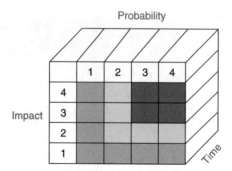

Figure 4.5   Both probability and impact vary over time

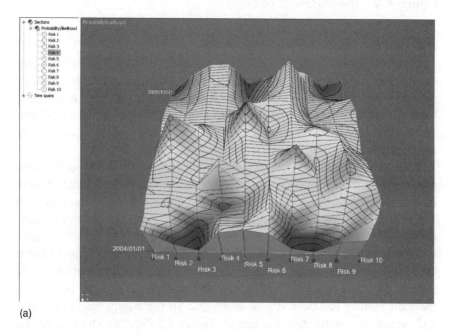

(a)

Figure 4.5a   Variation in probability of ten different risks over the duration of the project

both the probability and impact of each event have been assessed over an appropriate period. To take the example of a large project once again, appropriate intervals might be the end of the planning phase, the commencement of construction, the point at which 30, 50, 80 and 100 percent of the required capital has been drawn down, the commencement of operations and the expected point at which all capital invested has been amortized.

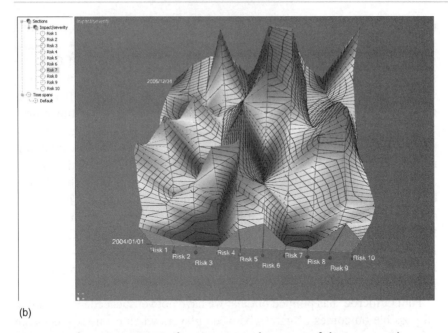

(b)

Figure 4.5b Variation in the anticipated impact of the same risks over the duration of the project

Just as important as making this initial assessment is subjecting it to continuous review. Both one's expectations and the measures one decides on when the initial assessment is undertaken may prove inadequate if circumstances change. If the review was rigorous and the individual biases and heuristics of the members of the team were tempered by robust discussion that minimizes herd behavior, the initial assessment will be a good point of departure. But environments change and, especially in volatile circumstances such as those which drive exchange rate fluctuations, few can claim to be prescient. Depending on the expected volatility of the environment, one must set periods at which the risk assessment of the project, or the company, will be reviewed with all the rigor that went into its construction.

4.3. Risk assessment tools

4.3.1. Assessing global risks

This leads us to the question of how to think about *exogenous* risks – risks that are largely outside the control of the firm, as they derive from the external environment in which the firm must do business. As shown earlier, we encounter these risks in all four layers or classes of risk – *strategic, financial, operational* and *project* – identified in chapter 3, and there are many different ways of addressing them. The problem is that in complex environments, the possible permutations greatly exceed our ability to calculate or comprehend them. One example is sufficient to make this point.

Chess is a difficult game to play exceptionally well, but the possible permutations in a game are far fewer than those that confront large multinational companies, governments, or even many globally engaged individuals in their professional lives. There are only 64 squares on a chessboard, two players, 32 (16 each) pieces – 16 of which (the pawns) are identical – and the movements and capacity of each piece (king, queen, bishops, knights, rooks and pawns) are constrained by the same rules. One would imagine that the power of the computers available to us today would be more than sufficient to create a digital catalog of all possible permutations. But this is not the case.

Paul Ormerod[6] has pointed out that we have not yet succeeded in defining all possible outcomes of games between players when even *six* pieces are left on the board towards the end of a game. We have cataloged the permutations leading to victory or draws in all games involving five or fewer pieces, but we have an awfully long way to go until we have exhausted the universe of games involving 32 pieces.

Now consider the challenges facing a global company that does different types of business (say surface-, underground- and marine mining, mineral beneficiation, industrial manufacturing, supply chain management, marketing and sales, as well as the related corporate finance and treasury functions) in 60 countries, each with environments far more complex than a 64-square chessboard. The company is confronted with different corporate, labor, contract and private law systems in each country, as well as a number of different accounting systems, all of which must be responsibly aggregated into financial statements and prepared in line with the accounting standards required by the jurisdiction in which it is listed.

Let us assume that this company is listed (or does business) in the United States, and is therefore subject to the Sarbanes-Oxley law.[7] This means that the CEO and other officers signing the accounts must certify[8] that the quarterly and annual financial statements are correct and complete, and fairly and accurately reflect the company's financial condition and results, and that the internal risk controls required by the company to address the material risks to which it is exposed, are in place. This undertaking is made under sanction of the criminal law of the United States.

There are several different dimensions of the dilemma we have outlined.

- First, no human being, not even the CEO of a Fortune Global 500 company, can know personally that the statement he (or she) is required to make under the Sarbanes-Oxley law, is accurate. All that he can know is that everything reasonably possible has been done to ensure compliance. As Professor Steve Kobrin of the Wharton School of Business observed at the annual meeting of the World Economic Forum in January 2004, while compliance can be required by law, it is dependent for execution on a supportive culture within the firm. What a legislation like Sarbanes-Oxley does is require that firms look more closely at all areas of the business, document what is taking place and thus provide a structured audit trail, and enable management to follow up and correct deficiencies. How successful this is depends on the capability, commitment and integrity of management.
- Second, firms must grapple with mounting complexity due to the increasing interconnectedness of the environments in which they operate. One cannot assess everything, so it is essential to try to know what matters. One good way to determine what matters is to use the power of networks. Good networks (i.e. networks composed by thought leaders with a broad range of insights and opinions) can give access to high quality analysis of many critical issues and prevent risk managers fall in into one of the greatest traps to which we are all prone: *group thinking*, which often leads to myopia, tunnel vision and denial. Networks constitute the best organizational response to the challenge of complexity.

Country risk indicators

Because they operate across the world, most global companies begin their assessments of the risks potentially associated with new investments in countries outside the OECD,[9] with *country risk indicators*, which are readily available from several rating agencies,[10] but are of varying quality. Typically, such reports consider political risk, macroeconomic risk, external economic risk and commercial risk, premised on a review of the trade and investment environments. The Dun & Bradstreet country risk indicators are defined as follows:

Political risk – internal and external security situations, policy competency and consistency, and other factors that determine whether a country fosters an enabling business environment.

Macroeconomic risk – the inflation rate, government balance, money supply growth, and all such macroeconomic factors that determine whether a country is able to deliver sustainable economic growth and a commensurate expansion in business opportunities.

External economic risk – the current-account balance, capital flows, foreign-exchange reserves, size of external debt and all such factors that determine whether a country can generate enough foreign exchange to meet its trade and foreign investment liabilities.

Commercial risk – the sanctity of contract, judicial competence, regulatory transparency, degree of systemic corruption and other factors that determine whether the business environment facilitates the conduct of commercial transactions.[11]

The Economist Intelligence Unit (EIU) also offers a country risk service which it describes as a quantitative rating of the risk of doing business in each country. This is based on a few factors:

Political risk outlook – analysis of the threat to political stability from factors such as war, social unrest and political violence;

Economic outlook – analysis of the state of government finances, economic growth and domestic financial indicators;

External finance and credit risk – analysis of the country's external financial position, including the current account, external borrowing, debt-servicing requirements and foreign-exchange reserves;

Specific investment risk ratings – assessment of the risk of investing in particular classes of financial instruments;

Two-year forecasts – in which variables are projected to a two-year forecasting horizon; and

Statistical appendices – up to 180 economic variables used in the country risk analysis, to provide a seven-year historical data sequence.

The EIU likewise offers a *credit* risk model which addresses the current account, debt structure, exchange rate policy, liquidity, monetary policy, fiscal policy, growth, savings, trade policy, regulatory policy, political efficacy, political stability and global climate. The EIU gives its credit risk assessment across 100 countries every month and claims to catch deteriorating or improving trends before the ratings agencies issue formal warnings. Its analysts are country experts who typically cover two or three countries in a region, while an employee at a rating agency will cover many more. In distinguishing its offering, the EIU states that its ratings are not commissioned and paid for by governments, unlike those of the rating agencies.[12]

Political risk reviews[13] typically assess the government, social elements, security and key aspects of the economy, in order to index national stability. The Deutsche Bank Eurasia Group Stability Index (DESIX) defines these factors as follows:

Government – such as strength of current government, rule of law and level of corruption;
Society – such as social tension, youth disaffection, and health education and other services;
Security – such as level of globalization, geostrategic condition, emergencies and disasters; and
Economy – such as fiscal condition, growth and investment, external sector and debt.[14]

Not surprisingly, given the difficulty of covering anything between 100 and 200[15] countries on a continuous basis, some reports – especially those not closely focused on particular classes of risk – are inaccurate and misleading. Many reports are useful means of tracking developments in countries in which a company has investments, or is considering investing,[16] but most are of little use in assessing the risk the external environment poses to a particular project. There are several reasons for this:

- **Inaccuracy of country data**

One should not underestimate the difficulty of collecting accurate economic data and sociopolitical information in many underdeveloped countries. If the data on which the model is based are inaccurate, the outputs of the model are inherently flawed.

- **Aggregation conceals the important information**

Rendering the outputs of complex circumstances (government, society, security and the economy, in the case of the DESIX) in the form of simple numbers – e.g. 62 as the Cumulative National Stability Score for India in March 2005,[17] invites what Maurice Tempelsman once described as the *bikini effect* – 'disclosing what is interesting, while concealing what is vital.' One needs the detail to assess risk to a project in most cases, *not* the index. Composite indices conceal vital differences between countries,[18] and can invite both overreaction and complacency, instead of encouraging diligent enquiry.

- **Impact depends both on the nature of the event and of the project**

Many examples can be cited, but one may be sufficient: Violent crime is a factor affecting business risk, but its probable impact on a car rental agency is very different to that on an advertising agency. A variation on this theme is the impact of distance. Lubumbashi, in the Katanga province of the Democratic Republic of the Congo is equidistant from Kinshasa, the capital of the DRC; and Pretoria, the capital of the Republic of South Africa; although Zimbabwe and Zambia lie between Lubumbashi and Pretoria. Due to the abominable state of the roads in the DRC, however, it is far easier to travel from Pretoria to Lubumbashi than it is to get there from Kinshasa. Although 'the widest interstate war in modern African history'[19] raged in the eastern areas of the DRC between 1998 and 2003, and even, in the early phases, in the capital, it never reached Katanga; and mining operations in that province continued on a limited scale throughout. The threats to these operations were government incapacity, debilitated infrastructure and supply chain disruptions, not war or even civil disorder.

4.3.1.1. Project-risk assessment

The most useful way of assessing and managing risk in *projects* is to use the *critical success factors* (*CSFs*) of the project as the drivers of the risk assessment. Achievement of the CSFs means success with the project; the frustration of any leads to failure. As a result, it is only those elements in the *external environment* that may lead to a failure to achieve the CSFs that are of concern in developing a risk assessment and a risk management framework. This helps define what matters, and narrows down what the project team and the company management need to consider.

A sensible approach to project-risk management thus begins with defining the CSFs for the project; then, in conjunction with country and regional specialists, identifying those elements in the external environment (political,[20] economic, social, technological, legal or environmental) that may frustrate their achievement. Building on these interactions, the team:

- defines the potential threats to the project from each;
- quantifies the probability of their emergence and the impact of each threat if it materializes;
- defines the consequences for the project if this occurs; and
- determines the appropriate risk mitigation or management strategy for each significant risk.

This gives a practical, useful profile of the risks associated with the project, enabling the board to decide whether to proceed and making possible sensible decisions about the blend of management and insurance strategies necessary to ensure success. It can also reduce the costs of *debt* and *political and commercial risk insurance* associated with projects.

Many otherwise viable projects in emerging markets are not undertaken because the cost of debt and political and commercial risk insurance make it impossible to generate NPVs[21] at or above the corporate hurdle rate. Equity investors require high NPVs to offset high perceived risk; lenders charge high margins above LIBOR[22] and insurers load premiums for the same reason.

Far less investment thus occurs in many emerging markets than would be possible if risk were more accurately assessed and priced. Sub-Saharan Africa, for example, attracted less than 2 percent of global foreign direct investment flows in the 1990s, but the projects in which these funds were invested, produced returns averaging 25 percent. This is not an anomaly; aggregate returns of this order are necessary to cover the high cost of debt and insurance premiums in projects with long payback periods, while still meeting the hurdle rate for investment.

If the debt and insurance premiums for viable projects in emerging markets are reduced – by *analyzing, assessing* and *managing the external risk* associated with potential projects effectively – more projects will go ahead with less exposure to risk for investors, lenders and insurers. Higher transaction volumes will offset the loss of revenue to banks and insurers as a result of lower margins, while the risk profile of the lending (or insurance) book will be improved, as institutions better understand the nature of the risks they undertake.

This methodology encourages project managers and corporate overseers, lenders and insurers to gain a common understanding of the external risk profile, and enables the project team to eliminate certain classes of risk, mitigate others, layoff those with high potential impact but a low probability of occurrence and manage, directly, or through subcontractors, those that must be assumed if the project is to succeed.

Once the project risk profile has been determined, regular, systematic risk reviews with project personnel and corporate management can ensure that changes in the external environment are observed, their potential impact on the project assessed, and the necessary adjustments made to risk management strategies and procedures. This also allows full transparency toward bankers and insurers.

4.3.2. Quantitative tools for risk assessment

Yet not all risks can be assessed or managed in this way. Financial risks, especially those deriving from portfolios of assets, need different techniques. Quantitative tools are essential in this area. Even though such tools cannot accurately price each risk, they foster rigorous thinking about risk if they are used well, and help senior business executives and boards to identify and understand the major risk drivers. As we said at the beginning of this chapter, risk management is not only about addressing the underlying risks, but also about understanding the links between them: Some risks offset one another, others are unrelated to each other and some compound others. An awareness of the intertwined aspects of risk and the way different risks aggregate, diversify or diminish our combined exposure is a prerequisite to making intelligent management decisions, and to challenging current assumptions where necessary.

Quantitative techniques also provide a common language that allows business executives, board members and others to communicate more clearly and understand each other's appetite for risk. They help senior executives rank and prioritize risks and focus on those most likely to affect the business.

An extensive discussion of the quantitative tools available to corporate finance departments and insurers to assess (and manage) risk is beyond the scope of this book, but a brief review of some of the most important categories will be helpful.

4.3.2.1. Sensitivity analysis

Sensitivity analysis is one of the simplest ways to evaluate risk. One uses it to examine how sensitive each value dimension is to one risk driver. Let's consider an investment banker specializing in mergers and acquisitions (M&A). He will develop an acquisition analysis with cross-sensitivities to two key drivers – the cost of capital and growth rates. A spread on the sensitivity analysis will make explicit the risks of the acquisition, such as the sensitivity of the price to growth assumptions. The simplicity of the method is also its drawback, however: sensitivity analyses give poor results when used to evaluate clusters of risks, or extreme risks.

4.3.2.2. Scenarios

Scenarios are not really quantitative tools, but are often used in conjunction with such tools to help make them become more robust in the context of future uncertainty. Scenarios are stories about plausible alternative futures. They help managers 'to get on top of what *might* happen, and to develop a better judgment of what this could mean, by working through the consequences of the different ways in which the business environment may change.'[23]

Scenarios are particularly useful in situations of uncertainty, when the extent of risks cannot be calculated on the basis of probabilities. This is especially true of complex and systemic risks, including those that are potentially global in scope. If decision makers use scenarios effectively, they are better able to judge reasonably whether the corporate strategy or a particular business decision will be robust across a range of possible futures. Business scenarios were first developed rigorously by Shell in the 1970s, at a time when oil-price forecasts had proved to be dismally off the mark as the old assumptions about *equilibria* between supply and demand had been turned on their heads by political developments in the Middle East. Uncertainty in an industry where investments are normally made over horizons of more than ten years required a different approach, and scenarios offered a solution.

Since then, scenarios have been used quite extensively in business[24] and in government, to both elucidate alternative futures and encourage particular outcomes. Both the US Defense Department and the US National Intelligence Council[25] have published long-range global scenarios, constructed after consultations with domestic and foreign experts. Shell has continued to make the outlines of its global scenarios available to the public,[26] and the Anglo American Corporation made extensive use of its 'High Road, Low Road' scenarios in South Africa in the mid-1980s to encourage South Africans of all political persuasions to understand that a managed transition could bring about a better future. Likewise, the Mont Fleur scenario project undertaken[27] in 1991–2 with a ten-year view toward 2002, contributed to the transition to democracy in South Africa with its four scenarios – *Ostrich, Lame Duck, Icarus* and *Flight of the Flamingos*. The Global Business Network[28] offers scenario services to companies across the globe.

Scenarios are good at encompassing multiple and extreme risks, but the efficacy of the technique is dependent on the quality of the assumptions the team makes about key drivers and key uncertainties. Algorithmic tools have been developed to facilitate structured thinking in scenario development, including the *Situation Analysis* and *Option Development* tools in the *Eidos* suite developed by the Parmenides Foundation,[29] but the quality of knowledge, insight and judgment brought to the exercise by the participants is the most important determinant of success. Finally, the real value of scenarios lies in understanding the implications of each scenario for the business and in ensuring that business strategies and risk management programs are robust against all scenarios. As Peter Schwartz, the Chairman of the Global Business Network, once said, 'the objective of good scenarios is not to make better predictions, but better decisions.' A few illustrative scenarios addressing global challenges are included in appendices 1 and 2.

4.3.2.3. Simulations or 'war-gaming'

Simulations are an effective way of developing an understanding of a company's ability to deal with systemic risks and of testing its resilience to them. Simulations use mock crises to evaluate how prepared business executives are to face serious business discontinuities. Structured exercises take place over one or two days and involve a series of simulated crises testing the reactions and resilience of critical components, or units, of a business. One group, often specialized consultants from outside the company, makes a series of moves while company officers respond in real time. Vulnerabilities are exposed and risk mitigation strategies elaborated. The great value of simulations is to generate ideas which participants did not have before the game started and to uncover solutions that were not previously obvious. The best-known quantitative application of this technique is the *Monte Carlo* simulation.

Monte Carlo simulation[30]

This is a much-used series of statistical sampling techniques used to approximate solutions to quantitative problems, relying on the ability of a computer to make millions of complex calculations exceedingly fast. As with many rolls of the dice, this technique generates random numbers to simulate possible outcomes. If the parameters are properly defined, the distribution of outcomes will plausibly simulate those that might occur in the 'real world.' In a simple trading strategy, the technique would identify two interdependent elements – a stock index and a bond index – and two random variables – an interest rate and an exchange rate. Running the simulation enables the analyst to understand how a mixed portfolio of bonds and equities will perform in circumstances determined by the movements of the two variables.

Monte Carlo simulations complement scenarios by combining hundreds of probability-weighted scenarios and engendering single outcomes. Although Monte Carlo is not subject to dimensionality,[31] its accuracy is affected by sample size. Increasing the sample size will reduce the standard error of a Monte Carlo analysis[32] but demands enormous computational resources. Variance reduction techniques, which incorporate additional information about the analysis directly into the estimator, make the estimator more deterministic and reduce the standard error more efficiently.

The main advantage of Monte Carlo simulations is clarity of outcome, but the parameters must be carefully calculated and the assumptions cannot easily be queried by management or board members. The underlying assumption, however, is that paths are linear and outcomes continuous. This is a very bold – and often inaccurate – assumption suggesting that the future will be like the past! Despite this, they are a valuable tool in the risk manager's toolkit.

Calculation of Value at Risk

Value at Risk (VaR), popularized by the investment bank J P Morgan in 1994 with the release of its *RiskMetrics*, has become a much-used software tool by which financial institutions and trading organizations measure their exposure to potential losses. VaR describes the market risk of a trading portfolio. It goes beyond an historical review and assesses the market risk to which the portfolio is exposed at that time. To manage risk, institutions must understand risks while they are being taken. If a trader miscalculates a hedge on his portfolio, his supervisor must know this before a loss is incurred. VaR quantifies market risk while it is being taken.

By assessing the probability of a certain level of loss or profit, VaR calculates how much money – value – is at risk in a bank or a firm at a given moment for a given period. The virtue of VaR is to reduce risk exposure to an easily digestible number, but like most quantitative methods of this sort, it hides many layers of risks behind the number. Consider this counterintuitive case: in certain circumstances, a desk trading Argentinean debt could come up with the same VaR figure as a desk trading US equities! Even the least seasoned market player will know that the risks of Argentinean bonds are very different to those of US equities. The similarity to the problem of comprehensive indices discussed under *country risk indicators* is apparent.

Valuation based on real options[33]

Real options extend financial options theory – based on binomial option pricing models epitomized by the Black-Scholes model – to nonfinancial business activities. A *real option* is a right, but not an obligation, to take a business decision, typically to make a capital investment. The opportunity to invest in a new factory is a real option, and once the decision has been made, the option to expand it, or link it into a different value chain, is another real option. In contrast to financial options, a *real option* is not tradeable – the company owning the factory cannot sell the right to extend it to another party.

Real options are a complement to the traditional discounted cash flow (DCF) method of valuing companies. The value of a company operating in uncertain markets can best be assessed by blending a DCF analysis of the value of the known businesses with an estimate of the portfolio value of its *real options*. In a paper in 1999, Credit Suisse First Boston analyst Michael Mauboissin, suggested that '[this] real option (value) can be estimated by taking the difference between the current equity value and the DCF value for the established businesses.'[34] He argued that real options thinking was most important where there were smart managers looking for new opportunities in market leading companies operating in markets 'where change is most evident.'

In Black-Scholes, the drivers of option value, in the most condensed form, are (i) the current price of the asset underlying the option, (ii) the strike price of the option, (iii) the time to expiry of the option, (iv) the prevailing risk-free interest rate and (v) the risk variance of the underlying asset. Timothy Leuhrman[35] offers real investment corollaries for these: (i) present value of the project's free cash flow, (ii) expenditure needed to acquire the project assets, (iii) time for which the decision may be deferred, (iv) the time value of money and (v) the riskiness of the project assets.

From management's perspective, the value of the *real options* approach lies in focusing on the options that are available and what is needed to create them; and understanding how and why option values change and how to capture their value. Seen from an investor's perspective, real options thinking demands a greater focus on business *potential*, rather than slavish reliance on NPV calculated from discounted cash flows. Mauboissin has argued that this approach explains the disparities between DCF valuations and the stock price of certain companies.

While this view has obvious merit, the pitfalls became abundantly clear in 1999 and 2000 during the *dot.com boom*. Companies with no value, according to traditional valuation methods, were assessed by analysts and the markets as having potential that justified price-earnings ratios in excess of 200. Not surprisingly, this 'irrational exuberance,' to use US Federal Reserve chairman Alan Greenspan's celebrated phrase, led to a market crash and the demise of most of these companies.

There is nothing surprising about the fact that models fail. As we showed in chapter 2, humans often do not behave the way rational models suggest they should. But the complexity of the working of the markets themselves brings a further challenge. Reflecting on the level of our understanding of the workings of financial markets, the 1973 Nobel Prize-winning economist Wassily Leontief, made a startling observation that in no field of empirical enquiry, he said, has so massive and sophisticated a statistical machinery been used with such indifferent results.

Perhaps even more remarkably, Benoit Mandelbrot[36] and Richard Hudson have cited Leontief's comment in a new book on *The (Mis)Behaviour of Markets*.[37] In an open letter to Alan Greenspan, chairman of the US Federal Reserve and Securities and Exchange Commission chairman William Donaldson, Mandelbrot has called for a major investment in 'fundamental research into the workings of financial markets' and in a financial risk management model that takes into account long-term dependency, or the tendency of bad news to come in waves.

> Even the most cursory glance at the economics literature will yield a perplexing cacophony of opinions – and more invidious – contradictory 'facts.' Consider one example. Proposition: Share prices are dependent over (a) a day, (b) a quarter, (c) three years, (d) an infinite span, or (e) none of the above. All these views have been presented as unassailable in countless articles reviewed by countless worthy peers, and supported by countless computer runs, probability tables and analytical charts.[38]

It is clear that we have a long way to go before certainty and predictability replace uncertainty in financial planning.

CHAPTER 5

Mitigating risk

Recognizing what we do not know, is the beginning of wisdom, and, of course, gaps in our knowledge universe are not an excuse for doing nothing. We are all familiar with the problem of *paralysis by analysis*. So what is a CEO to do? The first thing is to recognize that we know quite a lot, and to use that as a point of departure; the second is to build a capability to continue learning about what we do not know yet. Myopia and tunnel vision – failures to keep scanning what is happening outside the firm and its immediate market environment – is a recipe for decline, if not disaster. Think about the failure of Apple and Xerox, both of whom had enormous early-mover advantages in ground-breaking new technologies, to capitalize on those advantages. Microsoft's success is due, in no small measure, to its acquisition of DOS from IBM, and its mimicry and scaling of Apple's extraordinary 'point and click' operating systems and related graphic user interfaces; Apple is left with under 4 percent of the PC market.[1]

In chapter 4 we concentrated on correctly identifying the risks to which the company is exposed, and assessing the probability of these risks materializing, and their impact if they do. The aim, of course, is to be able to act intelligently to avert the risks or to mitigate their impact, either by laying them off through insurance or related instruments, or by managing them successfully. As we saw in chapter 3, boards and the managers that report to them have clearly defined obligations to the companies they manage, and to the shareholders whose funds are at risk in their ventures.

It would be a foolhardy chief executive, who, entrusted with running a complex business in many legal jurisdictions, decides to assume responsibility for managing all risks that a robust identification and assessment process had identified. Insurance-related instruments are thus vital in providing cover for factors that are entirely outside of a company's control. International exchange rates are a case in point, where the assumption that one knows the future smacks of hubris.

5.1. Insurance – The sound principle of risk sharing

The risk of future loss is why insurance exists. Insurance allows companies or individuals that do not wish to assume particular risks to pay a premium so that someone else carries the risks they do not want to bear. Insurance does not reduce the losses incurred if the insured event occurs, but it spreads their financial impact by enabling those at risk to pay a relatively small premium to secure protection against the risk of a large loss that has a small chance of occurring. For a risk to be insured, it has to be spread across many parties, so that the part that any one bears is negligible. The simple yet highly effective idea behind the principle of insurance is the *pooling* of risks. It is based on the law of large numbers, which has two important properties:

- the larger the number of separate independent risks, the more reliable the actuarial assessment of the overall risk and
- the larger the number of people across whom the total burden can be spread, the smaller the burden on each individual.

By requiring that the risks insured be both large in number and independent of one another, insurers apply the *law of large numbers* to good effect. Without abundant data in the form of actuarial tables, corporate balance sheets, employment information, tax records, credit histories and much more, insurance as we know it today would not exist. Since the insurance premium depends on the degree of uncertainty surrounding insurable outcomes, uncertainties must be reduced to probabilities, enabling an understanding of how the age of a car (and those of its drivers) may contribute to the risk of an accident, and how a person's medical history may affect the likelihood of her incapacity of death from disease. Only past records and abundant data permit precision. The *law of large numbers* allows the effective estimation and pricing of insurable risk while the absence of reliable data or its poor quality prevents our hedging it effectively.

Purchasing insurance is different to purchasing any other good or service.[2] The buyer of an insurance policy gets the right to demand a payment from the insurer of a prearranged amount during a specific period, if a predetermined consequence befalls an insured person or object. This can apply to a car, a building, or the health or life of a person. If a car breaks down, a building collapses or a person dies, the insurance company will pay the agreed value of the loss incurred to the buyer of the insurance. But if the car does not break down, if the building does not collapse and if the policyholder lives beyond the term of the policy, no payment will be made. The person who bought the policy will be out of pocket to the extent of the premiums he paid and will collect nothing. This does not mean that these payments had no value for the person who paid the premiums; they represent the price paid for the security desired against the uncertainty of the damage arising. Insurance is, in fact, a hedge against uncertainty and resembles a range of other financial instruments we can use to hedge against potential losses in conditions of uncertainty.

5.1.1. Insurance and global risks

Many potential events that can properly be described as global risks[3] present unique challenges to the insurance industry due to the long time horizons involved and the uncertainty associated with defining the probability of the event occurring and the potential severity of its impact. Many extreme (or catastrophic) events[4] that we classify as global risks do not satisfy the two conditions that define a risk and make it insurable: the ability to identify it before the event and to quantify its probability and severity. We can distinguish between two classes of such risks to make the point: natural catastrophes, like earthquakes or hurricanes, and global terrorism.

Insurers have considerable seismic data and a fair amount of geological and related scientific insight available when considering how to price the risk of damage arising from an earthquake. The level of uncertainty rises when we move to tropical storms, not least because the atmosphere is more volatile than the earth's crust and longer term climatic changes, like global warming or cooling, may tend to influence their occurrence and severity. But we are still in a realm where estimates of probability and severity are possible and the most sophisticated insurers collect detailed information and undertake event-based risk analysis relying on satellite imaging. The difficulty in both these cases is that the scale of the damage wreaked by an earthquake or hurricane may give rise, in areas where insurance is in demand, to claims that would exceed the cover available in the insurance pool for that class of risk.

Natural disasters of great scale can have very serious consequences for insurance companies. Using a very large dataset on homeowners' insurance coverage for 1984–2004, Patricia Born and W. Kip Viscusi reported the effects in different U.S. states on losses and loss ratios of both unexpected catastrophes and very large events they style 'blockbuster catastrophes.'[5] Insurers adapt to catastrophic risks by raising insurance rates which results not only in lower loss ratios after the event but also in the reduction of the number of policies written and the total premiums earned in that state, and lead to the exit of insurers from the market. Not surprisingly, firms with low levels of premiums are most adversely affected as their risk is poorly distributed.

It is also the inherent uncertainty about the precise probability and impact of what are generally recognized as low probability, high impact events like earthquakes, nuclear power accidents and serious environmental spills, that cause actuaries to raise the premiums required by insurers to assume these risks. This can result in the failure of insurance markets to mitigate such risks sufficiently. The premiums demanded by the insurers may exceed the price that property owners are prepared to pay;[6] and insurers will not provide coverage unless they can set premiums for which there is sufficient demand to allow the firm to cover its costs and make a profit.

The situation is even more difficult in the case of terrorism: When we are dealing with natural catastrophes or man-made catastrophes like environmental pollution or nuclear accidents, the available data allow for some calculation. The geology of a region, for example, permits us to estimate the probability of an earthquake occurring and the population density, building standards and emergency response capability of the local authorities allow us to estimate the potential impact of earthquakes of different intensities in that area. Terrorism, however, offers few reference points. There is no certainty who will strike, where, in what way or with what instruments of destruction. Individuals may have opinions on all or any of these topics; intelligence agencies may receive indications that prompt the authorities to raise alert levels from time to time, but the information needed to price the risk with any degree of precision is absent.

The uncertainty about the probability and impact of such events makes them poor candidates for insurance cover. Risks associated with natural events: earthquakes and weather-related catastrophes (cyclones, typhoons and flooding) are insured, though even here, the private sector signals from time to time that it cannot provide coverage in the aftermath of a major event. The State of Florida had to establish the Florida Hurricane Catastrophe Fund after Hurricane Andrew wreaked havoc in the state and led some insurers to decline cover for windstorm damage under the standard homeowner insurance policies.[7] The State of California had to take a similar path after the Northridge earthquake in 1994; it created the California Earthquake Authority to offer homeowners earthquake cover under a separate policy.[8]

The complexities on the supply side are compounded by difficulties on the demand side. There is plenty of evidence to suggest that when insurance is available to protect against catastrophic risks, many people do not buy it: many people do not buy coverage because they believe that 'it won't happen to me.' We saw in chapter 2 that denial is often the approach adopted by people confronted with large risks. Most individuals and companies display little concern about the risk of natural catastrophes or man-made technological disasters before their occurrence. Howard Kunreuther[9] notes that this was the case with Hurricane Andrew, the Northridge earthquake, the Chernobyl nuclear plant meltdown and the Bhopal chemical explosion. Only after the event do they want cover, and then only for a certain period. Kunreuther notes that people often cancel their earthquake or flood insurance after a few years if they have not experienced any damage. In Louisiana for example, where the risk of flooding is real and flood insurance is heavily subsidized, the percentage of homeowners with such cover just before Hurricane Katrina struck, ranged from 7.3 percent to 57.7 percent across different counties.[10]

As a result, insured losses represent only a fraction of the economic damage inflicted in any given catastrophe: the ratio of economic losses to insured losses will be very high when there is a limited insurance market (and tending to the infinite when there is none). In the case of Hurricane Katrina which we discussed in chapter 1, the insured losses amounted to $45 billion while the total economic loss was estimated at $150–200 billion. This amount does not take account of the collateral damage caused by the cascading effects we described earlier. In the developing world, the ratio of economic loss to insured loss is much higher because there is far less insurance cover in place. The tsunami that devastated South Asia in December 2004 cost the insurance industry 'only' $5 billion because only the tourism facilities were insured. The death toll was more than 280,000!

Most other *global risks* are not directly insurable. Take examples like state failure, if the state in question is a major source of global hydrocarbon resources; a hard-landing of the Chinese economy; or the possibility that research might indicate in future that new technologies – or the electromagnetic effects of well established technologies like power transmission lines or cell phones – pose substantial health hazards. All these involve potentially very high impacts associated with uncertain probabilities.

The uncertainties surrounding climate change suggest, moreover, that some events that are insurable today may not be so some years hence. At the moment, cover is available for most weather-related catastrophes, at least in the developed world. But the complex interplay of forces in the global climate ecosystem makes the future inherently uncertain. What if gradually warming sea-surface temperatures, triggered by climate change, lead to hurricanes of such force and frequency that insurers can no longer provide cover even to those who are prepared to pay? John Coomber, former CEO of Swiss Re (now the world's largest reinsurer), observed: 'Climate change is the number one risk in the world, ahead of terrorism, demographic change and other global risk scenarios.'[11]

5.2. Other instruments to manage financial risk

The financial industry has developed the most sophisticated risk assessment and management tools, to the point that some risk models are now so complex that they are like black boxes, effectively impenetrable by people without the mathematical skills to interrogate the assumptions and the algorithms. Not surprisingly in the light of all we have seen up to this point, these complex risk models have become risks in themselves.

As we explain in appendix 1, financial management of risk has made great progress over the past 50 years. This has been compounded since the 1980s by the extraordinary increase in computing power. Today, many kinds of new financial instruments have extended the principle of insurance to a wide variety of specific risks, ranging from weather disasters to pension funds and mortgages, bringing the world closer to – but as we shall see later, not yet to the point of – the ideal of Kenneth Arrow: a world in which all risks could be insured. Arrow's Nobel Prize in economics in 1972 was for his work on an imaginary insurance company able to insure against any loss of any magnitude. If we could insure against every future possibility of a loss, he thought, people would be more willing to take risks, making economic progress possible everywhere.

5.2.1. Derivative instruments

In their incessant quest for novel and more effective tools of risk management, market players developed *derivatives*, which are perhaps the most sophisticated financial instruments yet conceived. Derivative instruments had existed for several centuries,[12] but it was the breakthrough in the late 1960s by Black, Merton and Scholes that made their widespread use possible. In an article published eventually, in 1973, in the *Journal of Political Economy* (after several rejections by other prestigious academic journals!), they presented an elegant formula which allowed the use of mathematics rather than intuition to price an option, making the latter dependent on four elements: time, prices, interest rates and volatility.[13]

Derivatives derive their value from some other asset, and as such have no independent value They enable us to hedge the risk of any underlying asset whose price is volatile: oil, wheat, a currency, a government bond, a share or common stock. Like insurance, derivatives do not reduce the risk, but allocate it from those who want to avoid it, to those who want to assume it. Derivatives come in many forms and can be easily unbundled. Their diversity and divisibility mean that almost every risk can be separated out, priced and resold to the buyer with the greatest appetite for *that* risk. Derivatives comprise two main classes: *futures* and *options*.

Futures are contracts for future delivery at a specific price: they give someone the opportunity to buy or sell an asset at a prearranged price. A market actor who sells a *future contract* passes the risk of lower prices to someone else: He may miss out on some margin if the asset price rises above the agreed price, but the contract will protect him from lower prices.

Options are a sophisticated variation of futures: dealers can buy options known as *calls* when they want insurance against rising prices, and can buy *put* options that give them the right to sell to the other side at a prearranged price, thereby insuring against falling prices.

5.2.2. Securitization

The principle of securitization is creating an investment vehicle – issuing a security – out of the pool of loans or bonds given to lenders, or issued by borrowers. The security will provide a yield commensurate with the performance of the asset pool, and will normally be layered into different levels of risks and rewards so that it can meet the expectations of investors with different risk appetites. The recent wave of securitization has broadened the universe of risk-taking and risk management by giving poorly rated companies the opportunity to access credit other than bank loans. Similarly, it has allowed risk-averse institutional investors (pension funds and mutual funds) to buy into the highest and most secure layer of the security – the so-called super-senior tranche that is the last to bear losses if the companies in the pool fail to honor their payments.

5.2.3. Alternative risk transfer instruments

Alternative risk transfer (ART) mechanisms provide parties who bear a risk with coverage that supplements traditional insurance. They comprise a range of instruments that transfer part of the exposure to investors in the capital markets. Because they were initially developed to give insurers and reinsurers extra capacity against catastrophic risks, they have been used to date to protect against events with low probabilities and extreme consequences.

Catastrophe Bonds ('Cat Bonds') are one of the better known instruments in this class. They are issued by insurance companies or reinsurers in the form of debt with high coupons, to enable them to access funds if a disaster produces a loss beyond a predetermined level. 'Sidecars,' a more sophisticated version of Cat Bonds, are an innovative instrument developed after Katrina to provide reinsurance cover exclusively to their sponsors, through debt issued to investors. They differ from Cat Bonds in that they require an investment of at least $200 million, are of a shorter duration and are based on quota-share reinsurance, while Cat Bonds provide access to a reinsurance pool only required if excessive losses are incurred. Between November 1995 and July 2006, hedge funds invested more than $3 billion in sidecars to cover natural disasters in North America.[14]

New products and new markets emerge continuously in the highly competitive financial services industry. Risk-transfer markets will undoubtedly expand dramatically in future and will offer new investment and risk management instruments to institutions and individuals alike. For example, in 2003 FIFA (the world football governing body) issued a bond to cover the risk of terrorism and natural disaster during the 2006 World Cup. Under tightly defined conditions, the $262 million bond protected FIFA's investment from losses arising from events that might lead to the cancellation of the World Cup without the ability to reschedule it to 2007.[15]

More generally, the recent securitization of longevity risk, the creation of mortality swaps and longevity derivative contracts and the expansion of weather derivatives are a testimony to the remarkable vibrancy of the capital markets. This does not mean that all risks will eventually become transferable. There is still a great deal to be done, despite the successes achieved. Even today, with the partial exception of the United States, there is no market available to hedge the important risk of housing prices falling precipitously. Most geopolitical risks are likewise uncovered. Similarly, in our aging world, there is no capital market means of hedging against the risk of rising health care risks. Confronted with the lack of instruments to insure or hedge against some of these most intractable risks, enterprises are left only with the power of resilience.

5.3. Enterprise resilience – The goal of risk management

Some 10 percent of the six million economically active companies in the United States – approximately 600,000 at present – disappear each year.[16] The primary aim of risk management is to ensure that a company's business goals will be achieved and its assets safeguarded; in other words, it will be resilient against shocks in the competitive environment, and will continue to grow and thrive. Insurance and the tools available to corporate finance departments to hedge risks work well for those risks that can be anticipated and priced reasonably accurately, but many exogenous risks do not fall into this category. In the interconnected world of today, moreover, the risk of disruption may arise from many different quarters: A terrorist attack in a major financial center, the outbreak of avian flu, the collapse of a failing oil-producing state, a strike in protest against the effects of globalization that blocks national exports (or imports from large multinational companies) at the border, the failure of a single supplier that disrupts the entire supply chain; anything and everything in an almost infinite variety of permutations can result in disruption. Hedging instruments to protect one against these types of risks are – and may always be – poorly developed. Dealing with risks like these means that companies have to develop exceptional qualities of *resilience*.

Resilience is 'the ability and capacity of the firm to withstand systemic discontinuities and adapt to new risk environments.'[17] In a nutshell, it is about bouncing back from shocks, including those triggered by catastrophic events. In chapter 1, we showed that in our highly interconnected, nonlinear and volatile world, relatively small disturbances can combine to produce large discontinuities that result in severe disruption of business. Outcomes are unpredictable. Let's take Hurricane Katrina again: who could have predicted that a Force 4 coastal storm, closely monitored for days in advance, would result in an oil price spike over $70, when the entire production of the rigs and refineries in the Gulf of Mexico is just 2 percent of global output? Who would have expected that the same tropical storm would lead to a sharp dip in the approval ratings of a US president and a series of complex reappraisals of US capacity and reputation around the world? In cases like these, cause and effect are often not linear or one-dimensional, and sharp shifts in apparently unrelated areas can occur suddenly when conditions reach a tipping point, making it impossible to predict the nature or timing of outcomes. In such a world, companies are confronted with uncertain probabilities and incalculable impacts; they operate in an *uncertain* environment, rather than one characterized only by calculable – and thus manageable – *risks*.

The impossibility of predicting outcomes in these cases results from the *power-law* distributions associated with nonlinear events. Companies, governments and individuals are not able to plan effectively in the context of these distributions, although we manage normal – bell-curve – distributions, which assume independence among the components of a system, quite well. Power laws were first described by the Italian economist Vilfredo Pareto in the late 19th century. Pareto observed that the distribution of wealth was not bell-shaped, with most people clustered around the mean and an exponentially smaller number being either very rich or very poor. Instead, he found, there was a predictable imbalance, with 20 percent of the population holding 80 percent of the wealth. In fact, power-law distributions are found in most human – and many other – systems.[18] They reflect the reality of website usage: a small number of sites attract a very large number of viewers, while hundreds of thousands of others are rarely used or viewed. In language, the frequency of word usage displays a power law pattern, with a small number of words being used very frequently, and a very large number of others much less often.

In our present context, power-law principles make clear that the events that drive history display no mean or normal distribution. Tens of millions of occurrences have no appreciable impact beyond their immediate sphere of influence; a small number of others, usually in unpredictable conjunctions, change almost everything. As we shall see in appendix 2, the divine visions of a man in his 40ss in a remote area of the Arabian Peninsula in the 7th century CE,[19] led to the emergence of a new civilization stretching from China and India across southern Europe and the Mediterranean, to Iberia and West Africa. Likewise, almost 600 years earlier, the crucifixion of a man thought to be the son of a carpenter from Nazareth, set in motion chains of disparate events that include the present military hegemony of the United States and its determination to encourage others to apply its cultural norms. The same principles explain the disproportionate and often unpredictable impact of extreme, low probability events like hurricanes, wars, acts of terrorism or pandemics. This has always been true throughout history. But the factors we discussed in our first chapter – the extraordinary degree of global interconnectedness, near instantaneous communication, time compression and volatility – that define the present, pose new challenges. The potential for *perfect storms* has increased greatly and businesses (as well as governments, individuals and associations) operating in this environment have to develop and apply qualities of resilience not earlier demanded. Engineering for resilience has become the heart of risk management.

Resilient companies learn to 'embrace paradox,' as Gary Hamel puts it. They are both cost-effective and innovative, display flexibility without fragility and 'preserve order amid change and ... change amid order.'[20] Resilience involves learning how to adapt from earlier shocks, so as to avoid new ones, or absorb them without undue disruption. It assumes a capacity to reorganize one's resources and take appropriate action to ensure survival and advancement after a threat has emerged. A well-known example of this is Johnson & Johnson's response to the poisoning of its Tylenol capsules. In 1982, Tylenol had 35 percent of the US over-the-counter analgesic market and delivered about 15 percent of the company's profits. After someone laced the drug with cyanide, seven people died, panic ensued and the company's market value fell by $1,000 million. Four years later, the same happened again, but the company had learned its lessons; it swiftly ordered the recall of Tylenol from every outlet and did not reintroduce it until tamperproof packaging had been developed.[21]

Moreover, resilience is created by developing the ability to anticipate trouble before it strikes, and having plans in place to address it immediately. In 2000, a small fire in a Philips Electronics plant in New Mexico delayed the delivery of radio frequency chips by several weeks. Nokia reacted immediately and secured alternative sources of supply from other Philips plants. By the time that Ericsson, which was slower off the mark, made the same request of Philips, there was no spare capacity left. Ericsson lost $400 million in sales.[22] We shall return to this example later because it is a perfect illustration of the many qualities needed to successfully deal with global risk, or abysmally fail.

Developing resilience is the business of everyone in the firm. In this interconnected and fast-changing world, one cannot address risks in a fragmented way when the enterprise is 'networked' into its external environment. The CFO will still bear responsibility for managing the financial risk, the COO the operational risk, and the CIO the network security risk, but effective enterprise-risk management systems encompass all these tasks and allow both for preemption and rapid, well-targeted responses.

Too many controls may result in no control at all. Although the command-and-control ethos that dominated risk management in the past is starting to wane, most traditional models still rely on a highly centralized concept of the firm, with solutions that involve 'hardening' all potentially vulnerable spots. This approach risks bringing the enterprise to a standstill. Excessive control is counterproductive: it slows both initiative and speed of response and often fails to identify the truly vulnerable areas. In 1995, Nick Leeson destroyed Barings Bank – a highly reputable, centuries-old company – overnight by causing an exponential avalanche resulting from hedges on hedges. Like all investment banks, Barings had sophisticated risk management systems in place, but those systems failed to protect the firm against the actions of just one rogue trader.

Approaches that amount only to shutting the stable door after the horse has bolted are of little value. The only way to manage risk effectively is by instilling norms and values that are shared by all in the firm and then building systems and methodologies that reflect those norms. Risk taking is essential for success; the question is how to manage it. It takes a great deal of effort to create a coherent *risk culture* that is shared by an entire organization, in which all employees think all the time of the trade-offs between risk and reward.

If we think of a company as a living system, instead of an assembly of minds, boxes and machines, it is clear that building corporate capacity to resist shocks through *organic adaptation* is key. Change is now a continuous condition, rather than an episodic one, and the language of the life sciences is more suited to the task of risk management than the prescripts of the industrial age. Ninety-nine percent of all species that have inhabited the planet are today extinct, and, as in business, the 1 percent that have survived are not necessarily the strongest or the smartest, but those that have proven to be most adaptive to the changes they have experienced.

Jared Diamond,[23] famous for his Pulitzer Prize-winning work *Guns, Germs and Steel*[24] which explains the geographical and environmental factors that shaped the modern world, has written a new work,[25] exploring the experiences of communities as diverse as those in the US state of Montana, Australia, Rwanda and China, the Mayan civilization, the Norsemen in Greenland and the Pitcairn and Easter Islands in the Pacific, in order to explain why societies, as he puts it, 'choose to fail or survive.' He advances four reasons for failure, all of which are relevant for modern businesses:

- Failure to anticipate a problem;
- Failure to perceive it once it has arisen;
- Failure to try to resolve it once it has been recognized; and
- Failure in one's attempts to solve it.

All these classes of failure are familiar; companies are often trapped into complacency by past success and fail to recognize early signs of changes in the environment that threaten their survival. Even after such changes have emerged and sales are dropping, many executives fall back on comfortable explanations, suggesting that economic cycles, or high interest rates, or anything else that will regress to the mean in due course and restore earlier success, accounts for the decline. All too many companies – from the British motor industry to the European clothing sector – fail to deal with the underlying causes of decline, even after these are clearly apparent. Finally, not all threats can be warded off, especially if management did not foresee and hedge against them.

The experiences of the Wall Street companies that recovered rapidly in the period immediately after 9/11 are particularly illuminating. Most financial companies hit by the destruction of the Twin Towers got back on their feet with amazing speed, given the scale of the shock they suffered, but Cantor Fitzgerald, an international fixed-income securities firm, presents an astonishing example of resilience. Cantor Fitzgerald lost most of its workforce (657 people) and its headquarters in the attacks, but was able to resume trading when markets reopened less than a week later. How did they do this? There were two reasons:

The first – and obvious – one was planned redundancy. After the 1993 bombing of the World Trade Center, the firm mirrored vital information systems in two or more distant locations so that if one failed, another could take over. Cantor Fitzgerald staff in branch offices in Europe and Asia were also able to take on the workload of those who died in New York. Planned redundancy is a sound strategy in developing better resilience as long as the trade-offs between cost-effectiveness, flexibility and redundancy are well managed. How much redundancy is appropriate? How much should we invest in disaster planning? How much insurance should we buy? Many of the answers will emerge if one takes the systemic approach to risk identification, assessment and management that we discussed in respect of *projects* in chapter 4.

The second – and less obvious – reason for its extraordinary recovery was the quality of the social network at Cantor Fitzgerald. Traders and managers, of course, work in systems secured by passwords. To restore its operations, the company had 47 hours to discover the passwords to the systems of those who had died. The survivors sat in groups and talked through everything they knew about their dead colleagues until they discovered their passwords. Cantor Fitzgerald was saved because its people knew one another exceptionally well, because of the collegiality that flows from individual empowerment, because of the quality of its 'lateral teams.' That firm – and many others in Wall Street – were able to decentralize their locations and distribute their intellectual capital around the country and the world, without diluting the exceptional bonds of trust and mutual commitment that proved so critical in their responses to the crisis.[26]

The two key features of resilience that one can derive from the Cantor Fitzgerald experience are effective preparation and a way of organizing corporate systems that Paz Estrella Tolentino has called *heterarchy*.[27] In traditional – hierarchical – systems, relationships are characterized by dependence: power and knowledge flow vertically down through a fixed sequence of positions. *Heterarchical* systems, in contrast, are characterized by interdependent relationships, laterally distributed authority, empowerment at all levels, knowledge sharing and organizational forms that promote decentralization. Biotech ventures, private-equity funds, trading rooms in investment banks and advertising companies are among the organizations

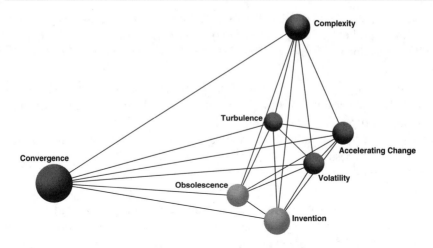

Figure 5.1 Defining elements of the competitive environment

that apply *heterarchical* systems successfully. This systemic behavior encourages resilience – there is no obvious engine room that can be destroyed, thereby crippling the firm[28] – and explains why Wall Street (where almost all companies act in this way) proved so durable in the face of crisis.

Figure 5.1 illustrates the challenge we face in these tumultuous times: *increasing complexity* and *accelerating change* are the defining elements of the environments in which all of us – individuals, companies and governments – are compelled to compete. The interaction between complexity and change generates *volatility* and occasional bursts of *turbulence* – a concept we borrow from chaos theory to describe conditions in which we cannot discern the way in which the system is working.[29] These interactions produce increasingly rapid *obsolescence* and sustained bursts of *invention* that continuously – or more accurately, *discontinuously* – transform the environments in which we operate.

The irony is that the response of many firms over the past decade has been to invest even more in *convergence* or *standardization* – think of the flurry of commitments to ISO 9000-related certification, and efforts, often involving thousands of consultancy hours, to conform to industry 'best-practice' standards. How ironical is that in an environment defined by volatility, turbulence and accelerating change, our response is to converge and stabilize! And yet it is entirely understandable from a psychological perspective. First, we rely on predictability in order to plan, and dislike uncertainty and enforced change, so standardization feels more secure. Second, in an uncertain world there is safety in numbers and the argument that McKinsey, Bain or BCG has assured the Exco that the company is now within 2 percent of global best-practice standards has assuaged many a CEO. But our preferences cannot be allowed to dictate behavior that will ensure our demise!

The companies who succeed in these tumultuous times are those that brace for the certainty of turbulence, and rise to the challenge of skillfully managing the risks attendant on operating in unpredictable environments. This has become a defining competitive advantage. The two key requirements for success are first-rate, relevant information, skills and knowledge, and an *organic*[30] ability to anticipate, where possible, exceptionally rapid and often discontinuous changes; and to adapt to, and manage one's way out of the shocks one did not foresee. Embedding this culture and appetite for risk taking in the firm is easier said than done, as most people have a limited ability to tolerate even continuous, let alone discontinuous, change, but the *heterarchical* approach certainly facilitates success.

As we saw in chapter 1, outsourcing, which is beneficial in many ways, poses particular risks to supply chain integrity as well as brand and reputation. It also confronts companies with challenges in building coherent risk cultures. Many firms are finding it difficult to ensure that integrated risk management and quality standards are applied across the extended supply chains. But there are lessons to be learned from Toyota: the Japanese automaker has succeeded in applying the Toyota Production System (TPS) which is premised on exceptionally high standards in *just-in-time* manufacturing and Total Quality Management, across its entire supply chain, reaching back into all its key suppliers. There is a catch, of course. Toyota has become famous for allowing all and sundry, even its competitors, to inspect its plants and interrogate its systems. It has no fear of losing its competitive edge, as its distinctive competences lie deeply embedded in its culture of quality and continuous innovation.[31]

The new corporate governance rules we discussed in chapter 4 are forcing companies to pay more attention to risk management. In the United Kingdom and South Africa, the combined code on corporate governance now requires companies to prove that they have put in place the processes needed to identify, assess and manage risks. As of the beginning of 2006, all 1,300 companies listed on the LSE will have to provide details of the nonfinancial risks they face, and how they intend to respond to them. In the United States, the Sarbanes-Oxley law forces companies to demonstrate that they can identify and measure risk on a continuous basis. This law requires that risk management procedures in the firm should address all risks, not just the financial ones. In the wake of the Enron scandal, moves to ensure compliance with the Sarbanes-Oxley Act has already led to

$1.4 trillion in net private costs, according to one study,[32] though this has been challenged by the SEC's director of corporation finance, Alan Beller.[33] But compliance with these laws and codes does not guarantee greater corporate resilience. The imposition of risk management procedures may come at the cost of adaptability; the issue is one of balancing *control* and *flexibility*.

Surveys of the World's 'Most Admired Companies' published by *Fortune* magazine over the past decade have identified CEOs with 'guts' and a propensity for successful risk taking; a policy of selecting, recruiting, developing and retaining the best people; a corporate culture of innovation, continuous improvement and acceptance of risk; a global vision coupled with a determination to address the specifics of local demand in every market and investment in society and the environment of which the company is a part as being the distinctive attributes of the world beaters. To be in this class, firms need to build excellent teams and organic, innovative cultures. Identifying, assessing, managing and mitigating risk skillfully and understanding its proper role in the success of the firm is a key factor in the quest for resilience and advancement.

Communicating risk

Why do we need to communicate risk? There are at least two obvious reasons: first, we need to ensure that the risks identified, assessed and intended to be managed within the enterprise risk management system are properly communicated to the people in the company (or the government) who need to know about them, so that they may act. As we saw, both in the 9/11 incident in the United States and more recently in the London tube and bus bombings during the G8 summit in Gleneagles, information that does not reach the people who can act to eliminate or mitigate the risk, serves no purpose.

But there is also a wider context in which risk must be communicated. As we have seen, concern about the impact on shareholders – and wider stakeholder groups, including employees and pensioners – of management's actions in seeking growth and profit, either for themselves, for shareholders or for both, has led to extensive regulation in many parts of the world that compels companies to assess and report on their exposure to risk.

Regulatory obligations on companies to communicate risks hit the headlines after the failures of Enron, WorldCom and Tyco in 2001 and 2002, but they date back to the 1980s, when they emerged chiefly from the need to educate communities and consumers about risks to their health. At that time, governments faced an array of potentially threatening issues such as air and water pollution due to chemical and hydrocarbon emissions as well as the use of pesticides, lead and asbestos, seepage from hazardous waste sites and radiation from nuclear power plants. The issue was whether management of the risks these factors posed to employees and local communities should be left to personal choice and behavior, or whether government should step in and address them through regulation.

The obligation to communicate risk was critical in both cases. If people are to be left to make their own decisions about how to deal with risk, they need to be able to make an informed choice. This means that the information available to workers, smokers, people living downwind from chemical factories and indeed the public about the nature of the risks they face as a result of the activities of companies, power utilities or other economic agents, must be accurate and adequate. Where communication is not an alternative to regulation, it is equally important that the risks on which laws prohibiting or regulating economic behavior are to be based, are well understood by companies, citizens and regulators. This is the only way to devise sensible regulations that are accepted as fair, to ensure that all parties understand them, and to enable their enforcement.

Risk communication, therefore 'is [a] .... process of exchange of information and opinion among individuals, groups and institutions ... It is essential in making decisions. It enables people to participate in deciding how risks should be managed. [It] is also a vital part of implementing decisions – whether explaining mandatory regulations, informing and advising people about risks they can control themselves, or dissuading people from risky behaviour.'[1]

The principle at stake in communication and regulation of risk is one of a *duty of care* for others: Just as the right of a driver to use his car on a road is contingent on his obligation to maintain it in good running order (evidenced by a roadworthy certificate), and drive it in a responsible way (encouraged by the obligation to have a drivers' license and obey the rules of the road), so as not to infringe on the rights of other road users; so a company, in the pursuit of its economic purpose, must not act so as to violate the rights of others in that society.

The first phase of enforced risk communication was therefore one in which companies and other economic actors like power utilities were required to communicate the potential risks that their activities posed to workers, consumers and local communities. The argument was that the damage inflicted was often too severe, even life threatening, to leave it to the courts to rectify the situation after the event. Both preemptive disclosures by the companies and intrusive inspection by government agencies were regarded as being needed to avoid irreparable harm. The great battles waged in the US Congress and the courts between lawmakers, aggrieved citizens and leading tobacco companies, however, illustrate just how difficult it is to reach agreement on the 'facts' informing the debate – *how harmful is smoking to one's health? how harmful is passive smoking?* – and on the boundaries of the rights of the parties.

The second phase, following the corporate scandals at the turn of the present century, extended the obligation to communicate risks affecting this *duty of care* to include shareholders. Shareholders, of course, earlier had the right to act against management after the event, either by firing them, or even, in egregious cases, by suing them in the courts, but the new regulations and codes[2] placed the onus on management teams to identify, assess, mitigate and publicly disclose both the risks the company faced and the measures implemented to address them. Perhaps the prime reason, apart from the shock the scandals brought, was that corporate shareholders were no longer a privileged class, deemed to know what was happening in the companies in which they were invested, or wealthy and diversified enough to survive the demise of one. The 1980s and 1990s has seen the emergence of millions of new investors in equities, either directly, or through unit trusts, or in equity-linked insurance products and in their pension funds.

In many ways, therefore we have now moved into an era where risk has become a common currency. As we have seen, in today's less risk-tolerant society, risks associated with food, drink, chemical and other hazards in the environment and even financial uncertainty, many of which our ancestors would have taken in their stride, are seen as unacceptable by many. So too, of course, are the risks associated with new technologies like those enabling gene-splicing and stem-cell research. Public anxiety is expressed through consumer boycotts and addressed through regulation; and consumers demand clear and timely explanations about the nature of the risks and the policies of those who create and manage them. Every business is affected. Stocks of companies that communicate effectively may trade at a premium, and the shares of those that miscommunicate often suffer disproportionately. Business executives are coming to recognize that one communication blunder can damage a reputation that took years to build. Once lost, trust is very difficult to regain. The conjunction of greater risk aversion by consumers and the complexity that companies have to grapple with in communicating properly about risk is having a profound effect.

Nowhere is the public's changing attitude to risk more starkly apparent than in the pharmaceutical industry. The Vioxx episode in 2004 showed how some companies had miscalculated the public's understanding of the risks posed by generally beneficial drugs.[3] Merck's handling of the claim of a woman in the United States that her husband's death had been caused by Vioxx, an arthritis and acute pain medication used by an estimated 70 million people around the world, had led, by May 2005, to the departure of Merck's CEO and wiped $30 billion off the company's market capitalization. On August 1, 2005, during a civil suit instituted against the company, a *Financial Times* report[4] observed: 'If Merck loses the trial, expected to conclude this month, the ruling could expose it to damages running into billions of dollars from nearly 4,000 other lawsuits.' The court later awarded punitive damages of $253 million to the plaintiff, sparking speculation that Merck's exposure could eventually be as high as $50 billion.[5] The regulatory scrutiny that followed the Vioxx affair also prompted the withdrawal of Bextra (owned by Pfizer) and damaged sales of Crestor (owned by Astra-Zeneca). Current scientific thinking is that Vioxx is probably safe for the vast majority of patients, but can significantly increase the risk of blood clots in a few. The problem is that there is no way of knowing in advance, at this point, who is at risk. *Personalized medicines*, new drugs that will be able to target unique pathologies in particular patients, are, however, being researched. The mapping of the human genome and the ability to identify genetic patterns associated with different forms of disease also makes possible far more specific treatment. Robert Goldberg of the Center for Medical Progress argues that if drug companies do not pursue this route more aggressively – 'go the route of understanding and responding to the tremendous genetic variations in how we react to medicine, you'll see more litigation, not less.'[6]

Vioxx was withdrawn from the market on September 30, 2004, but only after the company, whose ethics had been considered exemplary within the pharmaceutical industry, had sought to cover-up its side effects. The US Food and Drug Administration was criticized for its delay in adding worrisome cardiovascular data from a clinical trial in 2000 to the drug's label. Steven Galson of the FDA's Center for Drug Evaluation and Research said the agency had learned that it should give doctors and patients more information about drugs even while incomplete research results were still coming in: 'The most important lesson … is that the American public, practitioners and patients want to get clear and accurate information as early as possible so they can participate in their own health care decisions,' Galson said.

But it is not clear that this is the solution either. While the pharmaceutical industry and its regulators have responded by deluging consumers with information to help them make informed choices, the floods of scientific data have left many consumers feeling more, rather than less, anxious and isolated. Statistical categorizations of risks to health do not offer laypeople much insight into how this information should be used. In the words of Professor Michael Mehta of the University of Saskatchewan, ' … when drug makers communicate risks to consumers and doctors they often reel them off quickly in a list, in such a way as to imply that they have relatively no importance … There is a continuous failure of risk communication. Companies are not learning the lessons of the past.'[7]

6.1. The principles of risk communication

Risk communication needs to be *communication*, not just the provision of information. Information is a one-way street, while communication is a two-way process. Information often comes from 'on high,' while dialogue is needed to ensure understanding and gain trust. When someone simply delivers a message, there is often a discrepancy between what the informant said, or thought he said and what the recipients heard and understood. The gap between the sender's message and that understood by his audience can be a source of great confusion and misunderstanding.

Four principles underpin good risk communication.

1. Integrate risk communication within risk management
   This sounds obvious, but all too often risk communication is simply 'bolted onto' different parts of a business and undertaken as an obligation, instead of being seen as an integral and strategic part of the firm's risk-management process. The purpose of risk communication is first to enable the effective participation of *all* affected parties in making decisions on how to manage risks; and second, to support the effective implementation of these decisions. The problem starts with identifying the risks: the same risk is often identified differently in different parts of the company, resulting in confusion and inconsistent responses and communications. Resolving the problem means that corporate leaders need to define the major risks consistently and communicate these properly to shareholders, rating agencies and other affected stakeholders.

2. Listen to stakeholders
   Think about the following situation: People believe X and you tell them to believe Y. This provokes resistance, so you keep saying Y-Y-Y-Y more forcefully. This does not work because one cannot change people's minds simply by telling them they are wrong. The problem is especially acute when other sources of information are available to reinforce the belief that X is correct. Remember the *cognitive bias* heuristic that we discussed in chapter 3. All of us tend to select and believe information that confirms our prior belief, and ignore that which contradicts it.

   Effective communication requires careful listening and empathy. People who communicate risks and what is being done to manage them, need to identify and engage with all those who are potentially affected by the risks. They must try to understand the views of their audiences on the risks and what they think should be done, so that those views and preferences can be factored into the company's risk management strategy.[8]

3. Tailor the messages
   This follows logically from the last point, but many of those who communicate about risks do not follow through on simple principles: engage with the people concerned; respond openly to their emotions, fears and concerns; demonstrate credibility, competence and commitment;

and make the costs and benefits of different options clear, before saying what has been decided. Most people will support a decision that they feel has taken due regard of their feelings.

4. Manage the process

None of this will be done consistently and well unless clear and well-defined procedures have been set, and are followed, when communicating about risk. These must pay particular attention to goals, responsibilities, planning, implementation, monitoring and evaluation.

The critical role played by the media in risk communication and the formation of public views on risk justifies some further discussion. Media coverage is driven by novelty, presumed interest to readers, listeners or viewers and related commercial viability, rather than by a desire to present a clinical evaluation of risk. In addition, reporters and their editors are subject to the same cognitive heuristics as the rest of us, and display the same pattern of prejudices. Consequently, some issues that objectively pose infinitesimal risks in terms of impact may be amplified by the media to

---

The Seven Cardinal Rules of Risk Communication[9]

1. **Accept and involve the public as a partner.**
   The goal is to produce an informed public, **not** simply to defuse public concerns.

2. **Plan carefully and evaluate your efforts.**
   Different goals, audiences, and media require different actions.

3. **Listen to the public's specific concerns.**
   People often care more about trust, credibility, competence, fairness, and empathy than about statistics and details.

4. **Be honest, frank and open.**
   Trust and credibility are difficult to obtain, but easy to lose.[10]

5. **Work with other credible sources.**
   Conflicts and disagreements among organizations make communication with the public much more difficult.

6. **Meet the needs of the media.**
   The media are usually more interested in politics than risk; simplicity than complexity; and danger than safety.

7. **Speak clearly and with compassion.**
   Never let your efforts prevent you from acknowledging the tragedy of an illness, injury or death. People can understand risk information, but they may still not agree with you; some people will not be satisfied.

cause devastating effects on an industry without any sinister intent. Recent food 'crises' around *bovine spongiform encephalopathy* (BSE), known colloquially as 'mad-cow disease,' and listeria in cheese are good examples. Very few people died from either, but media coverage created great public concern about soft cheeses and beef, which led to sharp falls in the demand for both. Risk communicators are not often confronted with severe cases of risk amplification by the media, but where these occur, they appear to be triggered mainly by the following factors: (i) a perceived need to assign blame; (ii) alleged secrets or attempted cover-ups; (iii) the involvement of identifiable heroes, villains and dupes; (iv) links with high-profile issues or personalities; (v) strong visual impact and/or (vi) links to sex or crime.[11]

6.2. From risk perception to risk communication

As we saw in chapter 2, the perception of risk is often governed more by our emotions or instincts, than by pure reason. The communication of risk, driven by and responsive to risk perceptions, has to deal with this. Take two widely discussed examples: terrorism and corporate fraud. Television images, with their vivid immediacy, are able to push our emotional hot buttons, especially in relation to morality, notoriety, fame, sex and crime – all the factors just mentioned above – and to persuade us that a modest risk (very few people die in terrorist incidents, as compared with motor accidents; and very few leading CEOs practice corporate crime) is omnipresent. Many viewers' mental risk maps are thus further distorted, at least in relation to statistical reality.

Dealing with this means that risk communication has to be tailored to the way in which people *perceive* risks, taking into account the potential mismatch between the professional risk officer's definition of a particular risk and the understanding of it by other stakeholders. In a nutshell, scientists and professionals do their best to focus on measurable, quantifiable attributes of risks, while many in the public pay much less (if any) attention to these, and respond primarily to the value-laden perceptual attributes which the expert community tends to ignore. As a result, the risks that affect people are often completely different from those that alarm them. Hence, from a risk communication point of view, the correct formula for risk is *Risk = Hazard + Outrage*,[12] where *hazard* corresponds to the standard definition of risk (probability multiplied by impact), and *outrage* is the basket of factors that make people upset, angry or frightened about something. Seen this way, the public responds chiefly to factors that engender *outrage*, while risk managers address *hazard*. The opportunity for miscommunication is enormous.

Consider the following example: Hazard X kills 12,353 people a year; while hazard Y has a 50 percent probability of killing 247,060 people over the next ten years. Quantitatively, hazards X and Y are equivalent because both have the same expected annual mortality: 12,353 persons. Emotionally, however, the 50 percent probability that a quarter of a million people will die, resonates more strongly. Catastrophic risks provoke a level of *outrage* that chronic risks do not trigger. This is why an airplane or train accident causing 200 immediate deaths elicits a level of outrage that is not matched by a similar number of deaths on the roads over a weekend. Likewise, the risk of overeating and not exercising (one of the primary causes of death in most developed countries) does not cause *outrage*. Reverting to terrorism, which even most experts define as a major global risk, we encounter something similar: 12,353 people died in road accidents in South Africa in 2003, and a similar number in 2004;[13] by contrast, 10,000 deaths are said to have been caused by international terrorist attacks in the 31 years between 1968 and 1998.[14] The US State Department reports that worldwide terrorism casualties in 2003 were 625 dead and 3,645 wounded.[15]

Business is particularly good at seizing opportunities and developing new products when *outrage* outweighs *hazard*. Steven Levitt gives the example of child safety in the United States. Not much is done to save the life of the 400 young children who die every year in swimming-pool accidents in the United States, but almost five million car seats are sold each year costing as much as $200 each, even though accident data indicates that they are not particularly helpful in reducing mortality. Why? Because a child dying in a car accident provokes *outrage*, like a child burning in his pajamas – although flame-retardant pajamas save an estimated 10 lives a year in the United States – while swimming-pool deaths apparently do not inspire *outrage*.

Why does a car accident or a fire provoke outrage, but not a death in a swimming pool? Why does a comparatively small number of deaths from terrorism turn the world on its head, while a far larger number of traffic deaths is contemplated with apparent equanimity, except if children are involved? What are these *outrage* factors that impact so much on how people react to risks, and therefore determine how one must communicate about them?

They stem, of course, from the issues we discussed in chapter 3. *Outrage* is triggered by risks we experience as more disturbing. Although several are related, the most important are as follow:

Inequity
A risk which is seen to be unfairly distributed (some benefit, while others suffer the consequences) is a source of *outrage*, especially when the difference

is grounded in race, religion or economic status. We also experience more *outrage* at risks that result from human malfeasance, especially in pursuit of profit, and those that cause hidden and irreversible damage, than we do at threats that arise from natural sources. Our sense of outrage is also heightened when the damage strikes victims we know, or can easily identify with, rather than anonymous persons.

Involuntariness
A risk we assume voluntarily (e.g. as a result of a dangerous sport) generates no *outrage* while one that is involuntary (like exposure to severe pollution or terrorism) does.

Loss of control
A risk we cannot avert by taking personal precautions causes more *outrage*, even in simple cases. Most of us feel safer when driving ourselves than when riding in the passenger seat or in a taxi crammed with passengers. The same principle explains our outrage at bomb attacks in London tube trains. We experience more outrage when the sense that we are not in control is prolonged, as when responsible authorities make contradictory statements, either through inefficiency or because the cause of the threat is poorly understood.

Unfamiliarity
Risks that arise from an unfamiliar source provoke more *outrage* (like sniper attacks in Maryland, or tsunamis in Thailand) than those that sound familiar, like dying from heart disease.

Dread
Certain threats arouse particularly negative reactions (child rape, *muti* killings for body parts or cannibalism) and cause great *outrage*.

Immediacy
In a world that is impatient for short-term solutions and disregards events in the longer term, fear impacts most profoundly in the present. Governments all around the world secure funds to fight terrorism far more easily than to address heart disease, extreme poverty, HIV/AIDS, malaria and TB or the effects of hydrocarbon emissions on the atmosphere. Many factors play a role in this, but the fundamental reason is that terrorist attacks are occurring, and are publicized, now, while the other factors seem remote to most wealthy Western audiences, either in *time* (the fatal effects of heart disease or climate change) or *distance* (extreme poverty and diseases that afflict mainly poor people). Bob Geldof's use of Live-Aid and Live 8 concerts to draw attention to the ravages of poverty is an example of an effort to bring immediacy to the communication of this risk.

The way we perceive risk – we are excessively concerned about risks we cannot control, and far less about those we assume voluntarily – is of great importance in understanding how we should communicate about risk. When *hazard* (the objective probability of harm) is high, and *outrage* (the public sense of discomfort) is low, people will underreact; conversely, when *hazard* is low and *outrage* is high, there is a propensity to overreact. Communication about risk is used by different parties either to moderate or to exacerbate *outrage* in an effort to achieve their goals, with media coverage having an amplifying effect. Typically, businesses seek to reduce or manage *outrage* – calm people down after an event by 'putting matters into perspective' – while socially active NGOs aim to raise the level of *outrage* so as to make their points more effectively. When both *hazard* and *outrage* are high, it is time to shift to crisis communication.

6.3. Communicating in a crisis

Crisis communication has become a discipline in its own right: Public relations and crisis management consultancies have mushroomed to advise companies how to respond when crisis strikes.[16] Effective crisis communication is essential in preserving the value of a business.

> The characteristic quality of a crisis is that it has emerged without warning or at least without enough time to forestall it. The longer it takes to respond effectively, the greater the potential for damage, even more so in a world of instant communication. Proper advance planning for *crisis contingency* is thus of critical importance. To sit still and do nothing is the most dangerous thing, of course; yet paralysis is not infrequent. During the seven-day strike of its ground and cabin crews from July 22–8, 2005, South African Airways (SAA) seemed to have forgotten that it was an organization that existed to serve its customers, thousands of whom were widely distributed around the world. No direct communications were made to customers, not even those with platinum cards, the highest award for loyal frequent flyers. After days of confusion which left many passengers stranded, the airline issued an advice to the travel trade on July 27 asking agents not to book passengers on SAA for the next 10 days and advising travel agents that 'All passengers already booked for this period are advised to postpone travel dates or be rebooked on other carriers. SAA will refund tickets provided all relevant documentation is in order.' There was no mention of the airline assuming responsibility for rebooking its passengers.

After the strike ended on July 29, SAA's CEO, Khaya Ngqula, apologized to the *travel trade* for not communicating effectively about the strike. 'We could have done more to communicate with the trade.' He attributed the management's failure to do this to the strike being the first of its kind at SAA and said it was a 'big challenge.' No apology to passengers was recorded.

By contrast Singapore Airline's crisis response planning served the airline well after the tragic crash of flight SQ006 at Taipei's Chiang Kai-Shek airport on October 31, 2000. Eighty-three persons died in and after the crash, and 82 others were injured. The pilots had decided to take off although Typhoon Xangsane was whipping up strong winds and heavy rain, and other pilots from regional airlines had refused to fly. They took the Boeing 747–400, in error, onto a runway under repair, parallel to the one they were authorized to use, and crashed it into concrete blocks and construction equipment on takeoff. Senior Singapore Airlines' staff, including the CEO, were on local and international television channels within an hour after the crash and remained there throughout the night feeding information to the media as it became available. Airline executives effectively managed the story and gave an impression of exceptional competence.

This was not all. The Singapore government, ever conscious of the value of its reputation and the Singapore brand, leaped into action. Public-relations officers from the Ministry of Information helped airline executives process and deliver news to the media. Government ministers were sent to Taiwan to see the crash, support local authorities there and offer condolences to the bereaved and injured.

When Taiwan's Aviation Safety Council revealed on November 3 that the plane had been on the wrong runway, the Singapore government immediately staked its reputation on a transparent investigation and mentioned that it would be judged by how open we are about how the accident happened, how much we learn from it, and what systems we put in place so as not to repeat it,' the government said in a statement.

Singapore's communication strategy was particularly important as it transpired from the investigation that the pilots were legally responsible for the tragedy, opening the airline to a slew of civil suits over the next two years. The two senior pilots were fired, the great majority of the suits were settled out of court, accompanied by fulsome apologies; and the airline was left with its reputation intact.

These two contrasting examples illustrate the importance of businesses developing and documenting a plan for risk communication so that they are ready to deal with crises when they strike. To ensure effective response in a crisis, companies must determine who will do what in responding and what the communications strategy will be, vis-à-vis each group of stakeholders, including the media. The necessary communications infrastructure and procedures to get the information out and to respond effectively to questions must be put in place. An authorized spokesperson with evident authority and communication skills and experience of crisis communication is essential.

In managing communication during a crisis, a few simple, but important, rules apply. These are similar to those in standard risk communication, but the importance of applying them is even greater.

In terms of *content*:

- Keep the message simple, brief and straightforward;
- Avoid speculation – stick to facts;
- Respect and address people's concerns and requests for information.

In terms of *style:*

- Be frank and honest;
- Make it clear that the company recognizes the importance of communicating;
- Show empathy, concern and commitment.

This is not rocket science, although experience shows that not all senior executives understand that it is in their best interest to communicate honestly and directly, to avoid speculating in an effort to exonerate themselves, to listen carefully, to take responsibility for their actions and to treat their critics with respect. The rules of effective crisis communication conflict with the natural instincts of many business leaders and policy makers when they are under pressure. In crisis, many leaders tend to be even more determined and resolute, and their behavior under stress can lead outsiders to believe that they are arrogant, contemptuous, and dismissive of others' concerns. As a result, outrage is bound to grow.

Perhaps the worst thing to do in communicating in crisis is to convey the impression of overconfidence: 'The situation is under control – everything is going to be fine!' Unless the facts support the assertion, people find this alarming and disturbing. They sense dishonesty and become mistrustful before the outcome is known. The airline examples illustrate the point, but so do recent corporate scandals. When senior executives refuse to acknowledge the problems and address them effectively, the end is nigh. Indeed, it is much better to acknowledge uncertainty, share dilemmas, give people things to do so that they feel part of the solution, and sometimes, to apologize.[17] The balance struck by Mayor Rudy Giuliani[18] in rallying New Yorkers after the September 11, 2001, attacks on the World Trade Center, are a good example. In his book on leadership,[19] Giuliani lists five necessary conditions for effective leadership which offer the right balance:

- Know what you believe in;
- Be optimistic;
- Be courageous;
- Be prepared;
- Value teamwork;
- Communicate.

All these, but particularly the last four, are essential in communicating effectively in a crisis.

Peter Sandman has developed 25 key recommendations for communicating in crises. Some overlap, and not all will be applicable at any one time, but the list is well worth reviewing and keeping to hand when one is faced with crisis. Very few people are at their best when facing a crisis and needing to communicate effectively to others.

Risk communication is an uncertain field; it improves the odds of a good outcome, but there is no guarantee it will succeed every time. It will not, moreover, even when effective, solve all problems or resolve all conflicts. Despite its effective communication after the Taipei crash, Singapore Airlines faced some 140 lawsuits in the United States alone[21] and some had to be settled for what were described as 'record sums.' On the other hand, poor communication will almost certainly lead to a failure to manage the risk effectively. While the major challenge of risk communication stems from the intangibility of the benefit, its importance can only be ignored at one's extreme peril.

The Vioxx case, which we discussed first in this chapter, serves to remind us that the greatest challenge for a company, industry or government that has seen its reputation damaged in a crisis, is the rebuilding of *trust*, which is itself the most important factor in determining *reputation*. Proactive risk communication in a low-trust environment requires a cultural shift for most corporate or governmental organizations, to a mode that emphasizes openness, responsiveness, recognition of the importance of

The 25 key recommendations in crisis communication[20]

1. Do not over-reassure.
2. Put reassuring information in subordinate clauses.
3. Err on the side of alarm.
4. Acknowledge uncertainty.
5. Share dilemmas.
6. Acknowledge opinion diversity.
7. Be willing to speculate.
8. Do not overdiagnose or overplan for panic.
9. Do not aim for zero fear.
10. Don't forget emotions other than fear.
11. Do not ridicule the public's emotions.
12. Legitimize people's fears.
13. Tolerate early overreactions.
14. Establish your own humanity.
15. Tell people what to expect.
16. Offer people things to do.
17. Let people choose their own actions.
18. Ask more of people.
19. Acknowledge errors, deficiencies and misbehaviors.
20. Apologize often for errors, deficiencies and misbehaviors.
21. Be explicit about 'anchoring frames.'
22. Be explicit about changes in official opinion, prediction or policy.
23. Do not lie and do not tell half-truths.
24. Aim for total candor and transparency.
25. Be careful with risk comparisons.

public perceptions and participation and the acceptance of the central position of ethical issues. This remit applies well beyond the pharmaceutical industry: It encompasses all businesses and governments affected by the public's changing attitude to risk; that is to say, all powerful organizations.

CHAPTER 7

Managing global risks – Four examples

The strategic risks we referred to briefly in chapter 1 are global in scope, although businesses tend to experience their impact on a local level. Unless one understands risks of this sort in their global context, it is difficult to develop a perspective that allows us to assess them correctly. To help in contextualizing such challenges, we have selected four global risks that the World Economic Forum[1] has identified as being on the radar screens of global business and international experts today. Figure 7.1 below reflects the outcome of two sessions arranged by the WEF in 2006, in New York and London respectively, at which executives from leading global companies and a broad range of expert analysts assessed the evolution of global risks that would potentially affect the world over the next decade. A more extensive discussion of these risks and other activities of the Global Risk Network is available at http://www.weforum.org/en/initiatives/globalrisk/index.htm.

We have chosen not to address the economic risks identified – an oil price shock, a sharp decline in the value of the US dollar due to the widening US current account deficit, a hard landing in China, fiscal crises in the G8 countries, and the bursting of the asset price bubble in Western housing markets – in this chapter, as these have been the objects of extensive analysis and speculation in business and financial media, and most global companies understand how to factor these risks into their management strategies. Likewise, we have set aside the two technological risks identified – the breakdown of critical information infrastructure (CII) and the emergence of risks from nanotechnology. In the case of CII, most large companies – and their service providers – have invested in redundant storage capacity and communications channels, and developed robust data recovery and business continuity capabilities. The second technological risk class defined in the Global Risk Report 2007 – risks derivative of nanotechnology developments – seems too narrow for extensive discussion: the most challenging risks in this realm are likely to emerge from the convergence of the biosciences, notably pharmacology and genetic engineering, with information and related nanotechnologies.

Key:

↑	Increased overall risk
→	Stable overall risk
↓	Decreased overall risk
x	Expert disagreement

ECONOMIC RISKS	Reason for increased, stable or decreased overall risk
Oil price shock/energy supply interruptions ↑	Though some estimate capacity will increase to meet demand (forecast 25% increase by 2015), the energy market remains tight, and highly vulnerable to both physical and speculative shocks.
US current account deficit/fall in US$ ↑	Although the trade-weighted real exchange rate of the US$ has depreciated 23% since 2002, many believe this will continue, **in order to limit a widening US current account deficit.**
Chinese economic hard landing ↑	Chinese growth is both investment- and export-led. The expansion of exports may generate a backlash (particularly in the United States); high investment (over 40% of GDP) has generated excess capacity and fears of potential bad debts.
Fiscal crises caused by demographic shift ↑	The deterioration of fiscal balances in G8 countries, combined with continuing large deficits in other large countries renders a series of major fiscal crises possible, exacerbated by long-term challenges of ageing and equitable health-care provision.
Blow up in asset prices/excessive indebtedness ↑	House prices have doubled in most mature markets (and in some emerging markets) in real terms over the last 10 years, putting price-to-income ratios at all-time highs. Many experts fear a major correction, with differential impacts on consumption, economic growth and other asset prices.
ENVIRONMENTAL RISKS	
Climate change ↑	Carbon emissions are growing above trend and there are indications that feedback mechanisms, particularly increased heat absorption caused by Arctic ice-melt, will increase the speed and scale of warming. New research argues that the increasing intensity of North Atlantic hurricanes is due to global warming.
Loss of freshwater services ↑	Mitigation effects of improved water pricing have yet to have an effect; economic development and global warming have increased the risk to the sustainability of many already stressed freshwater systems worldwide, particularly in Asia.
Natural Catastrophe : Tropical storms ↑	The increasing risk from tropical storms includes two major components. The hazard itself may be increasing as global warming drives sea surface temperatures higher. Global vulnerability to tropical storms may also be increasing as a result of coastal development.
Natural Catastrophe : Earthquakes →	The threat of earthquakes, in terms of likelihood and severity, remains the same, driven by basic geophysics. Meanwhile, slight increases in the exposure of populations are matched by slight reductions in the vulnerability of assets.
Natural Catastrophe : Inland Flooding ↑	Increasing floodplain development and an expected increase in climate change-driven extreme weather events increase the risk of disruptive and costly inland flooding.

Figure 7.1   Global risk barometer, WEF global risk network

GEOPOLITICAL RISKS	
International terrorism ↑	The risk of future attacks has risen: threat levels in Britain consider an attack "highly likely", the US National Intelligence Estimate has argued that the Iraq war had heightened the risks, while the situations in Afghanistan, Somalia and Pakistan continue to cause concern.
Proliferation of WMD ↑	North Korea tested a nuclear device in 2006, Iran continued its programme, the US weakened its commitment to nonproliferation in a controversial deal with India, while some Middle East states said they would seek civilian nuclear technologies. All increased the risk of proliferation in the decade ahead.
Interstate and civil wars ↑	Civil war took hold in Iraq in 2006 while tensions fluctuated on the Korean peninsula and in the Middle East. The International Crisis Group identified November 2006 as the worst month for conflict prevention in 40 months. The risk of any of a number of hotspots causing a major conflagration in the decade ahead has increased.
Failed and failing states ↑	There is little prospect of immediate improvement in serial failed and failing states – notably Somalia, Afghanistan and Pakistan. The creation of the UN peacebuilding commission may improve mitigation but risks are increasing.
Transnational crime and corruption →	Transnational crime and corruption remain endemic in a number of developing countries and developed countries, damaging state authority, economic prosperity and weakening the ability to deal with other global risks.
Retrenchment from globalization ↑	Progress on the Doha trade round appears distant, while failures will be difficult to reverse after expiry of Presidential negotiation authority. Populist sentiment in Europe and the United States is set to increase.
Middle East instability ↑	Overall stability is deteriorating, despite rapid growth and moves towards stability in some Gulf countries. Grand bargains to stabilise the region may be possible, but underlying problems of Islamist extremism, political succession (as in Egypt) and fragile economic structures will make the region highly volatile.
SOCIETAL RISKS	
Pandemics →	Some measures (e.g. improved research and cooperation on early-warning) have improved response capability. However, the aggregate risk is constant as uncertainty remains over the timing and nature of any outbreak.
Infectious diseases in the developing world →	Though infection rates have stabilised in some countries, infection rates for HIV and other diseases are rising in others, presenting major risks to future prosperity. India passed South Africa as the country hosting the largest population of HIV/AIDS infected people.
Chronic disease in the developed world	Experts were divided on the balance between potential advances in medical science over the next 10 years and the increasing prevalence of "life-style" diseases.
Liability regimes	Experts were divided on the risks to global prosperity from liability regimes over the next 10 years: some argue liability regimes represent a legitimate policy choice, others suggest they represent a growing cost to business, while others suggest that US-style liability regimes are unlikely to make headway in other parts of the world.
TECHNOLOGICAL RISKS	
Breakdown of Critical Information Infrastructure (CII) →	Expert judgment suggested balance between increasing vulnerability arising from interconnectivity and growing awareness of security issues surrounding CII with investments in resilience and spare capacity in some key infrastructure areas.
Emergence of risks associated with nanotechnology →	In the absence of any major scientific discovery, experts estimated the potential risks arising from nanotechnology were unchanged.

Figure 7.1 *continued*

This has led us to select for discussion here, terrorism (together with conditions in the Middle East and issues of failing states), health risks (the risk of an avian flu pandemic and the reality of HIV/AIDS) and climate change and eco-system degradation. We have also included a brief discussion of systemic financial risk, derived from hedge fund activity, because this highlights the challenges of intense interconnectivity in complex environments.

7.1. Combating global terror

Most of what we address today in the West when speaking of *global terrorism* is, in fact, modern *jihadism*, a species of Islamist militancy that derives from the success of Osama bin Laden and a few of his close associates, notably Ayman Al Zawahiri,[2] through al-Qaeda, in propagating two simple messages consistently over the past 16 years:

- Barbarism and unbelief, based on rebellion against the sovereignty of Allah in earth ... and resulting in the 'oppression of his creatures' has taken hold and must be resisted and destroyed.
- Islam, Muslims and Islamic lands are under attack by the United States and its allies[3] and *jihad* is a moral imperative to repulse tyranny and restore justice and rights.[4]

We discuss the place of Islam in the evolution of modern human society in greater detail in appendix 2. As we point out there in greater detail, Islam poses no threat to the West. It is an integral part of the history of science and technology and the emergence of the modern. In this chapter, however, our aim is to place militant jihadism in its modern context.

The rise of the Muslim Brotherhood[5] by Hassan al-Banna in Egypt in 1928, provided a modern political context[6] for the *salafist*[7] ideals of three significant Sunni theologians over the centuries: Ibn Hanbal (750–855 CE), the founder of the Hanbali school of Islamic jurisprudence (*al fiqh*); Ibn Taymiyya (1263–1328 CE), a Hanbali theologian of Syrian descent, who lived during the Mongol invasion, the sacking of Baghdad and the destruction of the caliphate and who denounced the impact of Greek philosophy on Islamic theology; attacked esoteric sects as heretical and attacked the Sufis; and Mohammad ibn Abdul Wahhab (1703–92 CE), from Najd in the Arabian peninsula, who likewise rejected all 'foreign' influences on Islam as heretical and demanded a return to the *Qur'an* and *sunna*. Al Wahhab formed a military-religious alliance with Muhammad bin Saud, whose descendents came to rule the kingdom of Saudi Arabia in 1932 after the defeat of the Ottoman Empire – which had sided with the Germans in World War I – and the dissolution of the caliphate by Kemal Attaurk in 1924.

The rise of the house of Saud under Abdul Aziz al-Saud, after his capture of the cities of Mecca and Medina in 1924, led to a shift in the relationship between the Wahhabists and the al-Saud clan. The militant Wahhabists whose jihadist beliefs had helped the Saud clansmen achieve control of most of the Arabian Peninsula, had become a threat to the emergent secular power and its British backers. The more pliant members of the Wahhabist *al-ikhwan* or 'brotherhood,' were integrated into the Saudi National Guard after the militants had been defeated at Sabilah in March 1929. The Wahhabi *ulema*, or religious scholars, were given responsibility for the Saudi judicial system, religious education, the education of women and the 'preaching of Islam abroad.'[8] In 1962, the Saudi royal family endowed the *Rabitat al-Alam al-Islami*, the World Islamic League, to counter secular tendencies in the Islamic world and to 'invite' others to Islam. Nine years later, King Feisal provided the rector of al-Azhar University in Cairo with $100 million to extend the campaign. In the 1980s, following the coup in Pakistan by General Zia ul-Haq, the Saudi's funded the construction of the Shah Feisal mosque and the International Islamic University in Islamabad, and they and others from the Gulf invested heavily in extending Islamic education through Deobandi[9] medrassas[10] in Pakistan.

The Muslim Brotherhood often known in its ranks as *al-ikhwan*[11] has a simple, clear-cut credo: 'God is our objective; the Qur'an is our Constitution; the Prophet is our leader; struggle is our way; and death for the sake of God is the highest of our aspirations.' Hassan al-Banna's goal in creating the Brotherhood was to restore Islam to its origins, the *Qur'an, sunna* and a*hadith.*[12] Although influenced by the western political movements of his age, notably German National Socialism in the 1930s, al-Banna was essentially a gradualist. Sayyid Qutb,[13] a school inspector born in Musha in upper Egypt in 1906, who wrote the powerful indictment of modern society he titled *Milestones,*[14] was the man most responsible for transforming the Brotherhood into a radical militant organization. After Qutb's return from the United States in 1950, where he graduated with a master's degree from the Colorado State College of Education, and was shocked at the 'primitive' decadence of American society, he joined the Brotherhood and became the head of its propaganda division and a member of the Working Committee and the Guidance Council. The Brotherhood, whose underground wing was responsible for the assassination of Egypt's first prime minister, Mahmoud Fahmi Nokrashi in 1948,[15] was banned after an attempt to kill Gamel Abdul Nasser in 1954 and Qutb and many others were imprisoned.

He was released in 1964, rearrested in 1965 and hanged in 1966. The Palestinian group Hamas is as a wing of the Brotherhood formed out of a number of charities in the Palestinian territories which radicalized and militarized during the first Palestinian intifada from 1987 to 1993.

Osama bin Laden, born in Riyadh in 1957, of Yemeni descent, is the scion of a family from southern Arabia which became extremely wealthy from construction contracts awarded by the Saudi royal family from the 1950s onward. His mother was Mohammed bin Laden's tenth or eleventh wife, the educated, well-traveled daughter of a Syrian trader.[16] He studied management, economics and civil engineering at the Abdul Aziz University in Jeddah, graduating in 1979. Among the faculty he met several members of the Muslim Brotherhood who had been given refuge by the Saudi government, which used the university to counter the secular socialism then in vogue in much of the Arab world.

The year of bin Laden's graduation was epochal in the Islamic world. The Soviet Union invaded Afghanistan at the request of the Marxist People's Democratic Party of Afghanistan (PDPA) which had come to power in 1978 and was facing a revolt; a peace agreement was signed between Israel and Egypt; a shi'ite Islamic theocracy was established in Iran, leading to shi'ite riots in the Al Ahsa province of Saudi Arabia; and a radical Wahhabist group of 500, led by a former Saudi National Guardsman, Janaiman ibn Said al-Utaiba, occupied the Grand Mosque in Mecca until it was expelled after 14 days of fighting, by a force of 10,000 Saudi and Pakistani troops, supported by French counterterrorism units. Bin Laden was initially most moved by the entry of Soviet troops into Afghanistan and went to Peshawar in Pakistan to explore ways of assisting the religious authorities there early in 1980. Within four years he was established in Peshawar, and had become known for visiting wounded Afghan and Arab fighters and arranging for payments to their families. The Afghan resistance was funded both by the United States which channeled support through the Pakistani military intelligence service (ISI), and by Saudi money of equal or greater magnitude controlled by Turki al-Feisal, then the head of Saudi intelligence. Bin Laden was one of several channels through which the Saudi funds were disbursed.

The Afghan Islamists with whom he soon interacted were technically educated, provincial, professional men who had either studied in Egypt under the Saudi-funded programs at al-Azhar University or had been influenced by the writings of Sayyid Qutb and Sayyid Abdul a'la Maududi, translated into Dari. Two of these men, Burhanuddin Rabbani and Ahmed Shah Massoud, fled to Pakistan with a few followers after the first Afghan coup in 1973 and were received there by Hussein Ahmed, a Pakistani

Islamist of Pushtun descent, who was later to create Pakistan's *Jaamat Islami*. The ISI was told to keep an eye on the Afghan refugees and Gulbuddin Hekmatyar, who later established *Hisb-e-Islami*, was appointed as the Afghan group's contact person.

Seven Afghan mujahadeen groups operated out of Pakistan once the resistance was established; four of which were Islamist, the most radical being *Hisb-e-Islami*, the favored party of President (General) Zia ul-Haq, who had taken power in Pakistan in 1977. Rabbani, a Tajik, had created an Afghan *Jaamat Islami* and his military commander, Ahmed Shah Massoud, led the most effective anti-Soviet force. Abd al-Rab al-Rasul Sayyaf, who had been a colleague of Rabbani and Massoud, but was imprisoned in 1973 and unable to flee, later established *Ittehad-e-Islami*, which was funded heavily by the Saudis and other Gulf contributors.

The 'Arabs' came late to the fighting, their entry prompted by the preacher Abdallah Azzam, who had joined the Muslim Brotherhood at 18, fought the Israelis in 1967, completed his doctorate at al-Azhar and taught at Abdul Aziz university when bin Laden was there. He went to Pakistan in 1981 to teach at the Islamic International University funded by the Saudis and moved to Peshawar in 1984 to establish the *Maktab al-Khidamat* to coordinate volunteers and funds flowing from the Gulf. Azzam's personalization of the obligation to *jihad* by all Muslims was a critical element in the development of the militant jihadism. Jason Burke quotes his *Defending the land of the Muslims is each man's most important duty*. 'This duty will not end with victory in Afghanistan; jihad will remain an individual obligation until all other lands that were Muslim are returned to us so that Islam will reign again: before us lie Palestine, Bokhara, Lebanon, Chad, Eritrea, Somalia, the Philippines, Burma, southern Yemen, Tashkent and Andalusia.'[17] It was also Azzam who popularized the *hadith* suggesting that the Muslim martyr would enjoy absolution from his sins, permission to bring 70 members of his household to paradise and enjoy the attentions of 72 beautiful virgins. Azzam's impassioned religious metaphors came to define the language and mental frame of reference of jihadists in the decades ahead.

After 1985 when the United States provided the mujahadeen with 'Stinger' anti-air missiles and foreign volunteers began to flow in increasing numbers into Afghanistan from the Arab world and southeast Asia, the tide began to turn against the Soviets. Experienced Islamists from Egypt came to Peshawar and soon assumed leadership positions. Ayman Al Zawahiri took up a medical post. New bases were built at Zhawar Khili and Tora Bora, with reinforced tunnels into the mountains, and at Jaji and Khaldan. Bin Laden supported the construction of some of these with his family's construction equipment, and built a personal camp, al Masa'ada, near Jaji. The Egyptians built the Khalid bin Waleed camp near Khost. Bin Laden, fighting as Abu Abdullah,[18] saw combat frequently between 1986 and 1989.

After the Soviets withdrew in early 1989, the PDPA regime was greatly weakened. Pakistan's ISI sought to bring the war to a successful conclusion, securing the election of Sayyaf as prime minister of a new Afghan government and helping the mujahadeen launch a strike on Jalalabad in March 1989. Infighting and poor coordination caused the assault to fail, leaving more than a thousand mujahadeen dead and thousands more injured. Dissension spread: with the Soviets gone there was no common enemy. The different factions would fight on, with ISI support, for five years before the Taliban were installed in Kabul. But bin Laden's direct involvement with the Afghan struggle was over; disgusted at the infighting, he shifted his attention to new targets. Before withdrawing, he financed the compilation of the 'Encyclopaedia of the Jihad,' which codified the instruction given in the camps, making it more readily accessible to others.

Abdallah Azzam was killed in an air strike in November 1989, but his spirit lived on in a transformed radical jihadist movement committed to revenging Islam for centuries of hardship and restoring the salafist dream through jihad and martyrdom. Some Arab mujahadeen returned to their home countries and contributed to the birth of radical movements there, even as more were flooding into Pakistan and Afghanistan to continue training in Arab-run camps and engaging in combat. Tens of thousands of Muslims from other parts of the world continued to flow into the mujahadeen training camps in the first half of the 1990s. Bin Laden had no direct connections with any of these, though there is some evidence that he continued to provide money for one camp 'Kunar,' probably north of Jalalabad. Although official Saudi funding had been cut off after Sayyaf and Hekmatyar had openly attacked the Saudi government for permitting US forces to use Saudi bases during the First Gulf War in 1991, thereby 'defiling the land of the Prophet,' private funders from the Gulf continued to support the fighters generously. Abdel Omar Rahman, the Egyptian blind sheikh, succeeded to Abdallah Azam's mantle as the spiritual leader of the jihadists. Communism had collapsed and Islamist groups were rising in many countries. One of the most important Islamist leaders to emerge was Hassan al-Turabi in Sudan.

Toward the end of 1989, recruiting started for a group called *al-Qaeda*. The leader was bin Laden, the others were mainly drawn from the Egyptian Islamic Jihad, including Ayman Al Zawahiri and Mohammed Atef. The aim was to continue the jihad against the corrupt regimes of the Arab world.

7.1.1. The wider jihad

The bomb that exploded in the World Trade Center in New York in February 1993 was placed by Ramzi Ahmed Yousef, a Pakistani born in Kuwait in 1968, who studied electrical engineering in Swansea from 1987 to 1991 and spent his summer vacations teaching bomb making in the camps around Peshawar. He later trained militants from the Abu Safyyaf group in the Philippines, taught electronics and bomb making in Pakistan, planted the bomb in New York and injured himself while preparing a device intended to assassinate Pakistan's Prime Minister Benazir Bhutto. In 1994 he was in Thailand, preparing an unsuccessful attack on the Israeli embassy, then in the Philippines to plan the destruction of 12 passenger jets in the air, an aircraft hijacking and possibly an attack on a US target: in fact he succeeded in placing only one small bomb on a Japanese airplane, killing one passenger. Fleeing from Manila in January 1995 after a fire in his safe house, he returned to Pakistan where he was arrested in February and taken to the United States to stand trial. Although Ramzi is alleged to have stayed at guesthouses established by bin Laden and benefited from funding through the Saudi-based International Islamic Relief Organization, distributed by the husband of one of Osama's half sisters, there is no plausible link between the two men. Khalid Shaikh Mohammed, Ramzi's uncle by marriage, did play an important role in Ramzi's activities and became closely associated with bin Laden at the end of the decade and in the 2001 attacks on US targets, but had no links to bin Laden or al-Qaeda in the early 1990s. These separate activities and related networks offer a microcosmic insight into the numerous uncoordinated strands of jihadist militancy unleashed by the common experience of training in the camps in Pakistan.

After Ramzi's arrest, the Pakistani authorities were pressed to register the 'Arabs' and other foreign militants in Peshawar; the list comprised over 5,000 names: 1,142 Egyptians, 981 Saudis, 946 Algerians, 771 Jordanians, 326 Iraqis, 292 Syrians, 234 Sudanese, 199 Libyans, 117 Tunisians and 102 Moroccans.[19]

The year 1995 was another turning point in the evolution of militant jihadism as there were two attacks on Egyptian targets – an attempt to assassinate President Hosni Mubarak in Addis Ababa undertaken by al-Gamaa al-Islamiyya, and the destruction of Egypt's embassy in Islamabad by Ayman Al Zawahiri's Islamic Jihad. Between the spring of 1994 and 1997 things were also changing radically in Afghanistan. The Taliban emerged among the Pushtun tribes in the southeast of Afghanistan, from the Deobandi salafism learned in the medrassas of Pakistan, under the leadership of a simple mullah, later known to all as Mullah Omar. The infighting between the politicized Islamist factions had disillusioned the Pushtuns; their determination to return to a rural Afghan Islamic ideal, with the society obedient to the *shari'a*,[20] implied a rejection of modernity and foreign influences. The Taliban rejected not only the political Islamists, but also the traditional Khans and the leading figures of the ulema. When Mullah Omar called a meeting of 1,200 religious figures in Kandahar to select a leader and decide on the future of the Taliban, all previously politically connected persons were rejected[21] and Omar was elected 'leader of the faithful.' Kabul fell to the Taliban in September 1996 and Mazar-e-Sharif in 1997, leading Pakistan to become the first state to extend diplomatic recognition to the Taliban. By November 1999, they exercised nominal control over 80 percent of Afghanistan.

After Saddam Hussein crossed the border into Kuwait, potentially threatening the Saudi kingdom as well, Osama bin Laden saw his opportunity to raise an international Islamist force to protect the kingdom, averting the need to allow US troops into the land of the Prophet, contaminating *al-Haramain*, the holy places of Mecca and Medina. The Saudi royal family's rejection of this offer and its decision to allow the stationing of hundreds of thousands of US and other Western troops in the country, changed Osama's life and the history of the world. The *hadith* that attributed to the Prophet the instruction that 'there shall be no two religions in Arabia' had often been invoked to prevent the construction of churches or synagogues in the Saudi kingdom The senior *alim*,[22] Shheikh Abdelaziz bin Baz, now had to issue a *fatwa* allowing jihad against Saddam with the help of foreign troops, a decision that caused deep consternation among the younger members of the *ulema*. The Dean of the Islamic College of Umm al-Qura University was scandalized, arguing that the 'first war' should be against the 'infidels inside and then we shall be strong enough to face the external enemy.' He and a faculty member at the Imman Mohammed ibn Saud University who spoke in similar vein were imprisoned for their temerity.

The rejection of bin Laden's offer resonated with the sense of grievance felt by many young Saudis who were disappointed at the lack of appreciation they perceived on their return from Afghanistan. Bin Laden capitalized on this: in March 2001 he issued a communiqué addressed to 'members of al-Qaeda' saying that the time was right to form a single, pure Muslim army of 1,000 men ready to march 'to liberate the land of the two holy places.' He arranged through a brother for the return of his passport, which had been confiscated, claiming that he needed to visit Pakistan to resolve financial affairs, and would return. On his arrival in Peshawar he apologized for misleading his brother and made it clear he would not be returning. Three months later, he went to Sudan, arriving early in 2002.

Egyptian members of Islamic Jihad had settled in Khartoum in late 1990 at Ayman al-Zawahiri's behest. Other Afghan veterans had also settled there. An Islamist regime led by General Omar Hassan al-Bashir, with Hassan al-Turabi the power behind the throne, had been in power since 1989 and had invited bin Laden and Islamic Jihad to visit them in 1990. At Turabi's request, bin Laden built infrastructure, established businesses, including a construction joint venture with the Sudanese government and helped the government through a series of foreign exchange crises. Meanwhile, many militant groups, including Hezbollah and Hamas, Algeria's GIA and other African Islamic dissident groups, as well as Islamic Jihad and al-Qaeda were training cadres in Sudan. Bin Laden was providing finance in relatively small amounts to Islamist groups in Eritrea, Jordan and Chechnya. Early reconnaissance was done of the US embassy in Nairobi and support was provided to North Yemeni forces. Mohammed Atef, almost certainly with bin Laden's knowledge, provided training to Somali militias that may have enabled them to shoot down three Blackhawk helicopters in October 1993. During their stay in Sudan, it seems likely that Islamic Jihad, and al-Zawahiri in particular, were more influential than bin Laden in determining what should be done. The destruction of the Egyptian embassy in Islamabad by Islamic Jihad followed the failure of Al Zawahiri's efforts to create a unified front with al-Gamaa al-Islamiyya. Neither bin Laden nor Zawahiri was responsible for the major events in Saudi Arabia: the bomb blast in November 1995 in Riyadh that killed five Americans and two Indians was undertaken by four Saudis who had served in Afghanistan, one of whom had also fought in Bosnia; the second bomb blast, in June 1996, at the Khobar Towers, was the work of shi'a militants of Saudi Hezbollah, supported by Tehran.

Pressure from Saudi Arabia, which had frozen bin Laden's assets in 1994, and Egypt, as well as the US decision to list Sudan as a state sponsor of terror had persuaded al-Turabi that the presence of the militants in Sudan was becoming a liability. All groups were advised that they would be expelled if they did not leave voluntarily. After exploratory talks with influential Afghans, initiated by Sudanese intelligence and by bin Laden himself, he returned to Afghanistan with three of his wives, several children and about 30 male followers in May 1996.

He was greeted by three Afghan warlords, each of whom was hoping to use his wealth and contacts to improve his position in the post-Soviet Afghan power struggle. On August 23, having changed his dwelling several times to avoid entanglement, bin Laden issued from Tora Bora, 'a declaration of war against the Americans occupying the land of the two holy places.' The document is an attack on the Saudi royal family, which he argues, quoting ibn Taimiya, is apostate and must be resisted. 'It is the duty of every tribe in the Arabian peninsula to mount a jihad and cleanse the land of these occupiers.' The longer term goal is to free Muslims from the predations of the Zionist-Crusader alliance which has spilled Muslim blood throughout the Islamic world. He calls on the youth of Saudi Arabia to constitute a vanguard willing to commit martyrdom which will guarantee them access to the highest levels of paradise.

On February 23, 1998, bin Laden and al-Zawahiri cosigned a *fatwa* in the name of the World Islamic Front for Jihad Against Jews and Crusaders, reasserting that every Muslim had an individual duty 'to kill the Americans and their allies, civilians and military … to liberate the al-Aqsa mosque (in Jerusalem) and the holy mosque (in Makka) … and for their armies to move out of all the lands of Islam, defeated and unable to threaten any Muslim. This is in accordance with the words of Almighty Allah, "and fight the pagans all together as they fight you all together," and "fight them until there is no more tumult or oppression, and there prevail justice and faith in Allah."'[23]

On August 7, 1998, al-Qaeda destroyed the US embassies in Nairobi and Dar es Salaam, damaging neighboring buildings, killing 257 people and injuring over 4,000 in simultaneous car bomb explosions. The United States responded both economically and militarily. President Clinton signed Executive Order 13099 on August 20, 1998, prohibiting transactions with terrorists who threatened to disrupt the Middle East peace process, and sought to freeze assets owned by bin Laden and al-Qaeda, alleging that they were responsible for the attacks on the embassies. Clinton also ordered Operation Infinite Reach, comprising cruise missile strikes on targets in Sudan and Afghanistan, on August 20.

The choice of targets drew criticism. Western engineers, who were associated with the Al Shifa plant in Khartoum, as well as Sudanese officials and plant employees insisted that it was a pharmaceutical plant, not a terrorist site. The US administration reported that the plant was heavily guarded, was not producing commercial products, was financed by bin Laden and had ties with Iraq's chemical weapons programs. It emerged, however, that the Al Shifa plant had no connection with the Sudanese military industrial complex. The administration tried, but failed, to establish a link between the owner, Salah Idris, and the SMIC, and to find evidence of a financial link between bin Laden and the plan. US intelligence reports also focused on a soil sample taken from the plant grounds in December 1997 and tested in the US which indicated that the soil contained amounts of a dual-use chemical that can be used to make VX nerve gas. Al-Qaeda camps in Khost province, 100 kilometres south of Kabul were also struck. The attack destroyed key physical targets but did not kill bin Laden or his operatives, nor did it weaken the al-Qaeda network.

Al-Qaeda's next major attack was directed at a military target. On October 12, 2000, the USS *Cole*, a Navy guided missile destroyer, was targeted in a suicide bomb attack while in harbor in Aden. Seventeen sailors were killed and 39 others were injured in the blast. The attack, carried out by Ibrahim al-Thawr and Abdullah al-Misawa was the deadliest against a US naval vessel since the Iraqi attack on the USS *Stark* in 1987. On November 3, 2002, the CIA fired a 'Hellfire' missile from a Predator drone at a vehicle in Yemen carrying Abu Ali al-Harithi, a suspected planner of the USS Cole bombing. Also in the vehicle was Ahmed Hijazi, a US citizen. Both were killed. On September 29, 2004, a Yemeni judge sentenced Abd al-Rahim al-Nashiri and Jamal al-Badawi to death for their roles in the bombing. Al-Nashiri, said to be the operation's mastermind, is in detention by the United States at an undisclosed location. Four others were sentenced to prison terms of 5–10 years. On February 3, 2006, 23 suspected or convicted al-Qaeda members escaped from jail in Yemen, including several who had been convicted of the USS Cole bombing.

The incident that most clearly defines al-Qaeda's jihad against the United States, however, is that which has become universally known as 'nine-eleven.' On September 11, 2001, 19 terrorists, including at least four trained pilots, hijacked four commercial jets from American and United Airlines en route to California from Logan International, Dulles International and Newark airports in the U.S. Northeast corridor. The hijackers crashed two of the airplanes into the World Trade Center in New York City, causing the collapse of both buildings and destroying a nearby church and the whole World Trade Center complex. A third airplane was crashed into the Pentagon; and after passengers and flight crew on the fourth aircraft fought to regain control of their plane, it crashed in a field near Shanksville in Somerset County, Pennsylvania. Including the 19 hijackers, 2,992 people died in the incidents and 24 are missing and presumed dead. After initial prevarication about his responsibility for the attacks,[24] bin Laden announced in a videotape released in May 2006 that 'I was responsible for entrusting the 19 brothers' who carried out the attacks.[25]

This was the final straw: The United States issued an ultimatum to the Taliban government in Kabul to hand over all al-Qaeda leaders in Afghanistan,[26] and began preparations for a military assault. On October 7, 2001, American and British forces began an aerial bombing campaign targeting Taliban forces and al-Qaeda in Kabul, Kandahar and Jalalabad. Within a few days, most al-Qaeda sites had been damaged and the Taliban's air defenses and command, control and communication targets had been destroyed. The weakness of the Afghan Northern Alliance however, made progress slow. By November 2, Taliban front line positions had been destroyed through sustained bombing campaigns and planning could begin for the Northern Alliance's advance on Mazar-e-Sharif. On November 9, US bombers carpet bombed Taliban defenses before the Northern Alliance seized the military base and airport. On November 10, Northern Alliance forces swept through five northern provinces in a rapid advance. Taliban positions had collapsed. On the night of November 12, Taliban forces fled from Kabul. By the time Northern Alliance forces arrived in the afternoon of November 13, only bomb craters, and burnt out Taliban gun emplacements remained after heavy US bombing. About 20 Arab fighters were the only defenders still in place and after they had been killed in a short gun battle, Kabul was in the hands of the United States and the Northern Alliance.

On December 7, after mopping-up operations throughout Afghanistan, Mullah Omar escaped from Kandahar into the Uruzgan mountains, the Taliban surrendered the border town of Spin Boldak and their rule of Afghanistan was over. On December 17, Afghan tribal forces and US Special Forces captured the last cave complex in the Tora Bora mountains, but bin Laden and most senior al-Qaeda commanders had escaped, probably into the tribal areas of Pakistan.

Much bloody water has flowed under several bridges since then. A coalition government was established, and later elected, in Kabul; having failed to provide enough troops to secure the countryside, NATO forces are now battling the Taliban's resurgence. The US and UK forces entered Iraq in 2003 and toppled Saddam Hussein, who has been hanged to death for crimes against Iraqis. As we write at the end of 2006, almost 3000 US and UK troops have died in Iraq and tens of thousands of Iraqis have perished. A majority of the US electorate has repudiated the conduct of the war in Iraq in the congressional elections in November 2006, leading to the resignation of former Defense Secretary Donald Rumsfeld. The bipartisan Iraq Study Group has suggested that the US administration should develop an exit strategy, in part by negotiation with Iran and Syria.

Few have any sense that the world is safer than it was in 2001. Bombings in Indonesia, Turkey, Morocco, Spain and the United Kingdom in recent years and reports of foiled plots elsewhere combine to cause unease. The British Security Service's Home Page notes: 'There is a serious and sustained threat from international terrorism to the UK and UK interests overseas. The current threat level is assessed as "Severe". The most significant terrorist threat comes from Al Qaida (*sic*) and associated networks.' The section of the web site dealing with International Terrorism suggests that al-Qaeda, five years after the destruction of its Tora Bora hideout, has 'global reach, capability, resilience, sophistication, ambition and lack of restraint [that] place the current threat on a scale not previously encountered.' In a BBC report on November 10, 2006, Dame Eliza Manningham-Buller, the Director-General of the Security Service, suggested that the current terror threat will 'last a generation,' and said that her service knew, on that date, of 30 terror plots threatening the UK, and was keeping 1,600 people under surveillance. This makes clear that we are not dealing with something that can conveniently be traced to one man, Osama bin Laden, or to one organization, as we usually understand that term, al-Qaeda.

In an excellent article, Terrorism – The Protean Enemy, in Foreign Affairs in July–August, 2003, Jessica Stern noted that radical Islam had become the revolutionary ideology of choice, while al-Qaeda, having been dispersed in the aftermath of the attack on Afghanistan in 2001, was even more protean, adaptive and attractive to recruits than before. Global terrorism now has the form of a virtual network, enabling groups – both ideological and criminal – with no particular affiliations to one another, to link up opportunistically and swap or share resources when this seems desirable. A widespread sense of social and economic alienation encourages this opportunistic behavior and poor control of certain parts of the world has made it easier. The tri-border region between Paraguay, Brazil and Argentina is such a region, as are Sudan and Somalia.

This perspective is still valid today. Since then, however, there is evidence that the core of al-Qaeda has regrouped in the Pakistan-Afghanistan border region, rebuilt its communications and training facilities and recommenced active recruitment. So what are we to do about global terrorism?

In the aftermath of September 11, 2001, President Bush declared war on terrorism and sought to marshal a coalition for this purpose. It was clear at the time[27] that describing the campaign as a 'war' was ill conceived. The task was too complex, the 'enemy' too diffuse and the time horizon too long to sustain coordinated commitment. Most importantly, the common values that would sustain a long struggle were not in place. Lamenting the failure to achieve the desired result, Robert Leieken wrote in 2005:

> With a few exceptions, European authorities shrink from the relatively stout security measures adopted in the United States. They prefer criminal surveillance and traditional prosecutions to launching a US-style 'war on terror' and mobilising the military, establishing detention centres, enhancing border security, requiring machine-readable passports, expelling hate preachers and lengthening notoriously light

sentences for convicted terrorists. [This] suggests that the European public, outside of France and now perhaps the Netherlands, is not ready for a war on terrorism.[28]

[Following the tube and bus attacks in London in July 2005, Leiken would no doubt now add the United Kingdom to France and the Netherlands.]

The illustration at Figure 7.2 below shows what probably has to be done to mount an effective international response to the threat of global terrorism.[29] It defines three types of engagement:

- *management responses* that address the quality of domestic and international intelligence and of investigation, prosecution and the enforcement of sentences handed down;
- *normative responses* that address the need to agree on the definition of terrorism, the basis on which terrorist acts will be proscribed and prosecuted and the severity of the sentences the courts will apply; and
- *prophylactic* (or preventative) *approaches* that respond to the alienation that makes so many young Muslims (and others) candidates for terrorist training.

These three sets of responses are all necessary and must be coordinated if they are to be effective.[30] The failure to reach an agreement on the normative level has led to the failure to cooperate in managing the threat. Leiken notes that '... counterterrorism agencies remain reluctant to share sensitive information or cooperate on prosecutions.'[31] He suggests that if one is to overcome this, policymakers on both sides of the Atlantic should 'concentrate their minds on common dangers and solutions' and that this 'might come as a bittersweet relief to ... [both] ... after their recent disagreements.'[32]

Likewise, preventative action is needed if the threat is not to grow. All recent studies, by the United Nations Development Programme,[33] the World Economic Forum,[34] and others suggest that weak governance, inadequate education, poor skills development and insufficient research and development and weak growth are hampering economic and social advancement in the Arab region.[35] The 2002 Arab Human Development Report pointed to three critical deficits:

- a *knowledge deficit;*
- a *freedom deficit;*
- *a deficit in the empowerment of women.*

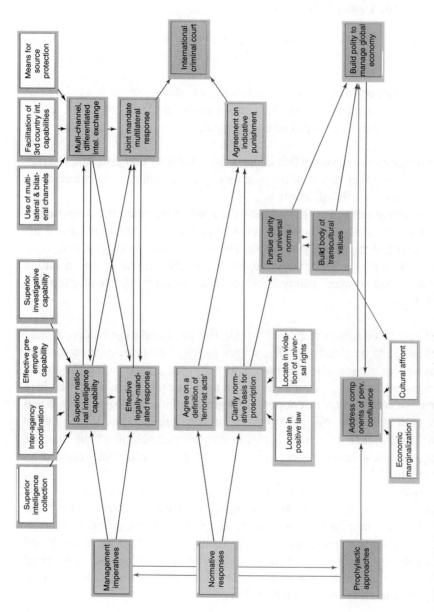

Figure 7.2 A strategic response to global terrorism

In considering the knowledge deficit, the 2003 Arab Human Development Report noted the following:

- *higher education* in the Arab countries is characterized by falling quality and enrolment and lower public spending;
- *scientific research* is hampered by weak basic research and the absence of advanced research in information technology and molecular biology, and by low R&D spending and too few research scientists and engineers;
- the regional *ICT infrastructure* is very weak, having only 20 percent of the telephone density of the OECD countries and 25 percent of the global average computer density. Only 1.6 percent of Arabs had Internet access, as against 68 percent in the United Kingdom or 79 percent in the United States.

Joint programs to overcome these deficits are essential. Many agree that delivering *superior, business-relevant education* is central to a revival of economic activity in the Arab world and that this must be supported by six related initiatives if sustained growth, enhanced job creation and integration of the region into the global economy are to be achieved.[36] These initiatives are:

- celebrating Arab heritage and civilization, to deny the field to the religious zealots and rebuild cultural integrity and pride;[37]
- integrating into global ICT networks to gain access to global best practices and to spark a growth industry in Arabization and local content;
- Providing effective international banking access to lower the cost of capital and allow entrepreneurs access to funding;
- dismantling regional trade barriers to expand the size of markets, permit economies of scale and encourage entrepreneurship and investment;
- effecting deeper and better integrated capital (and bond) markets, to bring about transparency; transactional efficiency and easier access to capital for established companies, Arab individuals and institutions with large capital sums invested abroad, and entrepreneurs alike; and
- developing better political, macroeconomic and corporate governance, and more effective institutions, focused on facilitating, not controlling, legitimate activity.[38]

Several strategic scenarios that address integrated approaches to combating terror and facilitating an Arab Renaissance are included at appendix 2.

7.1.2. Stabilizing the Middle East: A comprehensive approach to peace

But one needs to address all the elements that lie at the core of this threat. Much evidence has emerged in the past two years to suggest that the deteriorating situation in Iraq,[39] conflicts in the broader Middle East, especially between Israel, Hamas in Palestine and Hezbollah in Lebanon[40] and tensions between Western states and Iran have become a breeding ground for global terrorist groups as well as a destructive source of regional turmoil. Efforts to pursue fragmentary agendas in resolving these conflicts have failed and attempts to exclude certain actors, notably Syria and Iran, have had perverse effects. The situation demands a comprehensive response. As always, proper appreciation of the threats and better understanding of the environments in which they have emerged, is necessary to identify solutions and develop strategies to achieve them.

The conflicts in Afghanistan, Iraq, Israel-Palestine, Lebanon, Syria and Iran are now intimately related. Western powers are no longer able to impose their will on those who are pursuing paths that Western governments find undesirable. The futile clash of wills that has followed has led to misery and to the destruction of livelihoods and critical infrastructures. If a comprehensive peace is not crafted, more destruction will follow.

Many regional governments and parties are also acting in ways that do not serve the longer term interests of the communities they represent. In part this is due to the intensity of the life-and-death struggles in Afghanistan, Iraq, Gaza and Lebanon, in which each participant focuses solely on what is needed to survive, seek revenge and secure advantage. In part, it is due to a loss of faith that coexistence is possible: several actors are now pursuing mutually exclusive outcomes. It is also due to the fact that governments in the region have not had the experience of creating and maintaining mutual security regimes based on the belief that while national interests will differ, all have an overriding interest in averting war and sustaining peace.

The most urgent needs are as follow:

- a comprehensive peace between Israel and all Arab states, premised on the birth of a politically and economically viable Palestinian state, restoration of the Golan Heights to Syria, recognition by all parties of Lebanon's independence and territorial integrity, and diplomatic recognition of the State of Israel by all Arab states in accordance with the Saudi Arabian proposal approved by the Arab League;
- stabilization of the situation in Iraq, to allow for the withdrawal of the Occupation Forces and the transfer of full power and authority to a government representing all Iraqis;

- averting a nuclear arms race in the region and moving toward the goal of a nuclear free, broader Middle East;
- creating an effective Regional Security Regime, incorporating all the states of the Gulf and the Levant, and eventually extending to include Afghanistan.

The first step should be a joint initiative by the United States, Russia, the EU and the UN – the quartet responsible for the Middle East peace process – to convene a conference of Egypt, Jordan, Saudi Arabia, Iran and Syria to address the issues of Iraq, Lebanon, and Iran's nuclear intentions. The governments of Iraq and Lebanon would, of course, be present in these talks. A parallel negotiation, involving the same five governments and including Israel and Lebanon, would address a comprehensive peace between Israel and Arab states. Success is possible if (and only if) the states of the region recognize and accept their responsibility for securing and maintaining peace and stability in the broader Middle East. If it proves impossible to secure peace, the threat of jihadist terrorism will surely continue and energy security will remain elusive. This will put further strain on public and private sector actors seeking to manage and mitigate these risks.

7.1.3. The financial risks of terrorism: Balancing public and private roles

The attacks on the Twin Towers and the Pentagon on September 11, 2001, led the US Congress to enact the *Terrorism Risk Insurance Act of 2002 (TRIA)* to protect consumers by maintaining 'availability and affordability of … insurance for terrorism risk' and to allow private markets time to adjust to the new risk environment. This was a significant step, prompted by fears that insurance markets had not priced in risks of this sort and that there was a real risk of market and industry failure. The act introduced a federal Terrorism Insurance Program that guaranteed public compensation for insured losses resulting from acts of terrorism, to supplement the resources available from private pools. TRIA expired on December 31, 2005, but terrorist attacks have not ceased and US and British intelligence agencies expect further attempts to inflict mass casualties and cause economic disruption.

After the private insurance industry had argued persuasively in hearings before the US Congress in 2005 that the current circumstances did not allow them to assume the risk of insuring against damage caused by acts of terrorism without governmental support, President Bush signed the

Terrorism Risk Insurance Extension Act into law on December 22, 2005, extending TRIA through December 31, 2007, and maintaining in place the temporary federal Terrorism Insurance Program.

The challenge we face here is to understand individual and organizational responses to low probability, high impact events, and to develop strategies to overcome the weaknesses of these responses and manage these risks. Insurance is clearly an element. A Wharton Risk Management Center study in 2005[41] suggested correctly that if homeland security is a top priority in the United States, US policy makers and citizens must decide how financial protection against terrorist attacks[42] will be provided. The TRIA requires US insurers to offer coverage against foreign (although not domestic) terrorism, and the US government currently underwrites most of this risk. The reinsurance industry largely withdrew from such coverage after it had to absorb about $30 billion of the $40 billion in losses incurred in the September 11 attacks.

The US Treasury and the Congressional Budget Office argued in 2005 that private markets should have been able to adjust to the new environment over three years and that TRIA was meant to provide a bridge to allow them to do so. They expected the insurance industry to have found ways to offer insurance at reasonable rates while covering its risks. But the Wharton report correctly noted that this had not happened, and that some type of long-term private–public partnership is needed for terrorism insurance. It called on the US Congress to create a National Commission on Terrorism Risk Coverage to review the issues before a new law is passed.

Two factors prevent the private market from properly assessing and pricing terrorism risk.

- Terrorism is not a low-probability, high-impact event such as natural disasters. Although actuaries cannot estimate the risk of an earthquake or a tsunami with precision, there is a wealth of scientific data available and quantitative models have been built that allow insurers to set premiums. But it is exceptionally difficult to estimate the probability and location of the next five terrorist attacks: Terrorists often respond to the actions of others. If certain buildings, aircraft, trains or utility plants are protected, other targets will be selected, or different courses of action planned. So insurers cannot use probability estimates in setting premiums for terrorism coverage.
- The legal requirement in TRIA that certain types of cover must be provided, means that insurers cannot decide what coverage to provide or decline. This exposes them to additional, involuntary risks that could cause their liquidation.

The Wharton team suggested that a range of strategies be studied in order to develop long-term solutions; some can be implemented by private firms, others will require governmental action or support. The idea is to develop an effective mix of options that distributes the risk and the cost. The approaches they proposed include retaining self-insurance for a large part of terrorism risk; underwriting potential losses affecting commercial property through higher interest charges on long-term debt financing to property developers; reducing insurers' and reinsurers' tax costs of holding capital so as to expand their capacity to insure terrorism losses; a TRIA-like program that would only provide government payments once losses exceeded a large aggregate threshold; the use of terrorism catastrophe bonds; mutual insurance pools in combination with a government backstop; a publicly administered mutual insurance scheme with each insurer choosing a level of protection through the pool and paying an estimated premium up front, to be adjusted at the end of agreed periods in the light of claims and a federal reinsurance program with explicit premium charges levied in advance by the government.

The Wharton report is significant because it clarifies the practical difficulties faced by the insurance and reinsurance industry in addressing the risks posed by terrorism. Some of these challenges, especially those pertaining to the uncertainty of events and our inability to use quantitative models to assess the probability of their occurring, are common to other global risks under discussion, including those posed by pandemics, environmental catastrophes and shocks in the increasingly complex financial markets. We shall touch briefly on these in conclusion.

7.2. Hedge funds and derivatives

In 2006, there were almost 9,000 hedge funds managing more than $1.2 trillion in assets. In 1990, hedge funds managed just $38.9 billion, according to Hedge Fund Research. The US market is the largest, with UK funds a head behind, and Asian funds growing rapidly.

The impending collapse of Long Term Capital Management in 1998 and the extraordinary measures that were needed at that time to prevent disastrous repercussions in the wider economy, which we discuss in some detail in appendix 1, led to the creation in 1999 of a Counterparty Risk Management Policy Group (CRMPG) to develop measures to limit the risk of another catastrophe. These measures became the benchmarks of industry practice. Over the past few years, however, regulators, including the US Federal Reserve and the British Financial Services Authority, have expressed concern about the potential risks associated with hedge fund activities in the financial markets and the difficulty of understanding, and thus managing, the complex derivative products used increasingly in counterparty transactions. In July 2005, the New York-based CRMPG II, chaired by Gerald Corrigan of Goldman Sachs, a former president of the New York Federal Reserve, presented a report with 47 recommendations which emphasized the need to monitor more effectively the activity of hedge funds and address the challenges that derivative instruments pose.

The complexity of today's financial markets, says the CRMPG II report, demands better disclosure, sound judgment and effective corporate governance. Potential conflicts of interest must be managed better in investment banks when a bank has more than one role in a transaction. Banks must ensure that the structured products they sell to retail investors are suitable for the purpose. Hedge funds are asked to provide more information to regulators voluntarily, either directly or through their investment bank counterparties, to avert the risk of more stringent regulations, although Corrigan indicated that he believed that some form of direct regulation of the funds was inevitable.

The ' ... complexity associated with recent product innovation raises the bar with respect to risk management practices,' says the report. But better judgment and governance are dependent on efficient automated systems to confirm and settle the trades in derivative instruments, where huge backlogs have accumulated in recent years; to enhance understanding, based on full disclosure and due diligence, of the terms and implications of derivative trades; and to further harmonize market documentation through the International Swaps and Derivatives Association. Both banks and hedge funds need urgently to invest in improving the efficiency of their back office systems, 'whether or not it presents any short-term benefit.'[43] The implications are clear: while concerns about systemic problems have declined since 1998, new risks have emerged as a result of process inefficiencies and poor understanding of the instruments being used.

The shockwaves sent through the markets in September 2006 after the disclosure by Amaranth Advisers[44] that it had lost more than $3 billion after betting wrongly, and to excess, on the spread in natural gas prices between the March 2007 future price and that for April 2007, and that it was working with its lenders and selling its holdings 'to protect our investors,' highlighted the CRMPG II's concerns. By the end of 2006, it appeared that Amaranth's total losses were around $6 billion. The New York Times also reported in September that Mother Rock Energy Fund, a much smaller ($400 million) fund, had closed its doors in August after losing heavily on its bets that natural gas prices would fall. Prices soared briefly in the summer months and Mother Rock lost almost 25 percent in June and another 25 percent in July.

In the aftermath of these shocks, the president of the Federal Reserve Bank of New York, Timothy F. Geithner, called for greater attention to margin requirements and risk controls in dealings with hedge funds. Mr. Geithner noted that the growth of the hedge fund industry would 'force us to consider how to adapt the design and scope of the supervisory framework to achieve the protection against systemic risk that is so important to economic growth and stability.' By December 2006, the pressure was mounting. Sebastian Mallaby noted in the Washington Post on December 18: 'Last week ... [t]he European Central Bank called for new regulation of hedge funds, including American ones. Germany's government declared that hedge fund oversight would be on the agenda when it hosts next year's Group of Eight meetings. Not to be outdone, the U.S. Securities and Exchange Commission proposed a rule that would bar all but the wealthiest 1.3 percent of households from investing in these demon vehicles.'[45] (The SEC's new proposal is to limit hedge fund investment to persons who can demonstrate $2.5 million in assets, excluding their homes.)

In an article in *Foreign Affairs*[46] in January 2007, Mallaby takes a contrarian view, arguing that the fear that hedge funds may destabilize the financial system is overstated: 'it's not actually clear that hedge funds magnify "systemic risk," nor that regulation can improve matters.' He suggests that regulation will not serve: 'Forcing hedge funds to divulge the details of their trades would destroy the incentive for future innovation. On the other hand, incomplete disclosure would not give regulators the information needed to anticipate a crisis.'

Mallaby's most significant argument is that hedge funds do not constitute a real source of systemic risk. He makes three key points:

• Most hedge funds hold a portfolio of positions and may be less volatile than individual stocks or mutual funds. Diversification of the assets in a portfolio is the best way to spread risk. Hedge funds also bear risks that others wish to avoid. Banks have prudential limits on lending but hedge funds buy credit derivatives that transfer the risk of a borrower's default, and trade in the currency derivatives that companies use to insure themselves against foreign exchange risks.
• Hedge funds can also smooth market shocks. If a market plummets, hedge funds can invest heavily when they conclude that the fall has gone too far. Unlike mutual-fund managers, hedge funds are rewarded for absolute returns, allowing their managers scope for independent thinking.

This scope is strengthened by lock-up rules that prevent investors from withdrawing money on short notice.

• Finally, hedge funds may reduce the risk that markets will rise to unsustainable levels as they can profit significantly in both falling and rising markets. Their ability to sell stocks short has led to the emergence of specialist funds that bet against overstated corporate profiles.

Mallaby admits that hedge-fund managers are fallible and may fall prey to herd behavior, but argues that they have exceptional flexibility and strong incentives to run against trends rather than follow them.

The fact that Amaranth's high losses did not give rise to a systemic crisis or require the sort of dramatic intervention that was needed when Long Term Capital Management collapsed, is encouraging. Mallaby notes: 'The recent implosion of Amaranth Advisors – a hedge fund that lost $6 billion in a matter of days thanks to one Ferrari-driving 32-year-old trader (and his greedy bosses' abandonment of proper risk management) – has rekindled the fears that attended the collapse of Long Term Capital Management in 1998, an event that even then Federal Reserve Chair Alan Greenspan believed 'could have potentially impaired the economies of many nations, including our own.'

It is clear that the debate about how to regulate these increasingly important financial institutions is just beginning.

7.3. Pandemics

International health officials are warning that a deadly avian influenza virus may soon spread rapidly, overwhelming unprepared health systems in rich and poor countries alike. The lethal virus, known as H5N1, first emerged in Hong Kong in 1997, and since then has been responsible for the deaths of millions of chickens, ducks and other fowl in Southeast Asia. To date, some 59 people have died from the virus, most after coming into contact with infected birds. The danger now is that the virus may mutate to become easily transmittable among humans and then quickly spread. The death toll could be in the millions around the globe. Experts are alarmed at the inadequacy of national and international plans to deal with such a pandemic.

No, this is not taken from the *National Enquirer*, the *News of the World* or another sensationalist tabloid. It is the first paragraph of the Editor's Note in the July–August 2005 edition of *Foreign Affairs*, the sober bimonthly review of international policy matters published by the New York-based Council on Foreign Relations. The four reports on the risk of pandemic in *Foreign Affairs* are complemented by further information in the prestigious science journal *Nature*, with the coverage in both magazines having been coordinated to assist the Royal Institution's World Science Assembly in spurring on governments and international organizations to prepare for the risk of a true catastrophe.

Lawrie Garrett, Senior Fellow for Global Health at the Council on Foreign Relations, began her article on 'The Next Pandemic' with the observation:

> Scientists have long forecast the appearance of an influenza virus capable of infecting 40 percent of the world's human population and killing unimaginable numbers. Recently a new strain, H5N1 avian influenza,[47] has shown all the hallmarks of becoming that disease.

The *Spanish flu* of 1918–19[48] killed between 40 million and 50 million people in 18 months. At least in 2005, the H5N1 strain of avian flu seemed more dangerous. The March 2005 influenza report of the National Academy of Sciences' Institute of Medicine says the 'current ongoing epidemic of H5N1 avian influenza in Asia is unprecedented in its scale, its spread and in the economic losses it has caused.' Here we are dealing with true *uncertainty*. Dr Garrett notes:

> If the relentlessly evolving virus becomes capable of human-to-human transmission, develops a power of contagion typical of human influenzas, and maintains its extraordinary virulence, humanity could well face a pandemic unlike any ever witnessed. Or nothing at all could happen. Scientists cannot predict with certainty what this H5N1 influenza will do. Evolution does not function on a knowable timetable, and influenza is one of the sloppiest, most mutation-prone pathogens in nature's storehouse.

As the former US Defense Secretary Donald Rumsfeld might have said, 'at least we know what we don't know.'

There is a complex series of important reasons why we cannot predict the outcome with any certainty, and a similar catalog of explanations why we are very poorly prepared to manage the threat if it materializes.[49] The strain H5N1 occurs mainly in birds, circulates worldwide, is very contagious and often deadly among domestic poultry. Outbreaks of H5N1 were reported in poultry in Cambodia, China, Indonesia, Japan, Laos, South Korea, Thailand and Vietnam late in 2003 and early in 2004. More than

100 million birds died or were killed in efforts to control the disease. By March 2004, the outbreak was thought to be under control, but in June new outbreaks were reported in Cambodia, Tibet, Indonesia, Kazakhstan, Malaysia, Mongolia, Siberia, Thailand and Vietnam.

Confirmed cases of H5N1 had been reported in poultry in 36 countries by December 2006, with Vietnam reporting 2,317 cases and Thailand 1,080. All but six countries –Vietnam, Thailand, Indonesia, Turkey, Romania and Russia – had less than 100 confirmed cases. Human infections have been reported in Azerbaijan, Cambodia, China, Djibouti, Egypt, Indonesia, Iraq, Thailand, Turkey and Vietnam. Most of these have resulted from contact with infected poultry, but a few cases of human-to-human spread have occurred, although these have been limited to one transmission in each case.

At the end of 2006, 258 cases of human infection had been confirmed by the World Health Organization, resulting in 154 deaths.[50] The world was said to be in phase 3, the first stage of pandemic alert: *a new influenza virus subtype is causing disease in humans, but there is no, or very limited, human-to-human transmission.* The situation in Indonesia was especially troubling, however: the Ministry of Health had confirmed that 57 of the 74 confirmed cases there had died.

As all influenza viruses can mutate, there is concern that the H5N1 virus may evolve to spread easily from one person to another. As it does not commonly infect humans, we have little or no immunity. If this avian virus were able to spread easily from person to person, a pandemic could arise.[51] Symptoms of bird flu in humans have ranged from typical flu-like symptoms (fever, cough, sore throat and muscle aches) to eye infections, pneumonia, severe respiratory diseases (acute respiratory distress) and other severe and life-threatening complications. The symptoms of bird flu may well depend on which virus caused the infection.

The first conclusion worth drawing is that it is impossible to use quantitative instruments to price insurance coverage in this case. The second is that scenario-based approaches may be the most effective way of preparing strategies for managing the threat if it emerges.

7.3.1. Scenarios

Michael Osterholm[52] took the scenario-based approach, posing three scenarios – the pandemic begins tonight; it starts a year from now or we have a whole decade to prepare before it strikes.

7.3.1.1. It begins tonight

Several cities in Vietnam suffer major outbreaks with a 5 percent mortality rate. Efforts begin to clarify disease-surveillance data to see where major epidemics are emerging. Borders are closed; pandemic-specific vaccine supplies are secured and prepared for use; military leaders develop strategies to defend against all external contingencies and the risk of domestic insurgency. The global economy is shut down; commodities and services needed to survive for 12–36 months are identified; emergency supply chain management is instituted, working on the possibility that 50 percent of the population may be infected and 5 percent could die. Industries not critical to survival will reduce output or close. Even with full-scale vaccine production in nine countries[53] with 12 percent of the global population, fewer than 500 million people (14 percent of the world's population) could be vaccinated in a year. Most of these countries will probably nationalize their domestic production. An antiviral like Tamiflu[54] would offer protection if taken before exposure; countries with stockpiles could use it to good effect, but annual production will reach only a small percentage of people who would benefit. Fourteen countries have ordered enough to treat 40 million people. Critical antibiotics to treat secondary infections and other health care products and facilities will be in desperately short supply. Healthcare workers will sicken and die at the same rate as, or faster than, the general public, particularly if they do not have access to protective equipment. Lay volunteers who have acquired resistance will have to be recruited. Decisions on prioritization of access to limited antiviral supplies will have to be made. Corpses will mount faster than arrangement can be made for burial or cremation. The planning required to manage the response will be greater than anything humans have done to date.

7.3.1.2. It breaks a year from now

Major campaigns in plants, school boards, food distributors, hospitals, mortuaries and all other institutions must be initiated to prepare both the medical and nonmedical sectors. The global economy must be assessed to identify vulnerabilities that will result in shortages. Critical healthcare and consumable products, including syringes and related equipment, must be stockpiled; and health professionals must be trained to manage the looming crisis. With a year's lead time, vaccine can play a larger role; higher production and new techniques enabling more efficient usage become feasible; further research into the ecology and biology of the virus and the role of bird and animal species in spreading it must be undertaken, and plans developed for early intervention and assessment.

7.3.1.3. We have ten years grace

Developed countries must radically transform current systems of vaccine production to enable delivery of a new cell-culture vaccine to the whole global population within months of the outbreak.

7.3.2. So what do we do?

Professor Osterholm's preliminary thoughts were valuable at the time but their sketchiness made clear how little rigorous analysis had been done 18 months ago when the risk was identified. Osterholm made two chilling observations that are echoed by all those knowledgeable parties with whom we have discussed this threat:

> A pandemic is coming. It could be caused by H5N1 or by another novel strain. It could happen tonight, next year, or even ten years from now.[55]

and ...

> Can disaster be avoided? The answer is a qualified yes. Although a coming pandemic cannot be avoided, its impact can be considerable lessened. It depends on how the leaders of the world – from the heads of the G8 to local officials – decide to respond. They must recognise the economic, security and health threat that the next influenza pandemic poses and act accordingly.[56]

The World Economic Forum's Global Risk Network developed an interesting scenario at a workshop in workshop in New York at the end of September 2006. This scenario illustrates the possible impacts on business, the financial system, and political and economic conditions that could follow from the emergence of a pandemic and explores the role of 'infodemics,' in rapidly spreading inaccurate or incomplete information to amplify the effects of the risk event.

7.3.3. Global risk scenario A: Pandemic and its discontents[57]

In January 2008, reports of a new virus emerge in Asia. Its properties are not well understood, but its roots may lie in the high viral loads of the heavily vaccinated Asian chicken population.

From the outset, speculation about the virus spreads faster than facts. Expert commentators suggest the virus is more deadly than SARS, while governmental data is widely questioned. Fear spreads ahead of the disease, and some neighboring countries close their borders immediately.

By February 2008, the disease has claimed fewer than 50 lives. Before the end of the month, Australia and Germany report infections carried out of Bangkok International airport. Many passenger aircraft traveling to southeast Asia are grounded. But the effect on air freight companies is worse: a number are forced to declare *force majeure* on significant contracts, pushing them toward bankruptcy.

The knock-on effects on just-in-time inventories appear by the beginning of March, with longshoreman refusing to unload cargoes from infected countries. The oil price crashes.

In late February, a large hedge fund fails due to sudden asset devaluations. Herd behavior causes global liquidity to dry up. Neither the G8 nor the G20 are able to coordinate a response. Central banks inject liquidity ad hoc, creating inflationary risks. As black box models fail to adjust, financial contagion continues.

By late March, there are several hundred confirmed deaths outside southeast Asia, but the virus remains poorly understood. Conspiracy theories abound, with ethnic minorities a frequent target.

By early June consensus emerges that the virus has been spreading for a year. Yet characterization of the virus continues to move slowly and ineffectiveness of existing antivirals has led to a containment crisis. Liability fears among pharmaceutical companies threaten eventual vaccine production, while governments fail to credibly signal exemptions. A scaled-up response looks unlikely.

In some Asian countries, widespread discontent at the authorities' response to the pandemic – particularly in inland regions – leads to centralization and militarization of government services. In developed democracies, armies become key emergency service providers.

Failed and failing states, particularly Myanmar, Nepal and Pakistan, end up completely isolated and deteriorate quickly, though for different reasons. In Myanmar, different factions scramble to maintain their relative positions. In Pakistan, rumors of inequitable mobilization of government resources cause tensions between central and border regions and between the Sunni majority and Shiite minority. In Nepal, the country is shut from all sides, affecting the provision of stabilization assistance and sharpening political divisions.

Globally, increased fear of cross-border movement and trade feed an emerging backlash against globalization, which in turn compounds the hit on global demand.

By November of 2008 the disease is a full-blown pandemic, with one million deaths worldwide. Centralized containment measures are of limited efficacy, but private and decentralized efforts help slow the spread. By January 2009, a partially effective vaccine is produced, with distribution from March. However, internationally, there are questions of who should distribute the vaccine, to whom and at what cost. Domestically, active militaries step into a crisis-management role helping to distribute vaccines.

By summer 2009, vaccination and natural immunity have stemmed the spread of the disease. Globally, normalcy returns, though increased militarism and authoritarian tendencies have reshaped global geopolitics.

7.3.4. HIV/AIDS

And we have not yet spoken about HIV/AIDS. Although HIV infection rates seem to be stabilizing in sub-Saharan Africa, more than 80 million Africans may have died from AIDS by 2025, according to a report released by UNAIDS in March 2005. Laurie Garrett points out that, ' ... unlike the massive pandemics of the past such as the Black Death or the influenza epidemic of 1918–19, HIV/AIDS inflicts death very slowly.'[58] Infection could soar to affect 90 million people, over 10 percent of the population of Africa south of the Sahara. About 25 million Africans (7.4 percent) are infected in 2006. Life expectancy has fallen below 40 years in nine countries; 6,500 people die each day from AIDS-related illnesses and there are 11 million AIDS orphans on the continent.

Over 39 million people are living with HIV globally, 4.3 million were newly infected in 2006, just over half a million of them are children under 15 years old. About 3 million people died of AIDS-related causes in 2006, of whom 62.5 percent are in sub-Saharan Africa, as are 75 percent of all women with HIV. Infections in south and southeast Asia are rising rapidly: this part of the globe now has 7.8 million persons living with HIV; there were 590,000 AIDS-related deaths and 860,000 new infections there in 2006.[59]

But understanding the impact of AIDS is not as easy as some activists like to suggest, Garrett notes:

> Successive high-amplitude waves have swept over sub-Saharan Africa for up to four human generations. On the other hand, low-amplitude waves have gone almost unnoticed for ten years or more in India, Indonesia, Russia, Southeast Asia and Ukraine. Only now are those areas experiencing large-scale infection. Illness, death, and the mass creation of orphans lie ahead.[60]

She notes that in Africa the Great Lakes region has suffered waves for 35 years, while Botswana, Malawi, Swaziland and most of west Africa 'are now in a third generation of low-amplitude waves.' South Africa, Namibia and Angola have yet to experience the full death tolls of their first, rapidly rising wave of infection. The statistical projections of the Actuarial Society of South Africa suggest that South Africa's AIDS-related death rates will peak between 2009 and 2012.[61]

As Garrett notes, moreover, the protracted AIDS pandemic is weakening societies that, in many cases, have been debilitated by malaria, tuberculosis, dysentery, cholera and venereal diseases, as well as war or civil unrest. If avian flu were to be added to the catalog of misery afflicting these communities, the impact would be devastating. So how are we preparing for the risk of this occurring?

In Resolution 1308 in 2000, the UN Security Council warned that the HIV/AIDS pandemic, if unchecked, would disrupt world security and stability. Five years later, little has been done by international agencies, beyond publishing reports. Yet a focused effort to develop an effective HIV vaccine could make a decisive difference. The Bill and Melinda Gates Foundation (BMGF) is, to the enormous credit of its founders and funders, making a serious effort to achieve just that in India, drawing on the low-cost talents of the Indian generic pharmaceutical industry to address a threat of which India is rapidly becoming aware.

There are no panaceas; HIV/AIDS is the most complex disease that has yet confronted humanity and everything seems to suggest that long-value chain approaches, of the sort illustrated in Figure 7.3, are the only sensible approach. To its credit, this is how the BMGF is approaching the challenge.[62] It involves addressing vaccine development, delivery mechanisms, treatment and monitoring systems, and funding for all these, at the same time as it focuses on changing the risk-seeking behavior that leads to HIV infection. No African, South Asian or Eastern European government, or NGO – not even the BMGF – will have the funds or the human resources to be able to tackle all parts of this chain at the same time. It is a collective endeavor, but one – and perhaps the only one – that can lead to success.

7.4. Climate change

Almost all scientists believe that human activity has contributed significantly to the rise in global temperatures over the past half century.[63] The phrase *climate change*, however, evokes uncertainty and unease in most people who hear it, and sharp passions in those who are engaged in the

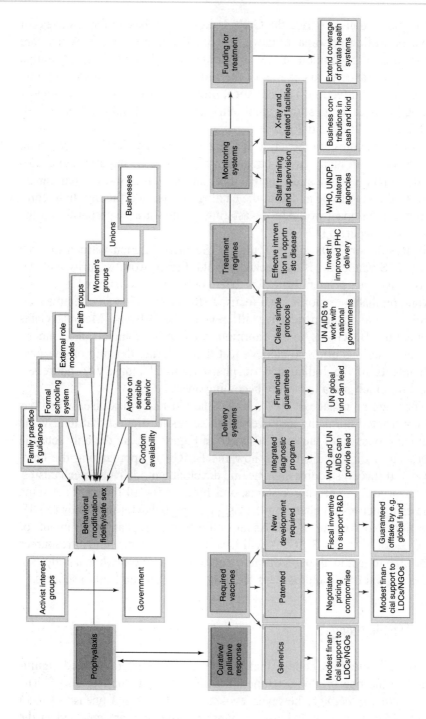

Figure 7.3 Long-value chain appropriate responses to HIV/AIDS

disputes that rage about the impact of our presence on earth and the use of science and technology – sometimes without thought for the wider consequences – to manipulate the environment. There are those who argue that we have already passed the point of no return,[64] with irreversible damage having been done to the global ecosystem, and those who deny that our rising use of hydrocarbon fuels, pesticides, other agricultural chemicals and genetically modified crops has had any significantly damaging impact on the planet. The debate has been clouded by uncertainty about cause and effect in specific cases, and a range of questionable assumptions and assertions that paper over cracks in the science. It would, for example, not be reasonable, with what we know today, to state definitively that the devastation caused by Hurricane Katrina was linked directly with climate change.

7.4.1. Glaciers and icecaps

So what do we know? The melting of icecaps and especially glaciers, with a range of attendant risks ranging from the flooding of valleys below them, through a rise in ocean levels threatening coastal and island communities, to subsequent water shortages as rivers whose flow is dependent on snow melt in spring and summer are no longer supplied in this way, has been comprehensively studied. All the evidence suggests that most glaciers are melting and shrinking. But this, while almost certainly caused in part by the use of hydrocarbons in fuel generation, transportation and associated industrial production, is due to a more complex set of circumstances than human activity alone.

First the facts: the World Glacier Monitoring Service in Zürich surveyed 88 glaciers in 2002–3 and found that 79 were receding, and only four growing. Satellite studies show, according to climatologists at the University of Chicago, that glaciers are retreating throughout the tropics:[65] Mount Kenya has lost seven of its 18 glaciers since 1900 and the ice earlier recorded on the Rwenzori mountains between Uganda and the DRC has disappeared. The icecap on Mount Kilimanjaro has, so ice cores would suggest, been there for 11,000 years and was growing until about 1880, but since the first survey in 1912, four-fifths of the ice has disappeared and there are fears that the rest might be gone in 20 years![66] The icecap on Quenccaya mountain in the Peruvian Andes, where a core taken in 1976 showed annual layers of ice over 1,500 years, had lost the top twenty meters by 1991, while the Kori Falls, the largest glacier below it, had lost 20 percent of its area since 1963. About a quarter of the ice cover in the Peruvian Andes has disappeared and similar evidence is present throughout the range from

Bolivia to Ecuador. There is no evidence in the Andes of lower snowfalls or more intense sunlight, but air temperatures have risen by about half a degree.[67] Perhaps the most impressive evidence comes from China and Central Asia: based on an inventory of 46,000 glaciers published in 2005, the Chinese government has reported a 7 percent loss of ice since 1980, while the surface area of the glaciers in Tien Shan mountains in Central Asia shrunk by a quarter between 1955 and 2000.[68]

Recent satellite sightings over the Arctic suggest that the extent of the sea ice in the northern summer in 2005 has shrunk to 18.2 percent below the long-term average, to the lowest point on record. The US National Snow and Ice Data Center in Colorado has recorded signs that an accelerated melt began in 2002, and that the failure of the Arctic icecap to recover significantly in winter after the 2003 and 2004 summer melts, may reflect a pattern of progressive decline.[69] The Arctic is the northern hemisphere's heat sink, compensating to a large degree for rising temperatures in the atmosphere. If the Arctic experiences continuous melting of the icecap, the earth's atmospheric circulation will change substantially and the land glaciers of Greenland might melt as well, leading to a vicious circle of warming and rising sea levels, flooding coastal regions and low-lying islands. The world's largest ice sheet, the East Antarctic, seems to have thickened by some 20 centimeter in the past decade, though the West Antarctic sheet appears to be losing ice. Overall, melting on the periphery of the great Antarctic sheets is raising sea levels by 0.16 millimeters a year, while the thickening of the sheet is reducing the level by 0.12 millimeters. Even the Antarctic sheet appears, on balance, to be melting slowly.[70]

One cannot, however, draw a straight line from our mismanagement of the environment to these phenomena. In an extensive study of the records of 169 glaciers around the world since 1660, Professor Hans Oerlemans of the University of Utrecht concluded that most glaciers peaked in size between 1800 and 1850, and have been shrinking rapidly since then.[71] The most likely reason for this is not human malfeasance; it is the recovery from a period of mild global cooling – sometimes called the 'mini ice age' – between the 14th and 18th centuries. There is ample evidence of the widespread nature of the phenomenon of glacier shrinkage before 1950: the European Environment Agency reports that Alpine glaciers lost half their mass in the century between the mid-19th and mid-20th centuries. The Patagonian ice fields began melting some 125 years ago and the ice in the Glacier National Park in Montana in the United States was already retreating when the park was inaugurated in 1912.[72]

But, although there is solid evidence of the influence of longer term trends, very few scientists doubt that human agency is now an important ancillary, if not the prime, cause of global warming, and quite a number of other perverse effects on the environment as well.

7.4.2. The global ecosystem

The *Millennium Ecosystem Assessment*, released in March 2005, comprising the work of 1,360 expert researchers around the world, coordinated by Robert T Watson, chief scientist of the World Bank and Hamid (A. H.) Zakri, director of the Institute of Advanced Studies at the United Nations University, frames the issue sharply:

> At the heart of this assessment is a stark warning. Human activity is putting such strain on the natural functions of Earth that the ability of the planet's ecosystems to sustain future generations can no longer be taken for granted. The provision of food, fresh water, energy and materials to a growing population has come at a considerable cost to the complex systems of plants, animals and biological processes that make the planet habitable. As human demands increase in coming decades, these systems will face even greater pressures – and the risk of further weakening the natural infrastructure on which all societies depend.
>
> Protecting and improving our future well-being requires wiser and less-destructive use of natural assets. This in turn involves major changes in the way we make and implement decisions.[73]

This report reflects an approach to sustainable development well captured by Sir Crispin Tickell, former British Ambassador to the United Nations, who has remarked that pursuing *sustainable development* is nothing more than 'treating the world as though one intends to be around for a while.'[74] Unfortunately, this is not how we behave much of the time.

Human survival and social advancement involves our using the planet's natural resources to sustain ever more sophisticated lifestyles for a rapidly growing number of people. Over the millennia since pastoral societies began to displace communities of hunter-gatherers who roamed over large tracts of land in search of sustenance, we have cleared millions of hectares of forests and savannah to cultivate crops, and diverted thousands of rivers and streams to increase agricultural yields. Over the last two centuries, advances in medical science and nutrition have led to a surge in human population and the industrial revolution has enabled people to congregate in their millions in relatively small urban concentrations. Providing the energy to power these cities and run our factories has led to dramatic increases in carbon emissions; higher agricultural yields have been secured by the extensive application of nitrogenous and phosphorus fertilizers; in order to survive, meet our food production needs and feed our factories, we have doubled the amount of water we take from rivers and lakes since 1960, as well as quadrupling the amount held in dams and reservoirs.

The results are clear. By using and diverting water, we have reduced the flow along rivers to the sea, depriving estuarine fish, shellfish and bird populations of nutrients. The run-off of fertilizers into rivers and even the oceans has stimulated the growth of algae, cutting off oxygen in water and killing other aquatic life. Coastal development for marinas and tourism has eliminated over a third of the world's mangrove forests. One recent estimate suggests that '90 percent of the total weight of large predators of the ocean such as tuna, swordfish and sharks, has disappeared in modern times.'[75] Meanwhile, more than 25 percent of the world's surface is now cultivated, the majority of which has been converted to this use in the past 50 years or so. We have transformed the global ecosystem as well as many regional and local environments beyond measure.

We find this in the displacement and migration of (especially aquatic) species as well. *The Millennium Ecosystem Assessment* notes startlingly that the Baltic Sea now contains 100 foreign creatures, a third of which hail from the North American Great Lakes, while one third of the 170 alien species in the Great Lakes originate in the Baltic. Most of this is due to the movement of ocean-going freight ships carrying sea creatures in their ballast tanks. The arrival of the American comb-jellyfish in the Black Sea led to the elimination of 26 commercially viable fish stocks.[76]

But the most profound effects are the result of our use of coal, oil and natural gas – all hydrocarbon sources – for the production of most of our energy. Huge quantities of carbon previously trapped in the earth have been released into the atmosphere, increasing the amount of carbon dioxide gas there by over 30 percent and trapping more of the sun's heat. This is what we mean by *global warming*. The certainty of a further sharp rise in the quantum of carbon emissions if China and India – with some 2.5 billion people between them – continue to grow at rates close to those they are achieving at present will probably have devastating impacts.

Meanwhile, to compound the challenge, the British National Soil Resources Institute at Cranfield University has found that the soil is emitting significantly more CO_2 than a quarter century ago, because rising temperatures are causing a higher rate of organic decay. The researchers have recorded that more CO_2 has been emitted from Britain's soil each year since 1978 than has been eliminated from industrial emissions in the United Kingdom in the same period.[77]

We do not know exactly what will happen as a result of all this, so hedging against defined risks is impossible. Successful species, and probably the entire ecosystem, are capable of evolutionary adaptation, but present indications are not encouraging. The *Millennium Ecosystem Assessment* concluded that 'the anticipated speed of climate change is greater than anything seen for at least 10,000 years, making it far more difficult for species to move to more suitable areas or adapt to the new conditions by evolving....'[78]

We are not making predictions about specific outcomes, but simply delineating what is known today about the circumstances that *could* cause large-scale shocks and the trends that are observable at present. The restriction of many plant and animal species to nature reserves – surrounded by human environments, whether urban and industrial, or agricultural – will necessarily change the way in which they can respond to environmental shifts. Such adaptation will, moreover, take place in an ecosystem in which biodiversity has been depleted by development. In the period defined by fossil records, it seems that the long-term average extinction rate among mammal species was less than one species per thousand, each millennium. Since the fossil period, it seems that the rate has increased dramatically, with the 'current extinction rate [of mammals, birds and amphibians being] up to one thousand times higher than the fossil record' while the 'projected future extinction rate [for all species] is more than ten times higher than the present rate.' The same study indicates that 'some 12% of birds, 25% of mammals and at least 32% of amphibians are threatened with extinction over the next century.'[79]

The *Millennium Ecosystem Assessment* suggests ways to check the damage and make sustainable development – which we can think of as optimization of the relationship between our ecosystem and human welfare – an attainable goal. It suggests changing the economic context of decision-making by bringing values not normally priced by the market into the equation;[80] improving the quality of environmental policy, planning and management; influencing individual behavior to encourage environmentally sensitive responses and developing and using environmentally friendly technology. Seen in the context of this book, the authors have offered the framework of a plan to identify, assess, manage and mitigate the risks associated with our economic behavior.

7.4.3. Conferences and conventions

There have of course been several earlier efforts to address these challenges. Some 180 governments gathered at the UN Conference on Environment and Development in Rio de Janeiro, Brazil, in June 1992 and adopted a Declaration on the Environment and Development, a Statement of Principles for the Sustainable Management of Forests, a Framework Convention on Climate Change (UNFCCC) and Agenda 21 – an action agenda for the 21st century. They also created a Commission on Sustainable Development 'to ensure effective follow-up.'[81] A decade later, the importance of these documents was reaffirmed at the World Summit on Sustainable Development in Johannesburg, from August 26 to September 4, 2002. Despite this, however, the *Millennium Ecosystem Assessment*, published in March 2005, presents a somber perspective.

Meanwhile, at the third session of the Conference of Parties to the Climate Change Convention in 1997, in Kyoto, Japan, a protocol was adopted, known, after its birthplace, as the Kyoto Protocol. The agreement came into force in February 2005 after Russia had ratified it three months earlier. By August 2005, 153 countries, collectively responsible for 61 percent of global emissions, had ratified the agreement, but the United States and Australia have refused to do so, claiming that implementation would cripple their economies. The Kyoto Protocol is a commitment by the industrialized countries to reduce their collective emissions of six greenhouse gases – carbon dioxide, methane, nitrous oxide, sulfur hexafluoride, HFCs and PFCs – by 5.2 percent below the figures for 1990. If the target is compared to the emissions expected in by 2010 when the protocol was drafted in 1997, this would be a 29 percent reduction. The fact that the United States has not ratified the protocol, however, makes it impossible to achieve the goal. US carbon emissions account for 24 percent of the global total and are growing by 1.5 percent each year.[82] The US Department of Energy has calculated that to meet Kyoto's goals, the US would need to reduce emissions by 540 million tons between 2008 and 2012. This is equivalent to closing 90 coal-fired power stations each year! The study estimates that meeting this target could cost $400 billion, reducing the US GDP by 4.2 percent by 2010.[83]

On July 28, 2005, however, representatives of the US, Australian, Japanese, Chinese, South Korean and Indian governments announced the formation of the *Asia-Pacific Partnership on Clean Development and Climate*, to develop and share more efficient, cleaner technologies that would reduce harmful emissions without causing economic hardship. The inaugural meeting of the partnership is in November 2005. The United States had, of course, been sharply criticized for its refusal to accede to Kyoto, and this initiative – especially as it involves China and India – may have impact. On their present growth paths and with current technologies, China will become the world's largest source of carbon emissions by 2025, with India only a little behind.[84]

The United States, meanwhile, has exceptional research and development capacity and could deploy this effectively in a concerted program that could first complement and then overtake Kyoto as a strategy to combat rising emissions and avoid further damage to the atmosphere. Two leading researchers from Princeton University, Stephen Sacala and Robert Socolow, published a paper[85] in 2004 identifying fifteen industrial-scale technologies whose wide use could stabilize emissions at present levels by 2054. These range from ensuring better energy efficiency in cars and buildings, to generating more energy from wind and nuclear sources. Carbon capture and storage[86] – the practice of pumping CO_2 that would otherwise be released into the atmosphere and contribute to global warming, into underground rock formations where it can be kept out of harm's way – is an essential component of such a strategy. John Topper of the International Energy Agency's Clean Coal Centre believes that this is one of only two options available to us if we wish to stabilize emissions, the other being a sharp shift to nuclear power generation.[87]

It is still early days for these new approaches and recent experience suggests that our responses may lag behind the need to act, confronting us with still greater challenges in the years ahead. The risks are, however, clearly identifiable and their potential consequences can be assessed. Strategies to mitigate and manage them are necessary.

The debate has been recently advanced due to the determination of British Prime Minister, Tony Blair, to confront his colleagues in the G8 Heads of State and Government with the challenge. Following Mr. Blair's decision to put climate change on the agenda of the G8 at its meeting at Gleneagles in July 2005, the chancellor of the Exchequer commissioned a review by Sir Nicholas Stern, which was published on October 30, 2006. The report suggests that: 'our actions over the coming few decades could create risks of major disruption to economic and social activity, later in this century and in the next, on a scale similar to those associated with the great wars and the economic depression of the first half of the 20th century.'

The Stern Report, the first by an economist on climate change, concludes that 'there is now clear scientific evidence that emissions from economic activity, particularly the burning of fossil fuels for energy, are causing changes to the Earth's climate.'[88] In his review of the report, Stern's predecessor as World Bank Chief Economist and Nobel Prize winner Joseph Stiglitz speaks directly: 'The Stern Review ... provides the most thorough and rigorous analysis to date of the costs and risks of climate change, and the costs and risks of reducing emissions. It makes clear that the question is not whether we can afford to act, but whether we can afford not to act.' The significance of this statement is sharpened further by the Daily

Telegraph's comment: 'Sir Nicholas Stern spells out a bleak vision of a future gripped by violent storms, rising sea-levels, crippling droughts and economic chaos unless urgent action is taken to tackle global warming.'

The report's main thrust is that failure to act immediately will exact far greater penalties in the future and that the cost to the economy of cutting emissions radically will be far less than the economic and welfare costs which climate change is likely to impose. Stern suggests that we need to spend one percent of global GDP – about £184 billion – annually to address climate change now, or face a bill between five and 20 times higher – up to £3.68 trillion – for the damage that unchecked change will wreak in future. Urgent and sustained action is needed within a decade if we are not to face a catastrophic global recession with up to 200 million forced to flee, after their homes have succumbed to drought or flood. The report urges doubling investment in energy research and advocates extending the European system under which carbon emissions are capped and businesses which need to emit more are forced to buy quotas from low-polluters elsewhere. The sense of urgency is underscored by Stern's call for signature of a successor to the Kyoto agreement on in 2007 and not in 2010 or 2011 as presently planned.

7.4.4. Grappling with the consequences

Insurers and reinsurers, who are exposed to exceptional financial risk as a result of meteorological and climatic occurrences, are naturally concerned at the threats posed by hurricanes and other coastal storms, tsunamis other natural disasters, whether they derive from climate change or other meteorological circumstances. They have responded to the challenge by developing sophisticated tools enabling actuaries to assess companies' potential exposure. A recent assessment of the 2004 hurricane season by Swiss Re, for example, begins with the observation that 'The number of events ... is indeed unusual. However, thanks to the use of event-based risk analysis, this series of storms found Swiss Re well prepared.'[89]

Despite the enormous variability of circumstances that can give rise to the storm, its path to landfall, the concentrations of people and economic assets it will encounter when it strikes and the scale of the damage it will wreak, the report concludes that simulation of all possible events in a year and linking these with economic values and costs is a – and indeed the only – feasible means of estimating reliably 'which losses a defined hurricane event will produce, how losses caused by multiple landfalls in geographically remote regions correlate [and] which aggregate losses can be caused by several events on one and the same year.'[90]

While no model can absolutely match reality, and continuing calibration is required, Swiss Re has found it possible to develop proprietary models premised on an events-based approach that allows its planners to reduce uncertainty progressively and optimize their models using the information gleaned from each event. Clear satellite images and detailed descriptions of individual buildings at risk give more sophisticated insight into the distribution of value, and allow actuaries to assess the impact of different construction methods and standards on probable damage under each simulated circumstance.

Swiss Re bases its business model on three pillars that we have discussed from many different perspectives throughout this book: *risk transparency*, *quantitative risk management* and *risk governance*. It recognizes and manages five classes of risk: insurance, market, credit, funding and liquidity and other (compliance and reputational) risks. Its key risk principles are controlled risk taking, clear accountability, an independent risk-management function and an open-risk culture. To ensure *transparency* – allowing it to understand its exposure – the company builds on a culture of disciplined risk taking, requires full financial and risk exposure and employs peer reviews to ensure compliance. A reliable capital adequacy framework, sound valuation and risk measurement practices and an effective system to monitor compliance with risk limits are the essence of its *risk management* approach. Effective *risk governance* is assured by clearly defined responsibilities for both risk taking and risk management; sound, well-documented policies and guidelines for risk management and operations, reporting, monitoring and control; regulatory compliance; and internal and external audit.[91] This is an object lesson that one might expect from one of the foremost global reinsurance companies in effective risk management.

7.4.5. Risk in context

We have sought, in this chapter, to put risk into context, to explore the tensions between risk and uncertainty and to make clear how complex some of the conditions from which threats like terrorism or coastal storms arise, really are. We have discussed other risks more cursorily, to suggest how to think about the assessment and management of risks like pandemics and to illustrate how poorly we are prepared to deal with some threats that are likely to arise and which will have a devastating impact if they do. We could have chosen many other topics to make the same points – management of the risks of nuclear proliferation in North Korea and perhaps Iran; the risks for the world economy of a simultaneous, or sequential, collapse of the housing market in several Western countries. Each of these would have disclosed some of the same lessons apparent from those we chose.

The management of risk is not a game, except perhaps in the Shakespearian sense in which life is a stage and we are all players.[92] Our insight and skill can make the difference between outcomes that are favorable and others that bring misery. That is the challenge and the extraordinary opportunity available to us in correctly identifying, assessing and managing risk. What is clear is that we cannot grapple with these global risks alone and that sophisticated partnerships between governments, businesses and citizens are essential if we are to succeed.

CHAPTER 8

Pulling it together: Key success factors (and reasons for failure ...)

This book began by identifying risk as a paradoxical notion. We might well conclude with the observation that dealing with risk successfully is also, in many respects, a paradox.

Since risk management is about mastering a future we cannot anticipate, how can business people manage what cannot be foreseen, especially when so many factors – such as the ones affecting risk perception we explored in chapter 2 – converge to make it impossible to calculate risk objectively? This confronts us with a daunting challenge, yet we all know of companies particularly adept at dealing with risk. So what are the (not so) secret ingredients that set them apart? In a world undergoing seismic changes and characterized by volatility and uncertainty, what can business leaders do to understand risks properly and bring more of them under control? Even though new instruments, tools and methods to mitigate risk emerge continually at a bewildering pace, global interdependence and the acceleration of change make risk management increasingly complex. Our effort in this chapter to explain why businesses succeed or fail in mitigating the risks they confront, and global risks in particular, is based not only upon current business literature, but on the lessons which business executives were willing to share with us and the conclusions they drew from them.

We should note firstly that risk management has emerged at the forefront of the concerns of CEOs and boards. The results of a survey of 271 executives conducted by the Conference Board and Mercer Oliver Wyman in 2004 indicate that 91 percent of respondents are either positively disposed toward, or have begun implementing, an enterprise risk management (ERM) system.[1] As a result, risk managers are moving fast up the corporate ladder. Boards are increasingly focused not just on meeting regulatory requirements, but on securing a return on their investment in risk management through better decision making, effective insurance and a clearer idea of which risks should be hedged and which not. The core task of the risk manager is to help CEOs and boards to ensure that the right balance is struck between risk taking, which is synonymous with value creation and risk mitigation, the prevention of value destruction.[2] As the old saying goes: 'the greatest risk is not taking one.'

Given the aversion to risk in much of the developed world today, how is one to get the balance right? There is no magic formula for managing risk, but there are certain sensible measures which must be taken to avert failure. We can divide these into two categories: *organizational* and *attitudinal* measures. The *organizational* measures are a set of well-defined policies that must be implemented by any company competing globally. They are often described as constituting ERM. While they are essential in building the ability to manage risk, they do not give firms a sustainable competitive advantage. The *attitudinal* factors are less tangible: they reflect the qualities and traits of those who lead the business. As they run counter to the instincts and habits of those who have made it to the top of many corporations, they can be a source of lasting competitive advantage.

The eight factors set out in Table 8.1 below reinforce one another through positive feedback loops. Implemented effectively, they reduce corporate vulnerability and strengthen resilience. The difference between preventing a threat from materializing and rebounding after it has struck is not as great as it may seem at first glance. Everyone who has experienced major shocks knows that measures designed to prevent disruption often build the resilience that permits recovery after a major crisis has occurred. We shall discuss some of these later in the chapter.

Table 8.1 Key factors for success

Organizational Essential, but unlikely to confer lasting competitive advantage	Attitudinal If implemented, bring sustain- able competitive advantage
1. Making risk thinking part of the culture	5. Building and using knowledge and networks
2. Aligning risk assessment, management and communication	6. Being aware of the cognitive biases
3. Assessing the vulnerabilities	7. Puncturing denial – being prepared and acting fast
4. Building partnerships	8. Displaying humility

8.1. Embedding risk thinking in the corporate culture

As we argued in the last chapter, risk thinking has to be made part of the company's (or institution's) culture. In the 21st century, command, control and compartmentalization of organizations is no longer possible. Simply 'preaching' or issuing *diktats* to staff in an effort to raise awareness and bring people on board is not a viable strategy. All members of staff need to understand the risks involved in doing business, the value of taking these risks in pursuit of opportunity and the ways the risks are being managed and mitigated. If only the CEO and the board have an overview of the corporate risk management strategies, things will slip through the cracks. Crises often result from the interaction of events in different areas, none of which seem serious enough on their own to warrant any business unit's changing tack, but which conflate to create 'perfect storms.' To get to grips with its exposure, the Australian bank ANZ developed a new program: 'In one way or another they had a third of the bank involved in developing it and that helped to circulate the issues, and to give all employees a sense they owned the programme.'[3] Companies that create this kind of *organic culture* are much more likely to succeed in measuring, understanding and managing the risks they assume. Appointment of a Chief Risk Officer (CRO) can help greatly in nurturing a culture of awareness. The CRO can focus both on reducing vulnerabilities, thus limiting the likelihood of disruption, and on building resilience. Many global companies are moving in this direction, and the trend will probably strengthen as insight into global and other systemic risks become more prevalent. The World Economic Forum's Global Risk Network has even suggested that governments should appoint CROs to coordinate each country's exposure to global risks and improve prospects for effective mitigation.[4]

8.2. Aligning risk assessment, risk management and risk communication

Ensuring that risk thinking has permeated the fabric of a company is essential but not sufficient; one also needs to integrate the systems for assessing, managing and communicating risk successfully. An integrated approach is essential because if one element fails, the whole system fails, as the tragedy of 9/11 illustrates so clearly.[5] For many reasons, key executives in large companies and governments are often better at analysis, measurement and management than they are at communication. Analytical rigor is essential; effective management is also a *sine qua non*, and monitoring and measurement of both the circumstances identified as significant risks, and the efficacy of the measures taken to manage them, are central to success. But we also have to ensure that the information, and the context that makes that information relevant, are communicated in appropriate ways both to the people who are responsible for dealing with the threat and to those outside the firm or the government who may be affected by it.

For all the publications and consulting hours devoted to knowledge management over the past decade, we are still not very good at ensuring that relevant parts of the knowledge accumulated in large organizations is available where and when it is needed. The challenge in ensuring that it is, is itself a subset of a much larger challenge. In too many organizations, knowledge is still seen as a source of power and is hoarded rather than shared. In particular, as failure is often interpreted as a sign of weakness, the valuable knowledge we can glean from failures is almost never shared.

The problems that these habits cause in the context of risk management are obvious. People are not inclined to admit mistakes in highly competitive environments, or in organizations where the culture is risk-averse. This leads to delays in communicating important information, either due to rationalization ('it's not important') and denial of responsibility ('I had nothing to do with it; it would have happened anyway'); and may lead to cover-ups, as when a trader whose positions are overextended, gambles on covering them with more extravagant trades. Only by overcoming these understandable but dysfunctional practices, and by providing incentives that encourage people to share relevant information and knowledge, in appropriate ways and under all circumstances, can one close the knowledge loop and allow an ERM system to work effectively. The competitive benefits to a company in a knowledge-intensive environment where knowledge efficiencies are generally low can scarcely be overestimated.

Understanding risk and assessing it properly, without falling victim to the many biases affecting our perception of risks that we discussed in chapter 2, will always be difficult. We shall not succeed in transcending our human condition! Building a corporate culture that values innovation and reflects the understanding that risk is inherent in the pursuit of value, but must be mitigated to secure the future, and putting in place an effective system to identify, assess, manage and communicate the risks we assume, are essential elements for success.

This integrated approach can be represented by varying very slightly the risk management model we used to introduce the topic in chapter 4. Figure 8.1 shows the relationships between the identification, assessment, mitigation and communication of risks – both to those within the company charged with managing different classes of risks and to those outside it who may be affected by its actions. All the elements we discussed in the previous

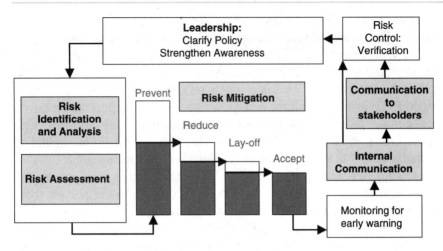

Figure 8.1 Dealing effectively with risk

chapters are included. The process is dynamic, continuous and systemic. If it is executed in this way, managing risk becomes seamless, a central part of the corporate culture and an effective means of directing and managing the company strategically. Risk management is not undertaken on the margins of great companies to ensure compliance with legislation; it is the means by which corporate leaders ensure an organic relationship between their companies and the challenging environments in which they must struggle and survive.

8.3. Assessing the vulnerabilities

In a speech not long after the 9/11 incidents and the ensuing anthrax attacks, Howard Kunreuther observed that the fact that a handful of determined individuals had succeeded in disrupting the activities of the world's most powerful nation, suggested that risk assessment should be supplemented by vulnerability analyses 'that characterize the forms of physical, social, economic, cultural and psychological harms to which individuals and modern societies are susceptible.'[6] A vulnerability analysis goes beyond an assessment of the risks to which the firm is exposed. It is a systematic analysis of the potential effects of these risks within the firm and its value chain, and of the effectiveness of the risk-management system in place in preventing or mitigating those effects. The aim is to reduce the vulnerability of the firm to both natural and man-made disruptions.

In assessing risks, one asks three questions: (1)What can go wrong? (2) What is the likelihood this will happen? (3) How severe is the impact likely to be? With these three in mind, managers can map the risks faced by their business and focus on addressing those that are most salient. We have illustrated this in chapter 4. This is a simple task for risks that are well understood and quantifiable but those risks whose potential impact on the firm is less certain, like most global risks, which are often low probability, high impact risks, are best considered by employing the scenario or simulation techniques we mentioned earlier. Simulations are an excellent way of examining vulnerabilities to threat, as they enable senior managers to play through the whole risk scenario in the context of the firm's responses, those of government agencies and of other companies in its value chain.

The closely connected supply chains of global business operations today mean that each company's efforts to build resilient systems are at the mercy of the chain's weakest link. Most global companies have no choice but to audit the risks to which their main suppliers and those for whom there are no substitutes are exposed, on a continuing basis, to reduce the risk of disruptions by detecting the risk early and taking appropriate steps to mitigate it.

Building-in redundancies is an obvious means of creating resilience against supply chain disruptions, but this is usually expensive in just-in-time manufacturing environments and spare capacity is not always available. It is also difficult to measure the economic benefits of risk avoidance and mitigation as the cost of the disruptions that we succeed in avoiding does not appear in the balance sheet or the P&L, unlike the costs of avoidance! Our dependence on information technology, however, makes this is one area where investment in redundant capability is taken for granted. Uwe Doerken, the CEO of DHL, the courier company that operates in 220 countries, set up three IT centers in three different time zones, each connected to two separate power grids based on two different power plants, to manage the risk of supply-chain disruption.[7] National Access Points (NAPs), locations where telecommunications carriers, Internet Service Providers and large telecommunications and Internet users meet to interconnect and exchange traffic, are required to provide triple redundancy of all key facilities to qualify for licenses. The NAP of the Americas, for example, a tier-1 NAP in Miami which provides carrier-neutral connectivity, peering and managed services in routing Internet traffic between the Americas, the Caribbean and Europe, is housed in what its web site describes as 'a telecommunications fortress with the most advanced security features available.'

8.4. Building partnerships

Building partnerships is a prerequisite if global risks are to be addressed. No stakeholder is powerful enough to mitigate global risks like terrorism or climate change on his own. Without the cooperation of all airlines the risk of a terrorist incident resulting in many deaths would be far greater. Geoffrey Heal and Howard Kunreuther have used the destruction of Pan Am flight 103 in 1988 to define key challenges in areas where the security of any actor is dependent on the actions of many others,[8] and to illustrate a series of important lessons.[9]

Pan Am Flight 103, traveling from London to New York on December 21, 1988, was destroyed by a terrorist bomb – a plastic explosive hidden in a radio cassette player in an unaccompanied suitcase transferred from another airline – over Lockerbie in Scotland. The explosion and crash killed 259 passengers and crew and 11 residents on the ground. In November 1991, the United States and Scotland indicted two Libyans for the bombing of the flight. After protracted negotiations, Libya turned over its two nationals to a specially constituted Scottish Court in the Netherlands in 1999. On January 31, 2001, the court found one accused guilty and sentenced him to life imprisonment, and acquitted the other.

The bag containing the bomb had been loaded onto a Malta Airlines flight in Malta, where there were minimal security systems in 1988, was transferred at Frankfurt, without inspection, to a Pan Am feeder line to London and loaded aboard Pan Am 103, again without inspection, at Heathrow. The bomb was set to explode at 28,000 feet, a height first attained over the Atlantic en route to New York. The faulty assumption that the bag had been properly screened at the airport at which it entered the baggage transfer system meant that no subsequent screening was undertaken at either transfer point. A security weakness at a small, technologically unsophisticated airport in the Mediterranean led to the destruction of a Pan Am flight out of Heathrow.

As Heal and Kunreuther show, an airline's incentive to invest in proper baggage screening system rises, in general terms, if other airlines in the same system invest as well, and falls if they do not. The same applies, of course, if the screening systems are provided by airport management companies. There is, however, a tipping point: one or a small number of airlines (or airports) may, if they elect to invest, shift the balance of interests so that all others will find it in their interests to invest as well.

There is a second problem: constructing private–public partnerships and partnerships between actors in different environments often runs foul of the difficulty of matching the beneficiaries of mitigation with those who must bear the cost. For climate change, as we have seen, all suggested mitigation strategies require substantial investment *now* for uncertain returns in the future. Leaving aside the issue of denial which we address later, many political or business leaders are reluctant to allocate resources to an issue whose dividends will only be seen when they are out of office. Global issues require global solutions, however: providing and managing the scarce resources that are available for risk mitigation requires collaboration between the private and public sectors at international, national and local levels, and between different stakeholder groups; as the International Risk Governance Council has observed: 'Global risks call for coordinated effort amongst a variety of players beyond the frontiers of countries, sectors, hierarchical levels, disciplines and risk fields.'[10]

Public policies that support private initiatives by providing incentives to those willing to take risk mitigation measures are an effective way to provide focused incentives. The private sector is in a much stronger position to address mitigation when the state provides the right regulatory framework or the requisite tax subsidies. The US Terrorism Risk Insurance Act (TRIA), where the US government has undertaken to cap insurance losses, has allowed insurance companies to insure more risk. Similarly, government limits on carbon emission in Europe have enabled the private sector to develop innovative responses to climate change.

Private–public partnerships (PPPs) in which all stakeholders bear a portion of the risk commensurate with their appetite and capacity, offer new opportunities for mitigation of global risks. The most interesting examples are emerging from the companies and institutions that are most exposed to specific global risks and who are willing to act as champions. In 2005, the reinsurance company Swiss Re collaborated with the UN Development Program and the Harvard Medical School to produce a report on Climate Change Futures: Health, Ecological and Economic Dimensions.[11] The aim was to raise awareness of a critical issue, and develop new risk mitigation approaches. Also in 2005, the World Economic Forum provided a platform to British Prime Minister Tony Blair at its Annual Meeting in Davos to speak on climate change, and launched the G8 Climate Change Roundtable. Chief Executives from 24 global energy, mining and minerals, transportation and banking and insurance companies met in a series of workshops over the course of a year and presented the prime minister with recommendations for performance-based technology incentives. The Climate Change Roundtable demonstrated broad-based business support for well designed mitigation strategies and shifted the debate from 'whether climate change is a problem' to 'how the problem should be solved.'[12]

8.5. Building and using knowledge and networks

Greater knowledge, insight and systemic understanding are needed to address the challenges of risk, and to balance threat and opportunity in a complex, interconnected world. When one considers the systemically integrated nature of the risk classes we have discussed under the heading of global risks, this is self-evident. Knowledge and insight make the difference between good and bad outcomes whether one is dealing with religious radicalism, the proliferation of weapons of mass destruction, natural catastrophes, financial market volatility or climate change. The leaders who succeed in rising above these challenges and deriving advantage from their understanding of them have developed insight into their origins and the relationships between them. Business and political leaders who grasp the essence of complex causal chains are better placed to reduce the probability of a risk materializing, and to reduce the severity of its impact if it does.

Given such knowledge and insight, however, firms must ensure that they enhance the quality of the flow of relevant information among those who have a stake in dealing with a particular risk. The process of assessment, management and communication must be seamless if well-considered responses are to be devised and implemented.[13] In 2002 Jean-François Rischard, then European vice-president at the World Bank, argued convincingly that *global issues networks* are the best way to move the understanding and the mitigation of global risks forward.[14]

How does one develop such knowledge and insight and ensure a proper flow of good quality information? Networks are the best instruments for this purpose because they offer the most effective organizational response to complexity. If they are sufficiently diverse and allow for a wide range of opinions, networks provide an excellent way of aggregating information and meaningful insights.[15] Good networks are built on the strength of 'weak ties.' By connecting people with other people they do not know, highly diverse networks become the channels through which fresh insights and perspectives are shaped, leading to relevant and useful approaches. Business leaders can use networks as effective early-warning systems to alert them to issues that are far out on the horizon or just over it, and to understand how these might affect their business. This is the best way to get a range of different opinions, thus compensating for one's own cognitive biases.

8.6. Being aware of the cognitive biases

Awareness of one's weaknesses is a good first step to overcoming them. One of our greatest human failings is the tendency to see the future like the past. When trying to anticipate the future, most of the mistakes we make stem from what psychologists call *structural extrapolation*: the tendency to represent a future state by analogy with what we can see today. This 'like-the-past' fallacy is associated with an inability, or disinclination, to question underlying assumptions. How often do we resort to the phrase 'that goes without saying?' Most attempts to anticipate the future, moreover, rely on mechanistic models. Too often the end result is predetermined by the methodology we use and ignores the fact that the business environment, like other aspects of our human condition, is governed by *complex* systems.[16] Complex systems (properly described as *complex, nonlinear, adaptive systems*) evolve by adapting to their environments, and thus frequently exhibit new behaviors that diverge from previous patterns. These systems are adaptive rather than deterministic in that the rules that govern their behavior change as a result of the behavior that the rules engender. Where does that leave senior executives and risk managers? Numbers and models are, of course, necessary, but one cannot simply substitute the computer for the Delphic oracle when seeking guidance in managing risk. Ultimately, the most sophisticated tools and methodologies are just tools; they are no substitute for good judgment.

All the heuristics we rely on, distort our ability to make good decisions in the face of uncertainty, but overconfidence plays an exceptional role. Strong leaders are particularly vulnerable to this bias. Overconfident people tend to exclude other voices and this often leads eventually to their downfall: smart people are more likely to do stupid things when they insulate themselves from advice and criticism. The problem can be acute when dealing with complex systemic risks. As they require mastery of detailed knowledge that few Chief Executives have readily available, some may fall back on unrealistic and optimistic scenarios. The notion that US troops would be met with rejoicing by Iraqis freed from Saddam Hussein's tyranny, and that the dictator's overthrow would usher in a new climate of democracy throughout the Arab world, has fallen prey to the complex reality of Iraq's and the Gulf's social networks and alliances, the relationship between Arab (and Muslim) sentiment and the unresolved situation in Israel, Palestine and Lebanon, and Iran's regional ambitions.

Climate change is another case in point. Although a majority of CEOs agree today that this is the greatest challenge we confront, few understood that two years ago. Some companies like Toyota, however, were able to transform the risk into an opportunity well before their competitors.

Many executives also show a strong herd instinct. Although highly successful in their own environments, they share the common traits of humanity. Most conform to the behavior and opinions of their peers. Our instinct for herding makes it preferable to be wrong collectively than right individually, a trait which is particularly apparent in the financial markets, where being right with the wrong timing (i.e. before everybody else) is punished in the same way as being wrong. As Warren Buffet remarked sardonically: 'Falling conventionally is the route to go; as a group, lemmings may have a rotten image, but no individual lemming has ever received bad press.'[17]

Senior executives who have identified these cognitive pitfalls have taken the first step to avoiding them, but structured policies are also needed. Excellent companies favor a *culture of challenge*, in which the management team encourages and thrives on constructive criticism. Several submit strategic decisions – in particular those which deal with issues of uncertainty and the management of risk – to robust checks and balances. In general terms, encouraging contrarians to express their views and encouraging frank debate reduces the perverse effect of cognitive biases.

8.7. Puncturing denial – Being prepared and acting fast

This looks like a mundane recommendation, and yet this is probably the most effective factor for dealing with risk successfully. It may be obvious that one should avoid denial, but is one of the most difficult challenges decision makers face. Jack Welch, former CEO of GE, knew that people love the status quo; 'It can feel like a warm bath. People never want to get out.'[18] Denial of the need to change is therefore the default response! Denial is the most common strategy when we confront threats: corporations often fall victim to the *boiling frog* syndrome. We tend not to react to fundamental changes until catastrophe is imminent, perhaps even unavoidable. Then, after the horse has bolted from its stall, we slam closed the stable door. In business terms, this translates into the tendency to be well prepared to deal with the last threatening event, but not the next one. Despite the encouraging figures in the Conference Board/Mercer Oliver Wyman survey cited on page 139, most companies, and especially small and medium-size enterprises, are not sufficiently risk-aware to act prudently before or even when things go wrong.

It is not only small companies that cannot afford a cohort of risk management specialists, who practice denial. The troubles that have plagued the Airbus A380 illustrate the problem of denial all too graphically.

The original problem stemmed from a typical project risk relating to wiring cables. Although assembly line managers reported the problem in the autumn of 2004, no one believed it was important enough to merit attention from top management. It was only in June 2005 that the company admitted that there were manufacturing problems and announced a six-month delay in delivery. That set the pattern. The first delay of six months grew to a devastating two years. 'People were in denial' said John Leahy, Airbus's chief salesman. Cultural rivalry between the German and French share-holders and their representatives in the executive also played a role, as did overconfidence born out of complacency. The success of the A320 family in the 1990s and Airbus's ascendancy over Boeing had encouraged a sense of invincibility and immunity from risk. The effect may be to strip about EUR 5 billion in profits from EADS over the next four years.[19]

The great scientist Louis Pasteur once observed that 'chance favours the prepared mind.' Two examples, one from the world of policy making and one from business, both related to the destruction of the World Trade Center in September 2001, drive this point home.

At the Annual Meeting of the World Economic Forum in 2002, Rudolph Giuliani, then mayor of New York, noted that he had thought that the hun-dreds of millions of dollars the city spent preparing for Y2K might have been wasted. On the morning of September 11, he realized that they had not been: the backup systems that allowed the mayor's office to get a new command center up and running within a few hours after the attack on the Twin Towers, had been developed to deal with Y2K contingency.[20]

The business example is even more startling. Four years before the 9/11 attacks, the US Naval War College organized a scenario review on the top floor of the World Trade Center with Cantor Fitzgerald and other Wall Street firms. The aim was to consider the potential impact of terrorist attacks on New York's financial center. According to David Rothkopf, then chairman and CEO of Intellibridge, who participated in the meeting, sev-eral firms decided at that time to move their back offices out of the Wall Street area.[21] Despite the destruction of 14 acres of lower Manhattan four years later, financial markets were back in business only four days later. Many observers correctly attributed the resilience of the markets to the remarkable spirit of American people, but foresight and planning played a critical role in building resilience.[22]

In lighter vein, South African Grand Slam-winning golfer Gary Player, on being congratulated on his luck in sinking a shot out of a bunker, acknowledged the 'luck' and then said, 'But I've noticed that the more I practice, the luckier I get.'

Nothing illustrates better the pertinence of all this than the example of two IT giants: Nokia and Ericsson. Both companies are renowned for the excellence of their technologies and the quality of their products. Both companies have superior ERM systems. Yet, when confronted with an identical disruption, one company seized the opportunity to strengthen its market position while the other faltered. On the evening of Friday, March 17, 2000, a thunderstorm struck a Philips's semiconductor fabrication plant in Albuquerque, New Mexico. The small fire was promptly extinguished by the staff before the fire fighters arrived. Nobody was hurt and the damage seemed superficial. Contamination by dirt had, however, destroyed the chips for millions of cell phones in a few minutes. The need for a completely sanitary manufacturing environment, moreover, meant that it would be a week before the plant could restart production. Nokia and Ericsson took 40 percent of the orders at that time.

The following Monday, Nokia's chief component purchasing manager was on the phone with his counterpart at Philips discussing the situation. Although one-week delays are common in global supply chains, the Nokia manager decided to pass the information to others in the company, including the top 'troubleshooter,' who put the issue in a 'special watch' list, requiring Nokia to make daily calls to Philips to check how the situation was evolving. Very soon Nokia realized that it would not take a week to restore production at the plant, but rather months. The delay was affecting the production of about four million cell phones. So Nokia assembled a team of 30 people to identify alternative sources and to develop close collaboration with other Philips plants.

Ericsson reacted to the call from Philips on the Monday in a far more relaxed way, assuming that everything would work out as planned. By the time it realized the magnitude of the problem, it was too late. When it turned to Philips for help, Nokia had already captured all the spare capacity and there were no secondary supplies for parts. Ericsson was unable to ship huge quantities of its high-end models. A year after the fire, Ericsson announced that it was abandoning the handset market; blaming component shortages, an incorrect product mix and marketing problems; and freeing Nokia from European competition.[23]

Why did Nokia succeed? Apart from its strong relationship with its suppliers, continuous monitoring of the supply of critical parts and a good command of the four organizational principles of risk management, its risk awareness culture and the mindset of its management gave it an 'attitudinal' premium. In the words of the troubleshooter, 'we encourage bad news to travel fast' and 'we don't want to hide problems.' Nokia showed no tendency to indulge in denial: it was able to act swiftly and effectively as soon as the risk was assessed. CEO Jorma Ollila, moreover, displayed humility, which we discuss below, by traveling to visit Philips' CEO in the Netherlands to emphasize the importance and urgency of the issue.

Why did Ericsson fail? It sat idle for too long and did not react as fast as its competitor. Its behavior showed a tendency to complacency in the face of uncertainty.

8.8. Displaying humility

The saying that 'humility is the only true wisdom by which we prepare our minds for all the possible changes of life' does not often lead experts to include humility in the arsenal of instruments of effective risk mitigation. It has rarely been discussed by business academics and many in practical business ventures underestimate its utility. One exception is the leadership expert Jim Collins, who, when researching *From Good to Great*, introduced the counterintuitive notion that humility is necessary for effective leadership.[24] Humility is particularly appropriate in the context of uncertainty and comes more easily to self-confident leaders who know their strengths and relative weaknesses. Such people usually surround themselves with people who complement and challenge them, and actively seek the insights of others with expert knowledge which they lack.

There is a thin line between self-confidence and overconfidence. Overconfident Chief Executives do not display humility, probably because it is not easy for successful leaders who deal successfully with a myriad of challenges, to acknowledge that events may expose their companies to risks that they do not understand or know how to manage.

The failure of Wal-Mart in Germany offers a startling example of how arrogance can damage a great brand and blight a promising business in a particular market. It was not that Wal-Mart had no experience in foreign markets; it has succeeded in many countries. Its experience shows that even the largest and most successful companies make some of the most obvious attitudinal mistakes. In such cases, first-rate ERM systems, which Wal-Mart has, are no substitute for senior management's lack of cultural understanding and sensitivity. The Wal-Mart case is an example of a project risk, triggered by a behavioral risk and exacerbated by a familiar global risk: the backlash against globalization and resistance to the homogenization of cultures. Although several other factors contributed to the demise of Wal-Mart in Germany, arrogance, ignorance and disrespect for local cultural sensitivities played an important role.[25]

When Wal-Mart decided to expand into Germany in late 1997, it appointed Rob Tiarks, a US citizen and senior vice-president who had previously supervised around 200 Super centers in the United States from Wal-Mart headquarters in Bentonville. Mr Tiarks did not speak German, like most other US managers Wal-Mart deployed to Germany. He made it clear that he had no intention of learning German and that English would be the official language of the company. After one year, he was replaced by Allan Leighton, an Englishman as ignorant of German language and customs as his predecessor. Leighton decided to run the German operation from his office in Leeds! These astonishing blunders in the first two years were fatal to Wal-Mart. A spokeswoman for Wal-Mart International later admitted that 'perhaps at first we had our stumbles in terms of finding the right way of meshing the two cultures, but I think we have caught on in recent years.'[26] But by then it was too late. Having failed to penetrate the German market successfully, Wal-Mart decided to abandon Germany in August 2006.

Wal-Mart's experience parallels the travails of other companies in other unfamiliar markets where a lack of cultural sensitivity can frustrate any chance of success. Both of us have spent many years in emerging markets and know of scores of deals that failed solely because of the cultural arrogance or incomprehension displayed by would-be foreign investors. Local governments and corporate officials are often equally obtuse, and the exchanges between foreigners and locals often resemble a true dialog of the (culturally, tone-) deaf. As we have shown in chapter 2, the perception of unfairness (or unfriendliness, or arrogance) often matters more than the maximization of utility to both parties. Whether this pertains to the pursuit of profit, or in managing risk, empathy is a vital ingredient.

This chapter would not be complete without mentioning luck! Ian Davis, CEO of McKinsey, has argued that 'those who say that business success is all about execution are wrong. The right products, markets, technology and geography are critical components of long-term economic performance. Bad industries usually trump good management: in sectors such as banking, telecommunications and technology, almost two-thirds of the organic growth of listed Western companies can be attributed to being in the right markets and geographies. Companies that ride the current succeed; those that swim against them usually struggle.'[27]

How does this relate to risk management? Assuming that one is in a good business – for Mr Davis is surely correct that few managers can make a silk purse out of a sow's ear – the capacity to adapt to new markets, technologies, a changing global environment and the emergence of new risks stemming from all these, is *the* element which will enable success. Carly Fiorina, former CEO of Hewlett Packard (HP) once described HP as an 'adaptive enterprise.' This was based upon Darwin's idea that 'the species that survive are not necessarily the strongest or the smartest, but those that are best able to adapt to change.' As Topsy famously said in Harriet Beecher Stowe's Uncle Tom's Cabin, 'sayin' don't make it so' – more than an assertion of adaptability is needed in order to succeed – but the principle is surely correct. The world is littered with examples of large, successful companies that became complacent and ended up insular, smug and slow. When the corporate culture becomes homogeneous and self-confirming, it acts as a shield against change and the company eventually falls prey to extinction. Resilience demands an understanding of all aspects of the competitive environment and the ability to rise to and triumph over the challenges it poses.

Conclusion: Leadership and resilience

We hope we have argued convincingly that models and well-defined processes are essential, but are not the only answer. Effective leadership is still more important.

Too many lesser companies manage risk as though all that mattered was covering the downside. This makes them dependent on complex mathematical models which most senior executives and board members can neither understand, nor query. Finely tuned models tend to operate superbly well within the parameters for which they were designed, but fail disastrously when the real world does not mimic the design.[1] And reality has a habit of making fools of us all! As the assumptions underpinning the model and the parameters defining it are not transparent, boards, and even CFOs, can be caught unawares. The warnings of the Counterparty Risk Management Policy Group (CRMPG) that we discussed in chapter 7 are very much to the point.

Models have their place, of course, there are certain things we could not possibly do without them, but the qualities needed to deal successfully with risk and ultimately to build resilience, are those required to succeed in business and in other areas of life. They are the qualities we associate with leadership. Even though the literature on the subject is overwhelming (googling 'business leadership' yields 205,000,000 entries!), leadership remains elusive. In a nutshell, leaders are distinguished by three characteristics:

- They have a *vision* of where the organization should go and a *core strategy* to take it there;
- They have *supporters*; and are able to induce others to buy into the vision and support the development of the strategy; to do this, leaders ensure that their people are *effectively empowered*; CEOs who fear and constrain their senior executives and practice strategies of 'divide and rule' are neither leaders, nor capable of sustained success;
- They do not take the composition of the firm, or the environment in which it acts, as a given; leaders work actively *to create environments* that will facilitate the success of the strategy and achievement of the vision.

Assuming and mastering appropriate risks is a critical component of achieving a shared vision of the corporation's future. In driving toward this goal, a leader must operate on many different levels at the same time: He (or she) must 'float like a butterfly and sting like a bee,'[2] as William Donaldson, former chairman of the US Securities and Exchange Commission, recently observed. But what skills and qualities, in the context of the uncertainty that is the essence of the challenge of appreciating and assessing risk, will lead to success?

Effective leaders both display confidence, and earn the trust of the teams who surround them. The balance between the formality of organizational structure and team involvement[3] and between a focus on production efficiency and a concern for employees[4] has been explored extensively, with grid solutions showing the importance of building committed teams with a clear understanding of company goals. In an important study in 1985,[5] Bennis and Nanus went further, distinguishing between the requirements that CEOs needed to demonstrate – knowledge of the industry and firm, well-established relationships in the industry, a superior reputation and track record, well-regarded abilities and skills, a high standard of integrity and personal values and a high level of energy and motivation – and the characteristics they need to display in their dealings with others in the firm – high self-regard with no evident need for external approval, courtesy to associates, evidence of acceptance and trust of others and a determination to evaluate others on their current ability, not their past mistakes. Manfred Kets de Vries, head of the Global Leadership Centre at INSEAD, argues that what differentiates great companies from merely average ones is the level of emotional intelligence (EQ) of their leaders and their capacity to instill this quality in their colleagues and associates. In a knowledge-based society characterized by sustained and discontinuous change, companies rich in leaders with high EQs not only have 'the best shot at creativity and innovation,' but they are also better equipped to build resilience.[6]

Leaders with these characteristics can demonstrate both confidence in their ability to master change and humility in the face of the unknown, to elicit a proper balance between assuming and managing risk so as to profit from it.

These are essential qualities at the level of the firm, but they are not sufficient to address risks of a global character. The risks whose management will define our future – climate change, the threat of terrorism, the need for cultural accommodation and the resolution of the abject poverty that still affects so many in different parts of the world – are still poorly defined, badly managed and cry out for leadership in addressing them. There are widely divergent views on how best to deal with these challenges and many different responses across national jurisdictions in the absence of a global strategy. We still lack both competent international institutions and an agreed framework within which to address them properly. In such conditions, a skilled business leader can build corporate resilience, exploit opportunities and secure competitive advantage by applying the strategies discussed in this book. The challenge of addressing the systemic risks that define the broader environment in which we all operate, is a larger task that demands the attention of all global leaders.

Appendix 1. The modern history of risk[1]

The idea that risks could be assessed *mathematically in terms of probability*, independently of particular people or circumstances, emerged in Europe only in the 17th century. This is not particularly surprising. Our agrarian forefathers were largely at the mercy of the environments in which they lived. The sun rose and set; the seasons changed, bringing heat or cold, snow, rain or drought. Hunting was successful, or less so; herds and flocks flourished or sickened, and crops thrived or withered on the lands. Religious orthodoxy discouraged speculation as to the reasons; it was safer to propitiate God(s) if fortune turned against the community or the individual; to thank Him (Her, or Them) if one was blessed and to offer prayers and sacrifices in supplication when seeking a boon.

Much more surprising is that, as far as we know, the mathematical and scientific instruments of the Egyptians, Greeks[2] and Romans, or the Chinese and Indian civilizations, were not applied to the great questions of probability and uncertainty. Nor were those of the great knowledge synthesizers, the Islamic caliphs who ruled most of the world between Transoxania on the borders of China and Sind – the lower Indus valley which abutted India, to the East and Iberia to the West between the 9th and 14th centuries. Their mathematics was far more sophisticated, integrating Euclidian geometry with Arabic numerals, and the Hindu concept of zero,[3] which became *sifr* in Arabic, to engender *al jabr* or algebra. The author of the first text that set out the rules of modern arithmetic was *al-Khowarizmi*, from whose name we derive the word *algorithm*.

Omar Khayyám, author of the quatrains known as the *Rubáiyát*, developed advanced algebraic notation and developed a triangular arrangement of numbers that allowed for calculation of the areas and other relations of geometric forms,[4] and was later used by Blaise Pascal[5] in his famous *theory of probability*. Despite extraordinary advances in algebra and astronomy – leading to sophisticated instruments for navigation – chemistry, medicine, botany and many technologies from paper and clock-making to irrigation and agronomy, the Arab scientists did not address probability. We can only conclude that belief in the transcendence of the Almighty discouraged such speculation. Only with the emergence and growth of humanism and a spirit of enquiry and experimentation in the European *renaissance* in the 15th century, was the scene set for the exploration of probabilities.

It is perhaps unsurprising that the investigation into probability that begins our story, which arose from a mathematical enquiry about a gambling problem.[6] In 1654, the Chevalier de Méré, an aristocratic gambler with an interest and facility in mathematics which impressed Leibnitz,[7] put to Blaise Pascal a gaming problem originally posed[8] by the Italian monk, Luca Pacioli in 1494. Pascal drew in Pierre de Fermat[9] and the two men, using complementary methods, devised a coherent mathematical *theory of probability* that lies at the heart of modern risk assessment and management. Pascal's triangle, a geometric structure he developed to clarify the underlying algebra, already had a distinguished history when he presented it,[10] but he arranged it in a way that transformed our understanding of probability and how to calculate it.

The path from this point is a steady one, punctuated with moments of genius. By 1689, Jacob Bernoulli[11] had published his *law of large numbers*;[12] in 1730, Abraham de Moivre[13] developed the *normal distribution (or bell) curve* and the concept of *standard deviation*.[14] His investigation of mortality statistics led to the foundation of the theory of annuities. In 1738, Daniel Bernoulli[15] made a breakthrough in decision analysis, introducing the concept of *personal utility*, proposing that the utility one ascribes to a small increase in wealth is inversely proportional to one's prior wealth. Bernoulli brought the individual, not the dice or the coin, to the center of the calculation.

A paper by Thomas Bayes,[16] published in the *Philosophical Transactions* of the Royal Society in 1763, two years after his death, greatly advanced *statistical inference* – which allows us to infer probabilities from rigorous observations. Bayes was the first mathematician to use probability *inductively* and establish how to calculate, from the number of times an event has *not* occurred, the probability that it will occur in future. Bayes ensured that information discovered through research would be used to revise earlier assessments of probabilities based on prior information. The core insight is that there is no single mathematically correct answer to questions of probability under conditions of uncertainty.

The contribution of Carl Friedrich Gauss[17] to the calculation of probability arose from his work in geodesic measurement in Bavaria. His observations over many years were clustered in a manner reminiscent of the bell curve identified earlier by de Moivre. Gauss's treatment of the *least squares' method* to reduce the impact of measurement error was based on the assumption of errors being normally distributed. By 1809, Pierre Simon

Laplace[18] had developed the *central limit theorem* – showing that the *average of averages* reduces the dispersion around the mean. Gauss and Legendre[19] had earlier used the *least squares method* for the combination of numerous observations, but Laplace later developed a formal proof of it, on which the *theory of errors* has since been based. For normal distribution to emerge from a very large set of observations, of course, the phenomena we are observing must be independent of one another.

All that we have described up to this point assumes the existence of a *norm* – a mathematically derived mean that enables the allocation of events around it in a predictable manner. Francis Galton's[20] passion for measurement led him eventually to an extraordinary discovery, that of *regression to the mean*. Galton's researches were based on heredity – his discovery was that both sweet peas and humans arranged themselves through several generations into *normal distribution curves*. His analysis led to the concept of *correlation* – the measurement of how two (or more) series vary relative to one another. It also transformed the static phenomenon of normal distribution into a dynamic process in which the outliers in sets of measurements inevitably gravitate over time toward the mean. *Aggregation around the mean*, and hence *normal distribution* as de Moivre and Gauss described it, is the only conceivable outcome. If this were not true among humans for example, evolution would have produced only giants and midgets. Instead we have what Quetelet[21] had earlier celebrated as a normal distribution around *l'homme moyen* – the average man.

The implications are profound, but how far can we take them? It has been suggested, quite plausibly, that the performance of companies over long periods,[22] of investment fund managers,[23] perhaps of capital markets as a whole,[24] are characterized by *regression to the mean*. If this is so, it has enormous implications for retirement planning, both for individuals and in state-sponsored programs. But how far can we extrapolate past experience?

The research of William Baumol, a Princeton university economist, into *long-term productivity trends*, suggests that what Baumol calls *convergence*, is applicable here too. In a study[25] of 72 countries from 1870 to 1979, Baumol showed that the productivity rates in market-industrialized economies have converged,[26] with those performing most poorly in 1870 catching up thereafter, and those with the highest productivity rates in 1870 showing slower rates of growth. One must apply caution here, however, as Brad de Long of Berkeley demonstrated in a comment two years later.[27] Baumol's set of 16 industrial countries are not representative of the world at large in either 1870 or 1980. They are, in fact, wealthy industrial countries, whose performance in 1980 predetermined the conclusion to which Baumol came.

Even if *regression (or reversion) to the mean* is a transcendent law, however, the question of time is material. As John Maynard Keynes[28] famously observed, 'In the long run, we are all dead.' There is no certainty in what period, or under what circumstances, such reversion will occur. Statistical analysis of the performance of the stock market over a century has little bearing on the time horizon of a retired person dependent on his portfolio for monthly income. Knowledge of the regularity of long-term exchange rate cycles does not enable the CFO of a gold mining company to decide whether to hedge the dollar price of gold over one financial year. We are often compelled to act, as Keynes observed, when the knowledge we have does *not* allow for a precise mathematical calculation.

Further consideration of utility

In parallel with the researches of Gauss and Galton into *normal distribution*, the 19th century saw further development of Jacob Bernoulli's concept of *utility*. Jeremy Bentham[29] saw utility as 'that property in any object whereby it tends [on balance] to produce benefit, advantage, good or happiness ....' His successor, John Stuart Mill, argued that 'actions are right in proportion as they tend to promote happiness, wrong as they tend to produce ... pain and the privation of pleasure.'[30]

William Jevons,[31] asserted that '*value* depends entirely upon utility' and argued that careful examination of the 'natural laws in the variation of utility, as depending upon the quantity of a commodity in our possession [permits development of] ... a satisfactory theory of exchange.' Although he makes no reference[32] to Jacob Bernoulli, he reaches a similar conclusion: the utility of (and thus the price one is prepared to pay for) an item, varies with the quantity of it that one already possesses.[33]

In 1900, Louis Bachelier[34] presented a thesis[35] defining the pricing of French government bonds, in which he developed a *distribution function* for the stochastic process underlying Brownian motion that Einstein applied[36] five years later in the famous paper in which he estimated the size of molecules. Bachelier's *option pricing model* predated the famous *Black–Scholes model* by 73 years.

Recognition of human limitations

Henri Poincaré,[37] who reviewed Bachelier's thesis and underestimated its importance, made important contributions in a related field. He argued that everything has a cause, though mortals cannot grasp all the causes of all events. Bernstein[38] cites Newman (1988a) on Poincaré as follows:

A mind infinitely powerful, infinitely well-informed, about the laws of nature, could have foreseen [everything] from the beginning of the centuries. If such a mind existed, we could not play with it at any game of chance, for we would lose.

But Poincaré's own words, from his 1903 essay on *Science and Method*, make clear that things are not that simple:

If we knew exactly the laws of nature and the situation of the universe at the initial moment, we could predict exactly the situation of that same universe at a succeeding moment; *but even if it were the case that the natural laws had no longer any secret for us, we could still only know the initial situation approximately.* If that enabled us to predict the succeeding situation with *the same approximation*, that is all we require, and we should say that the phenomenon had been predicted, that it is governed by laws. But it is not always so; *it may happen that small differences in the initial conditions produce very great ones in the final phenomena*. A small error in the former will produce an enormous error in the latter. *Prediction becomes impossible, and we have the fortuitous phenomenon.'* (Emphasis added.)

The consequence is that what appears to be mere *chance* is *the measure of our ignorance*. We overcome ignorance by reference to the *Laws of Probability* and *Great Numbers*, enabling efficient approximations that keep insurance companies in business. Poincaré uses the example of a cone perfectly balanced on its apex, which will topple in response to the slightest tremor, or breath of air, to illustrate why events that appear fortuitous are in fact caused by minute disturbances. The problem of understanding the likely effect of these minute occurrences is greatly exacerbated by complexity; meteorologists therefore are not very successful in forecasting the weather. The relationship to *chaos theory*,[39] a much later development that spawned the metaphor of the butterfly's wings in Peking (Beijing), causing storm systems a month later in New York, is readily apparent.

Reversion to uncertainty

Our ability to compute risk in human affairs had reached its natural frontier by the time of World War I. The confidence in reason and mathematics spawned by the Renaissance, the 18th century Enlightenment and the economic successes of the industrial revolution were shaken by the horrors that Europeans inflicted on one another with gas warfare in the trenches. The flower of a generation was cut down before it had bloomed and caution and cynicism grew in its wake. In 1921, Keynes observed soberly:

> There is a relation between the evidence and the event considered, but it is not necessarily measurable.

In the same year, Frank Knight[40] noted:

> There is much question as to how far the world is intelligible at all ... It is only in the very special and crucial cases that anything like a mathematical study can be made.

Faced in 1933 with the uncertainties of the Great Depression, Keynes was still gloomier:[41]

> We are faced at every turn with the problem of Organic Unity, of Discreteness, of Discontinuity – the whole is not equal to the sum of the parts, comparisons of quantity fail us, small changes produce large effects,[42] and the assumptions of a uniform and homogeneous continuum are not satisfied.

In his most distinctive work,[43] in 1936, Keynes was explicit:

> [Most decisions] to do something positive ... can only be taken as a result of animal spirits ... and not as the outcome of a weighted average of quantitative benefits multiplied by quantitative probabilities.

Bernstein supplies the explanation:

> Faced with the tensions of the post war years, only the most naïve theorist could pretend that all problems could be solved through the rational application of differential calculus and the laws of probability with well-ordered preferences. Mathematicians and philosophers had to admit that reality encompassed entire sets of circumstances that people had never contemplated before. The distribution of odds no longer followed ... [that which] ... Pascal had defined. It violated the symmetry of the bell curve and was regressing to means that were far more unstable than ... Galton had specified.[44]

Knight's most important contribution in this field lies in his distinction between *risk* – which he defines as *measurable uncertainty* – and true *uncertainty* – which cannot be *measured*. It is this insight that reconciles the discipline: certain things can be measured and calculated; others cannot. It is important to know which is which!

Knight believed that the usefulness of *mathematical calculation* in *forecasting by extrapolation* is limited to *large numbers* of observations of *independent, but homogenous*, events, like the throws of a pair of dice. In business, or other areas of human conduct, each event is so unique, he argued, that there are not enough similar instances in our past experience to allow us to use *mathematical formulae* to infer the probability of an outcome.

Keynes, whom Knight greatly disliked, reached similar conclusions.[45] Although he echoed Poincaré in believing that '[when] once the facts are known which determine our knowledge, what is probable ... in these circumstances has been fixed objectively and is independent of our opinion ...,' he did not believe that we are capable of knowing enough of the facts applicable at any time, to enable us to make more than a judgment, or an estimate, of what might occur in future. Keynes' economic work, which has influenced all generations since his own, was premised on *the uncertainty of future events*. This led naturally to his belief in the need for a more active role for governments in economic management. If the classical economic paradigm founded on spontaneous *equilibria* between supply and demand, and *regression to the mean* in the context of business cycles, was flawed because there was no intrinsic reason to believe that the future would reflect the past, then governments had a role to play in compensating for market failure and reducing uncertainty.

Keynes did not reject the work of Pascal, Bernoulli, de Moivre, Gauss and Galton on the mathematics of probability; like Knight he simply denied that these mathematical laws could be made applicable to forecasting events that involved human interactions – the probability of a European war, the price of copper, future interest rates or technological obsolescence – in the same way that they applied to the behavior of a coin, a pair of dice, a roulette wheel or sweet peas. 'About these matters,' he famously remarked, 'there is no scientific basis to form any calculable probability whatever. We simply do not know!'[46]

Kenneth Arrow,[47] a Nobel Prize winner for his work on the impact of insurance on risk-taking and economic advancement, had a similar view. In an essay published in 1992,[48] he observed:

> To me, our knowledge of the way things work, in society or in nature, comes trailing clouds of vagueness. Vast ills have followed a belief in certainty ... When developing policy with wide effects for an

individual or society, caution is needed because *we cannot predict the consequences*. (Emphasis added)

Arrow asked why we pay insurance premiums – which are set at levels that are intended to result in higher aggregate income for the company than it will have to pay out in claims. The reason, of course, is that one prefers the certainty of a small loss (the premiums) to the risk of a catastrophic outcome (e.g. the loss of one's house in a fire or of the impact on one's family if one dies at an inopportune time).

Arrow's sense of uncertainty led him to focus on insurance, and later, with Frank Hahn,[49] on the role of contracts expressed in monetary terms. Insurance and contracts are both ways of managing risk in a world in which uncertainty is pervasive. If we reflect on the *law of large numbers* and its relevance in the mathematics of probability, we realize immediately that we can almost never, as individuals, conduct enough trials to use the laws of probability to enable risk-free decisions. Because insurance companies aggregate the risks of hundreds of thousands of people, they act as intermediaries in enabling individuals to secure the benefits of the *law of large numbers*.

But insurers can only rely on the *law of large numbers* – and thus calculate both the risk and the attendant premium – when the risks to be insured are very numerous and independent of one another, and when one can mathematically calculate the odds. So, fire insurance does not cover destruction in time of war because the probabilities of damage to different buildings are closely interrelated and few listed insurers would offer a policy to be paid out in the event of a war between the United States and another state in 2015. We can only insure against a limited range of risks.

Arrow explored the potential benefit for overall economic activity if insurance were available to cover all potential losses, of any size, in a *complete market*. While he concluded that widening and deepening the scale of the economic activities we could take without unacceptable risk would expand our choices, promote opportunity and advance economic status and freedom, he warned that eliminating the consequences of risk-taking might also encourage irresponsible and destructive, antisocial behavior. A company that faces no risk of prosecution for pollution may be tempted to maximize short-term profits at the expense of the environment. The exclusion of risk can also, of course, result in complacency. If employees are guaranteed their jobs or their livelihoods, whatever their behavior, this may lead to lower productivity.

We try to limit these uncertainties and balance the outcomes through *contracts*, both those between individuals (or corporate entities) and *societal contracts* expressed in constitutions and laws. Arrow and Hahn[50] explored the relationships between contracts and money in limiting uncertainty, concluding that the reason we use 'money terms' in contracts is because we relate all decisions to a past about which we have some certainty and a future that is inherently uncertain. Contracts (and laws), founded on our experience of the past, are intended to limit our uncertainty about the future. Thus we agree a on price for delivery of a product with particular specifications at a future date, and often provide for what will happen if either party fails to perform.

New efforts at mathematical precision

The balance of the story of risk, from the Great Depression to the present, is defined by the intersection and entanglement of these two trends: our desire to secure the highest possible degree of mathematical certainty about the risks we face; and the recognition that much of human interaction in a complex cosmos[51] is inherently uncertain.

Optimism in the United States after its victories in Europe and the Pacific in World War II; the creation of global[52] and regional[53] institutions intended to remake the world and prevent a future war; and the recognition of the role of effective industrial and financial planning in ensuring the success of the 'war effort,' combined to spark a new wave of mathematical enthusiasm. The importance of precise calculations for nuclear weapons development and delivery, ventures beyond the earth's atmosphere ever deeper into space and the management of burgeoning air transport systems naturally encouraged a growing reliance on models and instruments promising precise forecasts. Increasingly sophisticated financial institutions, both banks and insurers, as well as those advising investors and managing their funds, eagerly seized on these instruments.

John (János) von Neumann[54] made outstanding contributions throughout his life in fields ranging from quantum theory to applied mathematics, and from computer science to development of the hydrogen bomb, but is perhaps most famous for the development of *game theory*. *Game theory* focuses on how individuals or groups of people interact, both when they cooperate and when they compete. *Non-cooperative game theory* deals with the interactions of rational individuals in an effort by each to achieve his or her own goals.

Von Neumann delivered his first paper on strategy games in 1926 to the Mathematical Society at the University of Göttingen,[55] demonstrating that *random behavior* was the only rational course of action in a simple competitive game of chance. He showed no further interest in the topic until he met the economist Oskar Morgenstern[56] at Princeton in 1938. Von Neumann and Morgenstern collaborated for six years in developing the mathematical theory of games and their economic applications.[57] Perhaps understandably, given their academic backgrounds, von Neumann and Morgenstern expressly rejected the idea that the social and psychological context of economic decisions made mathematical precision impossible. Morgenstern had sharply criticized Keynes' *General Theory* for its lack of mathematical rigor. Their aim was to bring the same precision to economic decision making that mathematics had earlier brought to the physical and biological sciences.

Although limitations in their mathematical framework originally made the theory applicable only under special conditions, since the 1980s it has become the most useful tool for an analyst confronting situations in which one actor's decision making depends on his rational expectations about what one or more other actors will do, while their rational decisions depend on their expectations about the first actor's behavior.

One well-known application in public policy, familiar to most, is Alan Blinder's[58] payoff matrix[59] which describes the trade-offs between fiscal (or budgetary) policy, which is in the preserve of the treasury and pertains to the balance between government expenditure and tax revenue; and monetary policy, through which the Federal Reserve Bank ('Fed') addresses money supply, chiefly by setting short-term interest rates. The aims of the two parties are often in conflict: the Fed often wishes to contain inflation, while the politicians seek to stimulate the economy.

Blinder's matrix resolves these conflicts by offering two *Nash equilibria*. A *Nash equilibrium*, named after John Nash[60] is a set of strategies, one for each player, such that no player has any incentive unilaterally to change his or her action. A change by any would lead that player to earn less than if he or she remained with the current strategy.

Game theory was also used extensively to model the negotiating strategies in arms control talks between the United States and erstwhile USSR in the 1970s and 1980s. Among the best-known applications in business are the spectrum auctions[61] for wireless communication rights, which raised $7.7 billion in the United States in 1993. The auctions for G3 mobile communication rights in Europe saw operators pay even more: the United Kingdom auction raised $33 billion in April 2000 and Germany received $47.5 billion later that year. At these levels, many commentators saw the high bidders suffering from the *Winner's Curse*,[62] having overpaid substantially. Finland later adopted a very different approach. This led to a wide disparity in license fees across markets, raising a number of issues related to market structure, pricing and service development.

Unfortunately, *game theory* has a great weakness: People do not necessarily behave the way it suggests they should. Merrill Flood,[63] who code-veloped the *prisoner's dilemma* game, became highly frustrated at the fact that rational people did not behave as the theories suggested, and eventually abandoned work in this area. Let's see why.

The framework of the *prisoner's dilemma* game is simple, though it is can be difficult to play in practice. Assume, in the simplest version, that you and a partner have conspired to commit a burglary and after leaving the crime scene on two motorcycles, have been arrested and held by the police for exceeding the speed limit and running a red light. You are being held in different cells, unable to communicate with one another, while you are both being interrogated. The police suspect you of the burglary, but there were no eyewitnesses and no fingerprints. You can either confess or deny the crime, but you do not know what your partner will do.

- If you confess and your partner refuses to do so, you will go free after testifying against him, and he will get a long sentence. (You *defect*.)
- If he confesses and you remain silent, the reverse will happen. You will serve a long jail term and he will go free. (He *defects*.)
- If you both confess, you will get a shorter sentence for displaying remorse and cooperating with the authorities. (You both *defect*.)
- If you both remain silent, you will not be convicted of burglary and will both get a very short sentence for speeding and running a red light. (You both *cooperate* with one another.)

What should a rational player – devoid of moral conscience – do? In principle, if only one round is played, the *best possible outcome for both players* would result from their *keeping silent*. But in the context of uncertainty about what the other will do, the *Nash equilibrium* for each is achieved by confessing. Each will be better off by confessing, irrespective of what the other does, than either will be if his partner confesses and he keeps silent. The problem is that the most rational strategy for each individual is not the best strategy for the group.

Flood's most famous experiment demonstrating that highly rational people do not necessarily seek *Nash equilibria*, involved two RAND Corporation analysts, John Williams and Armen Alchian.[64] Flood had devised a version of the *prisoner's dilemma* game in which the *Nash equilibrium* was for both players to *defect*, and Williams and Alchian were to play 100 repetitions of the game and record the reasons for their decisions. Despite the *Nash equilibrium* – of which neither player was aware as it has only recently been discovered – Alchian *cooperated* 68 times and Williams 78 times! At the outset, Williams had expected that both players would cooperate, while Alchian had expected both to defect; over time, however, both adopted a strategy of cooperation in most rounds.

When Nash was told of the result, his reaction was to criticize the players for being irrational, and inefficient in obtaining rewards! Several recent studies[65] show, however, how common it is even for players schooled in *game theory* to act in ways that are wholly irrational by game-theoretical standards. Similar criticisms of the gap between theory and human behavior by Nobel laureates Kenneth Arrow, Paul Samuelson and Henry Simon, a decade ago, also excited concern at that time.[66]

Despite this weakness, it would be wrong to conclude that *game theory* and other means of seeking to calculate optimally rational behaviors are a waste of time. We need the mathematics, even if we often do not – for reasons further explored in chapter 2 – respond the way the models predict. All financial institutions, for example, charged with investing the money of shareholders, policyholders or private banking clients, need means of peering through the clouds of uncertainty in search of predictable results.[67]

Harry Markowitz[68] and William Sharpe[69] made what are probably the most important contributions in the field of portfolio construction and were rewarded with the Nobel Prize for economics, with Merton Miller,[70] in 1990. Markowitz's contribution[71] was to introduce the need for diversification as a means of managing risk, suggesting that investors should concentrate on the risk–reward characteristics of a *portfolio* of investments, rather than individual instruments, when devising investment strategies.[72] Markowitz does not refer explicitly to *risk*; his focus is on investors who regard 'expected return as a desirable thing and variance of return an undesirable thing.' Volatility (or *variance of return*) is thus the proxy for risk in Markowitz's analysis, and *expected return* is the proxy for reward. Given the need to minimize volatility while maximizing return, diversification is the indicated strategy[73] and investors should select portfolios that lie on the *efficient frontier* where risk and reward are optimally balanced.

James Tobin[74] expanded on Markowitz's work by introducing a *risk-free asset*, making it possible to leverage a portfolio – magnify the risk and reward potentially associated with it – thus creating a *super-efficient portfolio*.[75] Through leverage, such portfolios can outperform other portfolios on the *efficient frontier*.

The potential problems with this mathematically precise approach are evident. Firstly, it makes rigid assumptions about the rationality of the institutions and individuals who invest. The construction of the *efficient frontier* and *superefficient portfolios* depends on the accuracy of the conclusions we can draw about the *reasons for* the historical behavior of markets. We have discussed this problem in chapter 2. Secondly, Markowitz explained that his aim was to develop portfolios that optimally balance *expected return* and *variance of return* or volatility. Do all investors regard volatility as a true proxy for risk, or does this depend on the time horizon of the investment? Thirdly, it is unreasonable to regard historical volatility (or return) as an adequate predictor of future performance? Fourthly, one must ask if return and volatility are *necessarily* negatively correlated?[76]

The scope of the research and the expertise required to construct portfolios on the efficient frontier is daunting. Markowitz worked with Sharpe in reducing this, replacing the need to calculate the covariances between all instruments on the portfolio with a formula assessing the variances of each instrument from the market as a whole.

In 1964, Sharpe used these insights to formalize his capital asset pricing model (CAPM), which makes specific assumptions premised on a greatly simplified world in which there are no taxes or transaction costs, all investors have the same investment horizons and hold identical opinions about expected returns, volatilities and correlations of the available investments. Not surprisingly, in this simplified and optimized world, the *market portfolio* is not only on the *efficient frontier*, it is Tobin's *super efficient portfolio*. All investors hold the market portfolio, and leverage or de-leverage their individual portfolios with positions in the *risk-free asset* to achieve the level of risk with which each feels comfortable.

The CAPM distinguishes between systematic and specific risk in each portfolio.

- *Systematic risk* is the risk of holding the market portfolio.
- *Specific risk* is the unique risk of an individual asset and can be eliminated by *diversification*.

Systematic risk is measured using *beta*, which describes the sensitivity of an instrument or portfolio to market movements. The market (represented, for example by the S&P 500 or the FT100) has a *beta* of 1.0. A portfolio which has a beta of 0.5 will move only half as much as the market, while one with a *beta* of 2.0 will rise or fall twice as much as the market.

The expected excess return of a portfolio above the *risk-free rate* equals the *beta* of the portfolio, times the market's expected excess return above the *risk-free rate*.

Given a *beta* and an *expected return* for an asset, the model assumes investors will bid its price up or down, adjusting the expected return. The

CAPM therefore predicts the *equilibrium price* based on the *assumption* that all investors agree on the *beta* and the *expected return* of every asset. In practice, of course, this assumption is unrealistic.

Portfolio theory provides a broad context for understanding the interactions of systematic risk and reward. It has had a great impact on the management of institutional investment portfolios. The mathematics of portfolio theory is used extensively in financial risk management, and has underpinned the development of value-at-risk approaches,[77] which we have reviewed in chapter 4.

Rational assumptions under fire

From the mid-1960s onward, a new wave of disquiet at the assumptions necessary to allow use of the sophisticated mathematical models employed for portfolio management, evidence of human behavior that departed sharply from the 'rational' *equilibria* defined in game theory, and advances in behavioral psychology combined to prompt the pendulum to swing back yet again from the extreme of its arc.

But this time it took a different path. Instead of merely discussing the respective merits of calculating the probability of independent events from very large samples and recognizing that much about the future is inherently uncertain, empiricists like Ellsberg, Kahneman, Tversky and Thaler, challenged the core assumption that underlay classical economics, and had made econometrics a plausible science, *that humans usually behaved in ways that economic theory had represented as rational*.

We have explored *Prospect Theory*,[78] the core of what has come to be called *behavioral finance*[79] in chapter 2. Here it is enough to note that Kahneman[80] and Tversky[81] sought to develop an alternative approach to *expected utility theory* which, as we have seen, discusses how decisions under uncertainty *should* be made. Prospect *theory*, by contrast, seeks to define how decisions *are* made in reality. Many insights have emerged from the experiments over 40 years, leading Kahneman and Tversky to observe in 1992, that 'Choice is a constructive and contingent process. When faced with a complex problem, people ... use computational shortcuts and editing operations.'[82] They suggested moreover, that: '... the experimental evidence ... confirm(s) a *distinctive fourfold pattern of risk*: risk aversion for gains and risk seeking for losses of high probability [and] risk seeking for gains and risk aversion for losses of low probability.'

In 1986, Richard Thaler[83] coauthored[84] a paper titled 'Does the Stock Market Overreact?'[85] It concluded that when new information became available to investors, they consistently overvalued that information and under-weighted information that they had earlier possessed. The result was that share prices consistently overshot the *objective* equilibrium by so far that reversion from the point they reached was predictable, irrespective of any subsequent changes in the fundamentals pertaining to the share.

While Thaler was attacked for his suggestion that the markets did not result – at least immediately – in rational pricing, a second paper[86] by Vakonishok, Vishny and Schleifer in 1993 reached a similar conclusion. These authors showed that 'value stocks' – shares priced below the index for earnings and other measures of value, tend to outperform higher-valued shares even after risk-based adjustments are made.[87]

The conclusion to be reached from much statistical analysis and many experiments conducted in the field of *behavioral finance* is that human behavior does not mirror the rational expectations of classical economics. Kahneman, Tversky and Thaler all accept, however, that 'human choices are orderly, if not always rational in the traditional sense of the word.' The tension between *objective rationality* and *perfect markets* on the one hand, and the foibles of human behavior on the other, does not lead to chaos, but should encourage us to caution and a modest appreciation of the limits of forecasting.

This is true even with the new advances made possible in recent years with superior computing capability, advanced algorithms and sophisticated derivatives, both futures and options. The powerful mathematics underpinning the *Black[88]–Scholes[89] option pricing model[90]* and the collective experience and genius of John Meriwether, the famed bond trader from Salomon Brothers, Nobel Prize-winning economists Myron Scholes and Robert Merton, as well as David Mullins, a former vice chairman of the Federal Reserve Board, did not prevent the impending collapse of Long Term Capital Management (LTCM) in autumn 1998. Only the intervention of the Federal Reserve Bank of New York brought LTCM's lenders together and facilitated its bailout, with 14 banks contributing about $300 million each to raise a $3.65 billion fund in exchange for 90 percent of LTCM's equity. That allowed it to withstand the turmoil in the markets until it had repaid its loans and had to be effectively liquidated in 2000.

Among the most profound lessons to be learned from this debacle is that the most sophisticated financial models are exceptionally subject to model risk and parameter risk, and need both to be stress tested and tempered with judgment.

Appendix 2. Global risk in historical and future perspectives

The essence of risk, as we saw in the Introduction, is captured by the symbiotic balance between *threat* and *opportunity* expressed in the Chinese ideogram. Our appetite for risk is tied to the opportunities we associate with it. Assuming calculated risks often translates into big rewards for people who accurately assess their scale and can see how to shape events to secure the advantages that others fear to grasp. Risks often mask exceptional opportunities for the advancement of wealth, reputation and human welfare. The whole of history is a record of obstacles overcome and hurdles leaped, because exceptional men and women rose above their fears and pushed back the boundaries of uncertainty, expanding the frontiers of knowledge. Skeat's[1] derivation of the word *risk* from the Spanish *arriesgar*, 'to venture into danger, [literally] to go against a rock,' is worth recalling. It provides the context of the voyages of discovery by Portuguese and Spanish navigators in the 15th and 16th centuries that transformed the uncharted waters of antiquity into today's familiar world.

Braving uncertainty – The origins of Portuguese exploration

How – and why – did they do it? Centuries of technological advancement preceded the decision by Dom Henrique, better known to many as Prince Henry the navigator, to explore the African coast. It is to his enthusiasm that the Portuguese owe their Golden Age. Henrique was the third son of King João I of Portugal and his English wife, Philippa, daughter of John of Gaunt, the Duke of Lancaster. In 1415, at age 21, while Christians and Muslims were struggling for control of the Mediterranean, he, with his father and brothers, captured the port of Ceuta[2] in Morocco. Three years later he created the first school of oceanic navigation and an astronomical observatory at Sagres to train sailors in mathematics, navigation and map-making. His aim was to send Portuguese sailors into the Atlantic, down the coast of West Africa, to find the limits of the Islamic world so as to defeat the Muslims in the Mediterranean by attacking them from the rear, and to find the mythical Christian empire of the priest-king Prester John.

At this time, no European seafarer had passed Cape Bojador on the Atlantic coast of Africa at latitude 27°N. The Portuguese called the ocean beyond the cape the *Sea of Darkness*. Henrique chose two captains who were not experienced sailors for the first expedition, apparently deliberately, for experienced captains who knew the legends would probably have refused. Portuguese mariners of the time, moreover, had no experience of sailing in open seas; their nautical knowledge was limited to coasting in sight of land.

Henrique sent 14 expeditions in 12 years in efforts to round Cape Bojador, before succeeding for the first time[3] in 1434.[4] In the following 16 years until his death in 1460, his ships had progressed southwards to Cape Palmas, in what is now Liberia. Not until 1488 did Bartholomew Dias sail around the Cape of Good Hope; Vasco da Gama's epic voyage to India was a decade later, in 1497–8,[5] 27 years after Henrique's death.

Seventy years passed between Henrique's decision to found his observatory and academy and Vasco da Gama's arrival in India. During all this time, under three kings, Portuguese seafarers continued to place their lives at risk, sailing further than their charts, and mapping new coastal and oceanic frontiers. What was it that motivated them and those who sent them? Azurara, a contemporary chronicler, summarized Henrique's aims in exploring the African coast, after the capture of Ceuta,[6] as being *to know the country beyond Cape Bojador, to establish trade relations advantageous to Portugal, to determine the strength of his enemies in the region, to seek allies in the battles against the enemies of Christianity, and to spread the Christian faith*. This mix of economic and spiritual motives lies at the heart of many dynasties seeking to expand their realms. It provides a powerful justification for the extension of political power. The cross and the sword (as well as the musket and cannon) were the instruments of economic colonization employed by the Portuguese and the Spanish in South America in the 16th century, and by the English in Africa and India in the 19th century. Different combinations worked for different people; what drove Kitchener[7] of Khartoum was not what motivated Livingstone, or the London Missionary Society,[8] or Cecil John Rhodes,[9] but all these people took extraordinary risks, motivated by religious or secular beliefs – and quite frequently both – in pursuit of opportunities that others may have felt were not worth the candle.

We turn back to Henrique to make a related point. Henrique's successes were due to more than his brave vision of discovery and the daring of his captains. Scientific knowledge, technology and innovation – what we think of today as the essence of the knowledge economy – defined his environment. As word spread of the Portuguese expeditions, astronomers, cartographers and geographers – Jews and Arabs, as well as Christians – flowed to Sagres to offer their services. What emerged there was less a school of navigation than a community of scholars who joined together to conquer the unknown.

Henrique had discovered the Arabs' superior navigational skills, while at Ceuta, years before.[10] But how had this mastery arisen?

Acquiring, disseminating and generating knowledge – The Islamic achievement

The political domain of Islam had its origins in 632 CE on the Arabian Peninsula, as an Abrahamic, monotheistic religion, based on the Qur'an, a set of revelations from the Angel Jibril (Gabriel) to the Prophet Mohammed[11] over 23 years from 610 CE. After the death of the Prophet, Islam began expanding under the Umayyad Caliph Umar from 634 CE and continued to grow under the Abbassids until the 12th century, when it extended from Transoxania and Sind to the Iberian peninsula on the western end of the Mediterranean.[12]

This extraordinary expanse gave the vibrant new polity access to the scientific and technological legacy of the Mesopotamian, Egyptian and Hellenic civilizations and allowed it to draw on the civilizations of China and India as well. This access shaped the scientific and intellectual capacity of the Islamic world and the Abbasid[13] Caliphs Harun ar-Rashid (786–809 CE) and al-Ma'mun (813–33 CE) acted so as to enable an explosion of learning. The outcome was a unique Islamic civilization which developed and grew the intellectual and technological legacy it had inherited, dominated the world until the 15th century[14] and unintentionally sparked the European Renaissance.

What did the Caliphs do to make this happen?

First, arguing that scientific enquiry was encouraged by the Qur'an, *sunna*[15] and *a'hadith*,[16] they provided intellectual patronage by establishing large libraries and facilities for research and academic exchange. A culture of intellectual enquiry was forged in Baghdad, Shiraz and Cordoba; caravans bringing manuscripts and botanical specimens covered the realm from Bukhara to Tigris, and Egypt to Andalusia. Embassies were sent to Constantinople and India to acquire manuscripts and teachers. Caliph al-Ma'mun established the *Khizanatul Hikmah* (the Treasure of Wisdom) and *Bayt al-Hikmah* (the House of Wisdom) in Baghdad, to encourage the translation of foreign texts into Arabic and research on their content. Scholars of many nationalities and religions translated Greek, Persian and Indian works on mathematics, logic, astronomy, philosophy and the exact sciences into Arabic, and wrote commentaries on those texts and produced original works of their own. A century and a half later the Fatimid[17] Caliph al-Hakim was still continuing the tradition; he created the *dar al-Hikmah* in Cairo in 1005 CE, which was open 'to everyone, without distinction of rank, who wished to read or consult any of the books.'[18] Caliph al-Hakam II of Andalus[19] built up a library of over 400,000 books in Cordoba in the same spirit.

Second, they overcame the barriers that different languages posed to the dissemination and development of knowledge across the realm. The political climate in the early Islamic period was favorable; Arabic was the *lingua franca* from Bukhara to Cordoba and even Jewish and Christian scholars in Andalus, and Syrian scholars in Egypt and Syria, were skilled in Arabic. In 711, Christian decrees against the Jews in Spain were reversed by the Umayyads and Jews were invited to join in the creation of a glorious culture. The Syrian scholars in Damascus were proficient in Greek and were retained to convert the whole *corpus* of Greek science into Arabic, with a special focus on Plato and Aristotle (philosophy), Euclid, Archimedes, Apollonius (geometry), Galen, Hippocrates, Dioscorides (medicine) and Hipparchos and Ptolemy (astronomy). Arabic thus became the language of science and technology all across the realm, making knowledge accessible to all.

The result was a huge boost to science and technology throughout the Islamic world from 750–1100 CE, and the rapid growth of innovative ideas which spread rapidly across that domain. A plethora of Muslim scientists emerged who built on the scientific achievements of their Greek and Indian predecessors and left a rich legacy, which underpinned the European Renaissance and the scientific and industrial revolutions that followed the Christian reformation. This is not the place to discuss all these remarkable men, though Farabi, Ibn Sina [better known in English as Avicenna], Al-Biruni, Ibn Shatir, Ibn Rushd [Avarroes] and Ibn Khaldun are names to conjure with in the history of science. Among their achievements were correction of Aristotle's misconceptions about human *embryology* and Ptolemy's errors in *astronomical calculation* and the development of new scientific disciplines and hypotheses, a few of which we list below:

• Al-Battani introduced Indian numerals with zero, and sines and cosines into Greek *mathematics* and transformed *astronomy* into an exact discipline;

- Modern *algebra* owes its origin to Al-Khawarizmi;
- Ibn Sina synthesized *medical knowledge*, supplanting Galen, Hippocrates and Dioscorides; his efforts led to teaching hospitals for in- and out-patients which provided free treatment without discrimination, separate wards for contagious diseases and psychiatric cases, pharmacies and libraries for students and teachers;
- Al Razi originated *clinical medicine* based on observation and experimentation;
- Ala al Din Ibn al-Nafis discovered that the blood moves into the left ventricle *via the lung*, not through a hole in the heart, as Galen and Ibn Sina had believed;
- Jabir Ibn Al Hayyan laid the foundations of *experimental chemistry* in the 8th century while Al Razi formalized them with laboratory experiments 100 years later;
- Modern *optics* owes its origin to Al Haitham; and modern *botany* to Ibn Al-Baitar who did his research in the Botanic Garden in Seville in the 13th century;
- Tyco Brahe's famous observatory used mathematical models of Nasir al-Din Tusi[20] and Ibn al Shatir[21] for observations and calculations. Tusi had introduced a planetary model that contained all the innovations of Copernicus's astronomy except the heliocentric hypothesis;
- The polymaths Al Kindi, Farabi, Ibn Sina and Ibn Rushd were the greatest exponents of Aristotelian rationalism, and translation of their commentaries into Latin in the 13th century, reignited European rationalism.

Not surprisingly, this scientific ferment led to important advances in technology, especially in navigation[22] and warfare,[23] but also in:

- Paper manufacture, which began modifying Chinese methods in Samarkand in 751,[24] and soon spread to Baghdad, Cairo, Fez and Jativa; the first paper factory in Europe was only established in Fabriano in 1276;
- Glass making, from where skills inherited from the Romans and employed in Syria from the 7th century onward were eventually transferred to Venice under treaty in 1277;[25]
- Weight-driven mechanical clocks, used by Muslims in Spain in 11th century, 250 years before they were introduced into northern Europe, and whose origins lie in water clocks and candle clocks described by *al Jazari*;[26]
- Windmills, first introduced in the Islamic world in the reign of the Caliph Umar (634–44) and first mentioned in Europe in a French text in 1105; and watermills;[27]

- Irrigation, which again had it origins in Roman machines, but was transformed in Iran into the *qanat* system, exploited water from aquifers, and reached Europe from Andalusia; *al Jazari* contributed greatly to this by developing sophisticated designs for double action pumps, among other solutions;[28] and
- Not surprisingly among people with a desert heritage who made a close study of botany and had developed sophisticated technology, exceptional advances were made in agronomy – especially in intensive cropping with up to four harvests a year, crop rotation to conserve fertility, the selection of crops suited to particular *terroir* and the use of fertilizers.

But the most important and lasting contribution of the Islamic period was the introduction and consolidation of *modern scientific method*. This came about because coordinated research was underway simultaneously in different centers, encouraging experimentation to test the validity of theories. Modern science thus arose from the new methods of observation, experimentation and measurement introduced into Europe by the Arabs. Ironically, given our concern about the destructive impact of anti-intellectualism in parts of the Muslim world today, the Islamic intellectual and scientific revolution of the 9th–13th centuries took place while Catholic Europe was still steeped in darkness because the clergy were opposed to science and secular thought.

Five key factors stand out when one reflects on what enabled the rapid transmission of new scientific ideas, and the transfer of technology, in this period:

- Enlightened, liberal *patronage* by the rulers, to ensure unfettered research;
- *Translation* into Arabic of the corpus of Greek and Indian scientific, astronomical and mathematical works;
- Encouragement of *centers of excellence* in mathematics, astronomy, chemistry, medicine, pharmacology, optics and agronomy;
- *Coordination* of research and rapid *dissemination* of knowledge within the Islamic sphere; and
- *Religious tolerance*, and support to both Muslims and non-Muslims in their academic pursuits.

The destruction of these enablers led to the decline of the Islamic realm. Three strands were key:

- *The Seljuk*[29] ascendancy (1077–1307 CE) led to the suppression of the diversity of thought that had prevailed under the Abbasids, Fatimids[30] and Buyids,[31] and led to the standardization of what was taught in the *madrassahs*, political consolidation and religious orthodoxy. In Baghdad, the Asharite scholar Al-Ghazali (1058–1111 CE) denounced the ancient Greeks as nonbelievers and attacked those who employed their methods and ideas as 'corrupters of the faith.' The Abbasid caliph closed the doors of *ijtihad* (interpretation of the *Qur'an* and *sunna*) in the Sunni tradition in the 13th century, restricting it to the heads of the *Maliki, Hanafi, Shafi'i* and *Hambali* schools of law. The motivation was political: experiencing challenges on many fronts, the Abbasids sought to outlaw other sects. Restricting *ijtihad*, however, led to intellectual stagnation as new solutions to new challenges gave way to *taqleed* (imitation).

- The *Mongol*[32] *invasion* from the east ended the Abbasid caliphate in 1258; and the Spanish Inquisition consolidated the expulsion of Muslims and Jews from Iberia[33] in the West.
- The success and advancement of the European paradigm established the superiority and dominance of what became the West. This process runs through the Italian Renaissance, the Portuguese and Spanish voyages of discovery, followed by those of the Dutch and the English, the Protestant Reformation, the Age of Reason in the 18th century and the Industrial Revolution thereafter.

There was a cultural renaissance in the East under the Ottomans,[34] under whose patronage the architect Sinan[35] designed the remarkable *Suleymaniye* mosque and 334 other buildings; the Safavids[36] in Iran, and the Moguls[37] in India, but the exceptional knowledge dominance that the Islamic realm had enjoyed for 500 years until the beginning of the 14th century, has not been recovered.

What can we learn from this experience? Particularly, in the context of today's risks, how is it that some of the descendents of these remarkable scholars, researchers and innovators have become *jihadists* and suicide-bombers?

Let's start with the first question.

The Islamic realm – Midwife of modernity?

A mix of religious and economic considerations encouraged successive Islamic dynasties to continue exploiting exceptional opportunities, despite the attendant hazards. As we saw earlier with our brief discussion of Henrique of Sagres, the Spanish conquistadores and a few British imperialists, these are powerful incentives. What is more remarkable, however, is the degree of *scientific discipline* that underpinned the Islamic effort. Unlike the ancient Egyptians, Greeks and Romans, the Umayyads, Abbasids, Fatimids and Buyyids placed little trust in priests and oracles. Although *Islam* implies submission[38] to the will of *Allah*, the sources of revealed truth, the *Qur'an and sunna*, are available to all. The Islamic (Sunni) orthopraxis[39] (*Islam*) is neither remote nor mystical; it involves a testimony of faith (*shahadah*) – what Christians call the creed, daily prayer (*salah*), charity (*zakah*), fasting (*sawm*) and (if one's circumstances permit) the pilgrimage to Mecca and Medina (*haj*). Islamic orthodoxy (*iman*) encourages one to seek God's truth though intellect; and its defining elements are common to Christianity and Judaism: belief in God, his angels, the scriptures, the prophets and the Last Day and the Hereafter. *Ihsan* – loving God and being open to union with him – is familiar to anyone with knowledge of the Abrahamic traditions; in Islam it is associated with cleansing the soul of greed, egotism, lust, gossip, envy and other sicknesses.

Although Muslims' belief in the transcendence of the Almighty discouraged speculation about probability, as we noted in appendix 1, the early Islamic advances in mathematics, the physical and life sciences, and technology, set the stage for comprehensive scientific appreciation of the complex world within which we assume and manage risk. Freed from layers of polytheistic uncertainty, in which the contests of the gods shaped and constrained human fates, there was no need for oracles and diviners. Rational enquiry and scientific experimentation enabled the pursuit of knowledge. At least until the 13th century CE, *ijtihad*[40] allowed interpretation of the *Qur'an* and the *sunna* to meet the changing needs of Islamic societies. This spirit of enquiry and experimentation had a profound impact on the Christian European societies in close contact with the Islamic realm – the Italians in particular – and stimulated Europe's own R*enaissance*.

The doors of *ijtihad* were closed after the 13th century in the Sunni tradition, with the right to perform it being restricted to only four scholars: Malik Ibn Anas, Abu Hanifa al-No'man, Muhammad Ibn Idris al-Shafi'i and Ahmad Ibn Hambal – the heads of the *Maliki, Hanafi, Shafi'i,* and *Hambali* schools of *sharia*, or Islamic law. The motivation was political: experiencing challenges on many fronts, the Abbasids sought to outlaw other sects in an effort to exercise control. Closing the doors of *ijtihad* led to intellectual stagnation as potential *mujtahid*[41] were prohibited from developing workable solutions to new challenges and forced to rely on *taqleed* (imitation).

Borrowings and scholastic emulation – The sources of European renaissance

Meanwhile, in the 13th century, as the Abbasids were near their nadir, their attention focused on Genghis Khan's advance from the East, and sectionalism rampant in the Islamic realm, the Catholic papacy was asserting itself, its aim being to establish control over the Christian realm. To achieve this, popes clashed with Christian kings and emperors. Relations between church and state and the doctrinal and legal issues they raised were debated in the monasteries and the new universities. These scholarly exchanges, informed by Latin translations of Aristotle and *Ibn Rushd's* commentaries, led to a new role for scholastics[42] like Thomas Aquinas.[43] These scholars facilitated an exchange of ideas and the progressive unification of Christian Europe. Latin, in the Christian realm, became the equivalent of Arabic in the Islamic, and new insights in theology, law, philosophy, liberal arts and architecture followed naturally as leading scholars traveled from monastery to court, and back, across many national boundaries.

Aquinas' greatest political contribution to the emergence of a new Europe was his use of Aristotelian methods to study both the natural and the political orders, thereby paving the way in Christianity for what eventually became the secular state. The other singular contribution was that of Robert Grosseteste[44] who introduced experimental method into science in Christian Europe, and emphasized the importance of exact measurement. Thanks to these two men, scientific method, exact measurement and an efficient secular world became, over the next few centuries, the defining features of Western modernity. As we have seen, however, it was the first two of these factors that had earlier characterized the Islamic realm; Aquinas and Grosseteste were deeply indebted to their Islamic predecessors.

By the end of the 13th century therefore, we can see two trends that changed the course of European, and eventually, global history. The Islamic realm was becoming more rigid and restrictive, and, as a result, notably less innovative. Meanwhile, Christianity was stirring; clerical scholars, equipped with a unifying language, Latin, were generating and disseminating knowledge in a way akin to that of their Arabic-literate counterparts several centuries earlier. Christian Europe was beginning to experience the same intellectual ferment that the Islamic realm had earlier known. Due to the tensions unlocked by competing schools – headed by Dominicans, Franciscans, Augustinians and scholars of other orders – and the rediscovery of Aristotelian rationalism, Christianity was becoming a more individualistic faith, weakening the power of poorly educated local clergy. Economic and social changes prompted by new waves of urbanization, weakened the hold of clans and tribes and strengthened a sense of individual accountability, while the emergence of science brought a measure of control and some capacity to predict events.

The first to break through were the Italian city-states, where the wealth amassed by merchants and bankers in the 14th century thereafter sparked the flowering of the arts we call the Renaissance.[45] The second explosion of wealth accrued to the merchant-adventurers, first from Portugal and Spain, whose lands had long been occupied by the Arabs and who had been exposed to their astrolabes, sextants, trigonometry and charts; and then to the Dutch, whose knowledge came from the Spanish who had occupied them until the 16th century and later the English, whose fortunes were intertwined with all three. The success of these states in exploring the globe and vastly increasing the reach of Christian Europe – though the power of Spain was later broken by the revolt of the Netherlands – built the foundations of Western economic and political dominance up to the end of the 20th century.

As the Abassids had earlier discovered in the Islamic realm, encouragement of a spirit of enquiry, extensive travel and the acquisition and dispersal of knowledge sat uncomfortably in Europe with Papal infallibility and Episcopal and monastic privileges. The emergence and growth of rational humanism, epitomized by Erasmus[46] and the reformation initiated by Luther[47] and Calvin[48] broke the monopoly power of the Catholic church and paved the way for the Enlightenment[49] and the triumph of rationalism in the 18th century. The great advances in scientific enquiry that this permitted, led to the industrial revolution and the advance of the British empire in the 19th century to the point where it could be argued that the sun always shone on some part of it.[50]

The central importance of knowledge[51]

This brief discussion of a millennium of history makes two things clear:

- First, the central importance of knowledge – its acquisition, dissemination and continuing generation – for the growth and development of societies. Both the dynamic Islamic civilization of the 9th–13th centuries and the rapidly evolving Christian (and later Western, secular) civilization that followed and eclipsed it, were built on philosophical[52] enquiry, enabling continuing learning, observation, analysis of data and experimentation, that permitted the formulation, elaboration and eventual falsification of the waves of competing scientific hypotheses that sustain and accelerate human advances. It is this that underpins what we call *risk identification*, *assessment* and *management* and allows us to *communicate* our understanding of the sources and quantum of risk, to others. It is this history that explains the origins of the words *risk* and *hazard*; and gives meaning to Peter Bernstein's splendid observation that mastery of risk is founded on 'the notion that the future is more than a whim of the gods and that men and women are not passive before nature.'

It also offers part of the answer to the challenge we identified in the first three chapters of this book, that of reconciling the dominance of the affective (emotive) elements of our minds over the cognitive in properly assessing risk, especially the exceedingly complex risks that are the product of the interconnected components of contemporary environments. We cannot overcome our human circumstance, but we can inform our decisions by basing them on the best knowledge available.

- The second insight is less sweeping, but perhaps no less relevant today. From the 13th to the 16th centuries, there is little that occurred in the renascent Christian realm in Europe that did not have its origins in the Islamic knowledge society that preceded it. The conflicts between Islamic caliphs and sultans and Christian princes and republics in the Mediterranean have obscured Westerners' understanding of our collective debt to the Islamic *Golden Age*.

This fact has an important corollary: The demise of the Islamic realm was due to more than the rise of the scholastics, humanists and rationalists, the waves of urbanization and the ascendancy of merchants and bankers that empowered Christian Europe. It was also due to the decision to close the doors of *ijtihad* and to force Islamic society to replicate tired formulae, devised in the 7th century, when addressing the challenges of a continuously changing world. The intellectual stagnation that followed was just as damaging to Islamic society, as the obscurantism and clerical tyranny in which the Catholic Church had been mired at the end of the first millennium had been to Christian Europe.

Iberia's experience provides a further footnote: After the defeat of Muslim forces in Spain in 1492, King Ferdinand's decision to use the Inquisition to eliminate Judaism and Islam in his domains, by forcing the Jews and Muslims who remained to convert to Christianity and burning (and confiscating the wealth of) those who recanted, led rapidly to the intellectual – and eventually the financial – impoverishment of the part of Europe that was best placed to benefit from Islamic science and technology. Sephardic

Jews and Muslims with knowledge, skills and money fled repressive Catholic Spain for more tolerant, Protestant, northern climes, settling in the Netherlands – which soon had fleets exploring the world, stock exchanges and sophisticated financial instruments – and along the Rhine, where the chemical and pharmaceutical industries of Basel are the successors of the alchemists who abandoned Spain. Swiss preeminence in watch making has its origins in Luther and Calvin's decisions that *Freiheit* included the right to personal possession of time pieces.

Islamist terror as a global threat

The question we asked earlier – why *some* of the descendents of the remarkable Islamic scholars, researchers and innovators of earlier centuries, have become *jihadists* – may thus not be so difficult to answer. Sustained, violent conflict, in the form of insurrection or liberation struggles, usually has its origins in threats that marginalized groups perceive to their *identity* and *collective security*.[53] In addition to the grievances that some Arab Muslims express about repressive autocratic or oligarchic governments in the Arab region, underpinned by the *mukhabarat*[54] whose task in some countries has been not only to preserve the political status quo, but also to suppress commercial, financial and intellectual innovation; the delays in finding a reasonable solution to the festering conflict between Israel and Palestine; and recently, the United States and British invasion and occupation of Iraq; there are other systemic sources as well.

Many militant Islamists resent Western political, economic and social dominance and reject what they see as corrupt, irreligious Western mores and consumerist values. This has led to a desire to reassert idealized 'traditional' identities and norms. As we saw in chapter 7, Western political and military power was sharply apparent after the first Gulf War, while the war in Afghanistan, in which a generation of young Muslims had been encouraged to fight the Soviet Army for the liberation of their country, had come to an end, with a radical government applying the *shari'a*, in power in Kabul. Thousands of experienced zealots were looking for new victories and new recruits to the cause. The ground was ripe for revolutionary messages, and al-Qaeda stepped into the breach a decade ago.

As Michael Scheuer has noted,[55] analysis of Islamist broadcasts and websites indicates that the call to *jihad* has been couched in terms that require devout Muslims to respond. The Islamists claim, with scores of examples, that Islam, Muslims and Islamic lands are under attack by the United States and its allies. *Jihad* is an imperative, according to Mohammed abd al-Halim of al-Azhar University, '… to repulse tyranny and restore justice and rights.' Attacks on Islam are said to be constituted by US demands for change in educational curricula and the monitoring of charitable donations; attacks on Muslims are said to be evident in US support for Israel's actions in Palestine, those of India in Kashmir, Russia in Chechnya, the Uzbek government in Uzbekistan, the Philippines government in Mindanao and in sanctions imposed over the years on Iraq, Afghanistan, Iran, Syria, Libya and Sudan 'to control oil production and dispossess Muslims.' Islamic lands under attack or 'occupation' range from Afghanistan, Iraq and Palestine (where Israelis are said to be intent on destroying Islam and establishing a Greater Israel from the Nile to the Euphrates), through the Arabian Peninsula, the birthplace of the Prophet, to the countries of the Gulf Cooperation Council (GCC), notably Qatar and Kuwait.

Systemic conditions have made some Muslims more susceptible to these messages. The reasons differ from one region to another – Muslims in Europe, Saudi Arabia, Indonesia and Afghanistan are not all similarly motivated – but many of those who identify with *jihadist* causes experience alienation from their secular environments and a sense of hopelessness, and are attracted by the prospect of glory and religious salvation. Prospects for young, poorly educated Afghans, Palestinians in the occupied territories or Syrians, have not been encouraging in the past few decades and anger and intense frustration can easily be channeled into utopian causes, if life holds no promise or meaning. Most European countries, meanwhile, have failed to integrate millions of their Muslim immigrants socially or economically. The result of this, according to Robert Leiken of the Nixon Center and Brookings Institution,[56] is that 'Jihadist networks span Europe from Poland to Portugal, thanks to the spread of radical Islam among the descendents of guest workers once recruited to shore up Europe's postwar economic miracle.' Leiken quotes a leader of the French Union of Islamic Organizations, cursing his new homeland poignantly:

> Oh sweet France! Are you astonished that so many of your children join in a stinging *naal bou la France*,[57] and damn your Fathers!'

This is a difficult topic, infected and confused by poorly researched and emotional generalizations, and we do not want to compound the problem here. This book is also not the place for a detailed discussion of the many strands that account for the widespread, militant Islamist[58] resentment of Western political, economic and social dominance; the rejection of what are seen as corrupt, irreligious Western mores and secular, consumerist values; and the reassertion of idealized 'traditional' identities and norms.[59]

But the scale of the threat posed both by those who plan, or employ selective readings of verses of the *Qu'ran* to justify and incite, guerrilla attacks on Western security forces and targets, and acts of terrorism[60] that kill thousands of civilians from Iraq and Indonesia to Madrid and London; and those who, enjoying no hope of a *normal* future in a globalized world, become their cannon fodder, demands consideration.

For several years before September 11, 2001, it was clear that the world was on the verge of a systemic crisis.[61] The convergence of information and communication technologies, the exceptionally rapid growth of market economies after the Cold War and the emergence of global financial markets operating at electronic transaction speeds had created a volatile new environment, management of which confronted us with unprecedented challenges.

The world's largest economies, with their exceptional reservoirs of skills, were poised to gain, though domestic stresses were inevitable; Europe in particular faced – as it still does – serious structural obstacles to globally competitive performance. China was already moving onto a sustained growth path. A number of smaller countries were positioned to exploit profitable niches. But there were few reasons for optimism about the future of most central Asian, African, Andean or Middle Eastern states.[62] The new concept of *emerging markets* made it clear that many of the lesser developed countries were not advancing, at least in relation to the leaders. Bridging the digital divide posed – as it still does – an enormous challenge and the poor skills at the disposal of most underdeveloped states consigned them to the margins of the debate about new global paradigms. The world has changed greatly since the pillars of our global architecture were built after World War II, and the global institutions – the United Nations, the World Bank, the International Monetary Fund and the World Trade Organization (born out of the General Agreement on Tariffs and Trade) – have lagged behind. The collapse of scientific socialism in 1991 led to the belief that liberal markets and democracy had triumphed and the new global market economy that emerged was (and is) unmediated by an accountable system of global governance.

Although *jihadism* seems, at first blush, unrelated, its sources are similar. Economic and social uncertainty feed fear, and fearful people are often attracted to religious radicalism. As Ernest Hemingway famously remarked, 'There are no atheists in a foxhole.' Fundamentalism has been on the rise in all religious traditions for over a decade. The elimination of physical distance by global broadcasting, branding and advertising, had, moreover, by the end of the century, exacerbated cultural friction by aggressively promoting secular consumerism and other modern Anglo-Saxon values.

In 2000, the Arab Middle East was in a distressing state.[63] Because of rapid population growth and most economies' high dependency on oil revenues,[64] *per capita* incomes had stagnated since 1975, performing worse than all regions other than sub-Saharan Africa. Levels of knowledge, innovation and technological advancement were poor; while the macroeconomic environment, the quality of governance and public institutions, the functioning of goods and factor markets and the integration of the region into the global economy discouraged entrepreneurship. Nonoil merchandise exports from the region contributed only 6 percent to GDP, as against 20 percent in Southeast Asia. The ratio of FDI to GDP was only 0.5 percent, while in Central Europe and Chile, FDI/GDP ratios had risen to between 5–6 percent. Fifteen percent of the labor force – and perhaps 30 percent of those between 16 and 24 years of age – were unemployed. Growth in real output of at least 5 percent a year was needed to prevent unemployment rising still further.

Professor Bassam Tibi at the University of Göttingen had warned that 'political Islam and its concept of order' were hostile not only to the globalization of Western state models, but also to the 'universalization of Western values':

> The Islamists target the nation-state, because they despise its basis of popular sovereignty, and even ideologies like pan-Arab nationalism are perceived to be influenced by secular tendencies.[65]

The Islamists' prime argument is against the secular order in which state and religion are constitutionally separate. Christian Europe became secular in the wake of the 18th century Enlightenment, the process accelerating as empires gave way to nation-states in the 19th and early 20th centuries. This was not inevitable, however; it was the result of a particular historical experience of protracted religious wars[66] following the Protestant Reformation, and the signing of the Treaty of Westphalia[67] in 1648. As the West became politically and economically dominant, the system of nation-states was recognized throughout the world, culminating in the decolonization process after World War II. But no Arab state has secularized – even Lebanon at its peak in the 1970s was a religious consociation which collapsed into externally sponsored sectarian civil war after Israeli and then Syrian troops crossed its borders – and in Turkey and Iran, neither of which is Arab, Islamists continuously threatened the secular advances initiated by Ataturk[68] and Reza Shah[69] in the 1920s. Since 1979, following a referendum in which 98 percent of those who voted approved the transition, Iran has been an Islamic Republic, whose institutions now reflect both theocratic and democratic traditions. Pakistan, meanwhile, owes its existence to London's decision in 1947 to separate an Islamic state from the larger part of what had been British India because of social and political tensions there, and in Bangladesh – the former East Pakistan –loyalties are divided and identities fractured.

The democratic political culture that underpins the nation state, which prioritizes the *individual* as the bearer of fundamental rights,[70] and the *sovereignty of the people*[71] as the normative foundation of the state,[72] has therefore not acquired political legitimacy in much of the Islamic world, where religion is still the main source of norms and values. But the world is structured in accordance with dominant Western paradigm and globalization has increased pressures on all states to align themselves with this model! Structural and institutional globalization thus coexists with diverse and, in part, divergent, political cultures and norms. Two are of particular importance:

- In the teachings of the Islamists, the Islamic state, *al-dawla al-Islamiyya*, is founded on God's rule (*hakimiyyat Allah*); it cannot be secular.
- As the state is not secular, but founded on the rule of God, to whom Muslims submit,[73] the notion of *individual rights against the state* is foreign to Islam. Instead Muslims have obligations (*fara'id*) to the community (*umma*). This principle is identical to that in the Christian (and Judaic) injunctions[74] to 'Love thy neighbour as thyself'[75] and 'Do unto others as you would have them do unto you.'[76] It is common to the three Abrahamic faiths and mirrored in most other organized belief systems. Such reciprocal obligations are, in fact, the essence of *community* and they underpin the Islamic *orthopraxis* we discussed earlier.

Efforts to dismiss these alternative approaches and impose Western models under the rubric of universal values have, at least in part, been counterproductive. During centuries of European expansion and the growing political and economic dominance of the West, especially in the 19th and 20th centuries, many Muslims encountered modernity as *hegemony*. The emergence of a globally integrated world dominated by the United States has sharpened that feeling among those who resent it. Efforts to oppose practices in traditional Islamic societies that Westerners find offensive,[77] by invoking the concept of *universal human rights*, also runs foul of the Islamic concept of *asalalh*, the notion that intellectual and normative values of each people arise from their own culture. Culture, as Clifford Geertz, succinctly notes, is the context for '... the social production of meaning'.[78] Western pressure, in the absence of an inclusive 'dialogue of civilisations',[79] has led to a deepening conflict with Islamists over concepts of social and political order, power and norms.

There is no reason for a clash of Western and Islamic civilizations if mutual respect can be restored. Islam is an Abrahamic faith with Hellenistic roots, and was the prime source of the European Renaissance. Nor is pride in the cultural heritage of Islam, and the evident search for *authenticity* that one can observe in many Muslim societies,[80] a problem. It can be a source of exceptional strength and an important element of global coexistence as long as the cooperative and competitive components between the cultures are balanced, and competition is not allowed to spill over into violent conflict. Hedley Bull reminds us that a global society must be premised on:

> ... a group of states, conscious of ... common interests and common values ... conceiv[ing] themselves to be bound by a common set of rules in their relations to one another.[81]

Perhaps the most important element in developing these common values is recognizing the importance in all societies of an appropriate balance between *individualism*, which emphasizes the atomistic and competitive elements of existence, and *community responsibility*, which stresses the collaborative and collegial. While leading Western societies, in the traditions of the Protestant Reformation and the Enlightenment, now emphasize the primacy of the individual; and most others, whose cultural histories have taken different paths, tend to focus more on community harmony; no successful society can ignore the need to balance the two. Nor is an emphasis on either dimension a barrier to success; Toyota Motor Corporation's dedication to Japanese cultural values, which are far more community-oriented that those of Anglo-Saxon societies, has not constrained its growth or profitability. Indeed, the elements of Toyota Production System (TPS), just-in-time manufacturing made possible by Quality Circles and other elements of Total Quality Management – are envied and copied throughout the world.[82] The legendary US retailer, Walmart Stores, meanwhile, despite its errors in Germany, is the largest company in the world based on revenue, with net income of US$10.3 billion on US$285.2 billion of sales in fiscal year 2005.[83]

It is worth noting, however, that over 80 percent[84] of the people in the world – about 5.5 billion – still live in societies that stress the importance of community over that of the individual. The population of the *developed world* is just 1.2 billion and some 200 million people there, in countries like Japan and Korea, are more communalist that individualist in orientation.[85] Before the Industrial Revolution, an individual acting independently had little chance of survival, and harmony in the community was essential for success. Those societies, in Asia, the Arab world, Africa and many parts of Latin America that were bypassed by the European and North American experience of Christian reformation, Enlightenment and, in that context, early Industrial Revolution, did not develop the preoccupation with the welfare, excellence and protection of the *individual* that Western nations prize. The Islamic notion of obligation to the community resonates more strongly in most of the world, than does the West's emphasis on individual rights. One has only to consider the importance of *ubuntu* – properly *umuntu ngumuntu ngabantu*[86] – in Southern African tradition,[87] to grasp this point. In the words of Constitutional Court Judge Yvonne Mokgoro: '… the individual's whole existence is relative to that of the group: this is manifested in anti-individualistic conduct towards the survival of the group if the individual is to survive. It is a basically humanistic orientation towards fellow beings.'[88]

As we saw in chapter 7, when discussing the management of global risks, these strands mesh in challenging and fascinating ways. Individual interests are often at odds with those of society at large[89] – the sense of responsibility that any one of us bears for the *global commons* is well captured by the familiar refrain of NIMBY – not in my back yard! Many wealthy people agree without hesitation that poor people living precariously in squatter camps ought to be relocated to efficiently planned, low-cost townships, as long as the township is nowhere close to where they live. But what Samuel Huntington called the *Clash of Civilizations*[90] would be disastrous in the closely interconnected world of the 21st century. Indeed, it is not sufficient to avoid a catastrophic cultural clash: managing global risks, whose scale exceeds the grasp of any company, and indeed any government, requires that sense of common interests and common values that Hedley Bull notes are essential for the global society.

We will only achieve a global society if we abandon our desire to impose our values by force, and cease to cloak the pursuit of our interests in moral garb. No ethical singularity is evident, or readily available. No people, state or civilization will always be right, morally or scientifically. We need to reexamine some of our own premises and then work to craft the balance and the normative framework – the *doctrine of limits* to which Henry Kissinger has so often referred – without compromising our deeply held values, or requiring others to do so. Coexistence demands compromise, as every married couple knows. A willingness to craft a *détente* does not imply surrender, only recognition that the sustained application of force in a particular situation is likely to be economically, socially and morally debilitating. With the benefit of hindsight, imperial overreach is never seen to have been prudent or moral.

Kofi Annan noted in 1999 that '... globalisation is a force for both integration and fragmentation ... which has brought ... obvious, though increasingly unequally distributed, benefits to the world's peoples.' A few challenges in this regard should be singled out: the need to manage the growing economic disparities between societies when access to information and a sense of relative deprivation is near universal; the need to address the changing nature of threats to regional and global security, including climate change, environmental degradation, refugee flows, and the pandemic spread of viral disease, as well as the proliferation of nuclear weapons technology and the risk of biological warfare by rogue states or nonstate actors; the need to accommodate cultural diversity in a systemically connected world; and to learn how to apply the principles of individual freedom, popular sovereignty and the rule of law on a global scale. We have done poorly in all of these to date.

The West will continue to play an important role and the values of the Enlightenment will continue to influence the way the future evolves. But we have passed the peak of the Western, post-Cartesian paradigm that has shaped the world since the end of the 18th century. The next hundred years will not be made solely in the Western image.

Despite the United States' overwhelming military superiority – the Quadrennial Defense Review 2007 suggests a budget of $439 billion, up 7 percent from 2006, before the cost for Iraq and Afghanistan of $70 billion in 2006 and $50 billion in 2007 – Washington cannot shape the world to its liking. Firstly, as Kissinger observed,[91] the international system is 'far more complex than any previously encountered by American diplomacy' and no self-evident legitimate order is to hand. Or, in Huntington's sharper formulation: 'Western intervention in the affairs of other civilizations is probably the single most dangerous source of instability and global conflict in a multicivilizational world.' Secondly, as Joseph Nye has noted'[92] the United States' preeminence in the military sphere is not matched by a similar capacity to shape the international economic system, or address the challenges of the global commons.

The IMF reports[93] nominal global GDP at $44,433,002 million in 2005. Of this, the 25 countries of the European Union contributed $13,446,050 million and the US$12,485,725 million. Eight other countries had a GDP of over one trillion dollars: Japan $4,571,314 million; Germany $2,797,343 million; China $2,224,811 million, Great Britain $2,201,473 million, France $ 2,105,864 million; Italy $1,766,160 million; Canada $1,130,208 million; and Spain $1,126,565 million. South Korea at $793,070 million was slightly larger than Brazil at $ 792,683 million; India at $775,410 million; Mexico at $768,437 million; and Russia at $766,180 million.

A recent study by the *Economist Intelligence Unit*[94] suggests that real global GDP growth averaged 3.8 percent per year from 2001–5, and will average 3.5 percent from 2006–20, making the global economy two-thirds larger in 2020 than in 2005. China will contribute 26.7 percent to global growth, the United States 15.9 percent and India 12.2 per cent. Asia's share of global GDP, measured by *purchasing power parity*, will rise from 35.7 percent in 2005, to 39.5 percent in 2010, and 43.2 percent in 2020. The United States will see its share fall slightly from 20.8 percent to 20.3 percent and 19 percent over the same period. Europe's share – with expansion of the EU from its present 25 members to 28 in 2010, and 33 in 2020 – is forecast at 21 percent, 20.2 percent and 19.1 percent, respectively. China's share will rise from 13.7 percent to 19.4 percent over the 15 years, while India's will advance from 6.2 percent to 8.8 percent. Most other regions and countries within them will be unchanged. It is too soon to proclaim an Asian century, but the center of economic gravity is shifting rapidly from the Atlantic to the Pacific. The geopolitical and social implications of this shift are considerable.

Huntington suggested that the United States and European countries should act 'to preserve Western civilization in the face of declining Western power,' by maintaining Western technological and military superiority, integrating closely, consolidating Christian Europe in the EU, encouraging Latin America's alignment with the West, constraining the development of the military power 'of the Islamic and Sinic countries,' slowing Japan's drift toward China and accepting Russia as 'the core state of Orthodoxy and a major regional power with legitimate interests in the security of its southern borders.' Even if Washington had not intervened so directly 'in the affairs of other civilizations' in the past five years – a debilitating act in Huntington's analysis – this ambitious agenda could not be achieved. Kissinger's more modest Bismarckian approach – ensuring that the United States establishes close relations with many parties, builds overlapping alliance systems, and uses this influence to moderate all claims – would be possible, if political leaders were able to calculate coolly and consistently.

In its *development path to a peaceful ascendancy*, China may outflank Huntington and accommodate Kissinger. In a recent article in Foreign Affairs, Zheng Bijian[95] stressed that, despite its rapid growth, China would become a modern and medium-level developed country only in 2050. Its challenges were a shortage of resources, environmental problems, the need to coordinate its economic and social development goals and balance reform with stability. He referred to a strategy of three 'transcendences': replacing the old model of industrialization with new technology, economic efficiency, low per capita resource consumption and pollution and efficient use of human resources; emerging as a nonthreatening great power by rising above ideological differences in a search for peace, development and cooperation; and replacing outdated modes of social control in a harmonious socialist society in which self-governance would supplement state administration and democratic institutions and the rule of law would be strengthened in 'a stable society based on a spiritual civilization.'

The greater challenges in East Asia relate to tensions between China, Japan, Russia and the Koreas in the context of China's growth and rising resource needs and nationalist tensions in Southeast Asia. Japan will have to adjust to the presence of an economic peer, unconstrained by constitutional restrictions on its military spending, with whom it will compete for hydrocarbon and other resources, and trade. It will have to decide how best to coexist with two (and possibly three) regional nuclear powers. No multilateral treaties presently underpin Asian security; there are only bilateral arrangements between Washington and Japan, South Korea and Taiwan. This is inadequate: treaties committing Asian states to reciprocal security founded on an acceptance of limits are needed for stability. Japan's weakened economic growth has reduced its strategic significance. South Korea's rapid advancement has led to assertive independence in regional policy. Taiwan has been politically marginalized and integrated into the Chinese economy: Although one cannot exclude a miscalculation, a peaceful accommodation with Beijing is likely. North Korea's fractious propensity for disruption can best be contained through a united stance by its regional seniors. The United States has already reduced its role as the unique balancing power in East Asia. Francis Fukuyama has suggested that Washington, using the six-party talks on North Korea, should encourage the creation of a permanent five-power organization to address regional security issues. This could be linked to ASEAN (and the ASEAN Regional Forum on Security Matters); the ASEAN-plus 3 group, which includes China, Japan and South Korea; and the Asia-Pacific Economic Cooperation forum (APEC), which includes the United States. This is a sensible idea.

Russia, particularly in its efforts to leverage its oil and gas production and reserves to restore its global standing, poses a further challenge. Dimitri Trenin has written[96] that Moscow has 'left the Western orbit,' seeking to claim 'its rightful place in the world alongside the United States and China rather than settling for the company of Brazil and India.' Despite Gorbachev's notion of a 'common European home' two decades ago, the idea that Russia would be 'integrated into Western institutions ... was stillborn from the beginning.' Russia would only join the West if it had 'co-chairmanship of the Western club – or at the very least membership in its Politburo,' says Trenin. Despite its inclusion in the G8, this has not happened. Putin succeeded neither in developing a special relationship with Washington after 9/11, nor in sustaining a French-German-Russian axis after Iraq. In the past year Moscow arranged military exercises with China and with India, ended gas subsidies for its neighbors and cut off Ukraine, disrupting European supplies, after demanding a four-fold price increase. Its Middle East policy has diverged from that of the West: it invited Hamas leaders to Moscow and offered them financial support. It rejected sanctions against Iran for as long as possible and has continued its nuclear cooperation and arms trade with Tehran. It is also expanding into its 'near abroad' for economic and political reasons.

Despite this, Russia will not confront the West and will cooperate in key areas, like the war on (Islamic) terror, when its interests so dictate. Trenin points to an area of short-term tension: Kosovo's separation from Serbia will serve as a model in Moscow's view for Georgia and Moldova, where the West insists on maintaining territorial unity. But sensible *realpolitik* will rise above this and above the challenge of Putin's succession in 2008. The risk lies in miscalculation by any or all sides in Central Asia and the Caspian, where Russia, China, Turkey, Iran and the United States have overlapping and competing interests and where statehood is immature; and hydrocarbon deposits rich and local tensions rife.

Secretary of State Condoleezza Rice reorganized the State Department's South Asia Bureau to include Central Asia after her tour of the region in October 2005, and announced a United States–Greater Central Asia program to wean the Central Asian states from Russia and China. But the Shanghai Cooperation Organization (SCO), created in June 2001 with China, Russia, Kazakhstan, Kyrgyzstan, Tajikistan and Uzbekistan as members, has admitted Mongolia (in 2004) and Iran, India and Pakistan (in 2005) as observers, and called on US forces to pull out of Uzbekistan. The SCO's priority is to combat 'terrorism, separatism and extremism as well as illegal drug trafficking,' but its scope now includes economic cooperation and joint military exercises. China and Russia, while wary of one another, and conscious of their competing interests in Central Asia, both resent the US military presence there. Moscow fears political interference in its 'near abroad' and Beijing sees the US presence as part of Washington's containment strategy. After Indian media suggested in March that the US administration's offer to formalize India's nuclear status but not that of Pakistan, was due to its desire to tie India into its efforts to contain China, Pakistan's foreign minister said that Washington had not been a 'constant friend' like Beijing. Mismanagement by Washington might even tempt China to support nuclear programs in Iran and Pakistan.

Russia, meanwhile, sees US goals in Iran as being to replace the regime, establish control over Iranian oil and gas resources and pipe hydrocarbons from Central Asia and the Caspian Sea across Iranian territory under US control, bypassing Russia and China. In Kazakhstan, it believes the US wishes to control the Kazakh oil reserves and pipe them from Baku to Ceyhan. Kazakh President Nazarbayev's visit to Moscow in April was thus focused on his commitment to continue to use Russian pipelines. Careful management of these competitive relationships is essential.

We are reverting, as often in the past, to a search for new reference points that will allow us to share the earth. Three strands are emerging: a revival of faith,[97] challenging, but not displacing, the post-Enlightenment paradigm of scientific modernity; the need to accommodate a set of different – and sometimes divergent – cultural claims and societal forms in a more comprehensive *weltanschauung*; and a syncretistic search for that which is common across cultures. Its roots may lie in the two core Abrahamic principles (love thy God, and thy neighbor as thyself), Aristotle's Golden Mean, the Buddha's Middle Way and Confucius's imperative of Propriety, all of which address the need to balance individual rights and responsibility to the community, to enable societal harmony.

On the way to that point, competing belief systems are clashing, and will continue to clash, in the struggle to define the new synthesis. These will impact directly on many challenges, four of which are already evident: energy security in the context of sustainable resource usage; containment of proliferation of chemical, biological and nuclear weapons' technologies and revision of the nuclear nonproliferation bargain; the conflation of economic marginalization and cultural disaffection in parts of the world, leading to state failure and the strengthening of nonstate actors; and the ethics of biotechnology, which also has the potential to divide secularists from religionists in all developed societies. All these issues pose strategic and normative challenges and will be hotly contested. A conscious decision to tackle them openly in an inclusive global debate, showing respect for the diverse perspectives such discussions will elicit, may help reduce tension and enhance understanding. This is the core need if we are to manage global risks with greater success.

Several paths to Arab *renaissance*

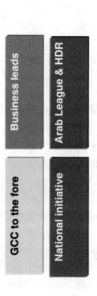

Framework

The interactions between ten factors have been considered: rediscovery of Arab heritage and civilization; delivering superior secondary and tertiary education; expanding school enrolment; dismantling trade barriers; effecting regional ICT integration; expanding banking access; creating effective capital and bond markets; encouraging entrepreneurship; refocusing the bureaucracy; and improving governance.

The core assumption is that an Arab renaissance requires integration of the region into the global economy, a great improvement in education and skills training and better financial intermediation to encourage investment and entrepreneurship. Improved governance and refocusing of the bureaucracy are necessary to enable this. Undertaking this transformation in the context of a renaissance of historical Arab and Islamic attainments, may facilitate the task of reformers.

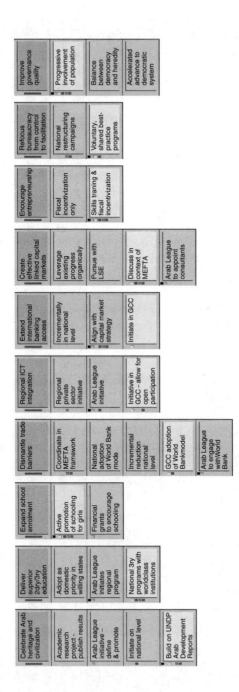

GCC to the fore

Building on the Arab Human Development Report, the GCC takes the lead in an Arab renaissance by encouraging superior educational programs, the education of girls and skills training and financial incentives for entrepreneurs, while actively encouraging regional ICT integration and improved access to international banking and other financial services. Drawing on the U.S. Middle East Free Trade Initiative, the GCC explores further integration of the region's capital and bond markets, and adopts the unilateral tariff reduction model advocated by the World Bank in *Global Economic Prospects 2004*. Citizens are increasingly involved in governance and exchanges of best practice experience, characterize efforts to reorient the bureaucracy from control to economic facilitation.

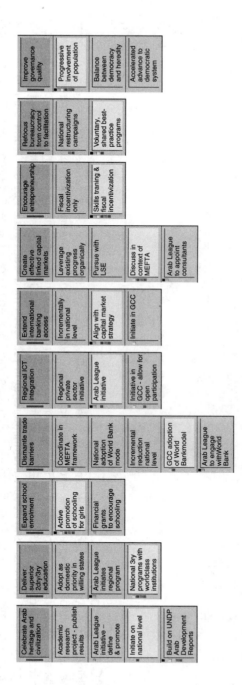

National initiative

National initiative

Enlightened Arab states lead an Arab renaissance by encouraging greater involvement of their citizens in governance, superior educational programs with leading global institutions, the education of girls and skills training and financial incentives for entrepreneurs. This leads the Arab League to develop a program for regional ICT integration. Drawing on the U.S. Middle East Free Trade Initiative, further integration of the region's capital and bond markets and improved access to international banking and other financial services are facilitated. The GCC states adopt the unilateral tariff reduction model advocated by the World Bank and exchanges of best practice experience, characterize efforts throughout the region to reorient the bureaucracy from control to economic facilitation.

Business leads

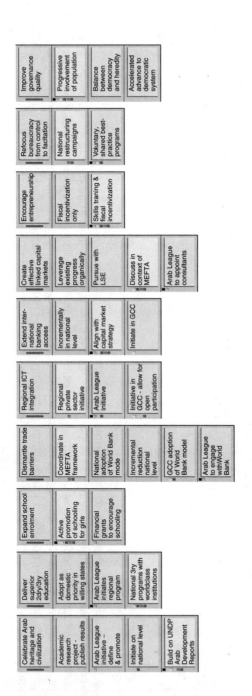

Business leads

Arab business leads the Arab renaissance by developing a program for regional ICT integration and engaging actively in the U.S. Middle East Free Trade Initiative with the support of enlightened Arab governments. This enables integration of the region's capital and bond markets and improved access to international banking and other financial services. Progressive governments encourage greater involvement of their citizens in governance, superior educational programs, the education of girls and skills training and financial incentives for entrepreneurs. Trade barriers are lowered as states begin to participate in the Middle East Free Trade Initiative and progressive states begin national programs to reorient the bureaucracy from control to economic facilitation.

Arab League takes up the Human Development Report

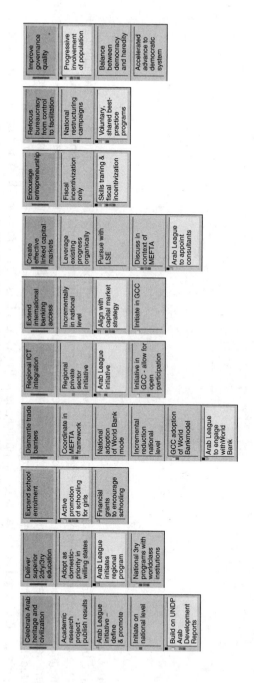

Celebrate Arab heritage and civilization	Deliver superior 2dry/3ry education	Expand school enrolment	Dismantle trade barriers	Regional ICT integration	Extend international banking access	Create effective linked capital markets	Encourage entrepreneurship	Refocus bureaucracy from control to facilitation	Improve governance quality
Academic research project - publish results	Adopt as domestic priority in willing states	Active promotion of schooling for girls	Coordinate in MEFTA framework	Regional private sector initiative	Incrementally in national level	Leverage existing progress organically	Fiscal incentivization only	National restructuring campaigns	Progressive involvement of population
Arab League initiative – define & promote	Arab League initiates regional program	Financial grants to encourage schooling	National adoption of World Bank mode	Arab League initiative	Align with capital market strategy	Pursue with LSE	Skills training & fiscal incentivization	Voluntary, shared best-practice programs	Balance between democracy and heredity
Initiate on national level	National 3ry programs with worldclass institutions		Incremental reduction national level	Initiative in GCC - allow for open participation	Initiate in GCC	Discuss in context of MEFTA			Accelerated advance to democratic system
Build on UNDP Arab Development Reports			GCC adoption of World Bankmodel			Arab League to appoint consultants			
			Arab League to engage withWorld Bank						

Arab League takes up the Human Development Report

Building on the Arab Human Development Report, the Arab League takes the lead in promoting an Arab renaissance by encouraging superior educational programs, the education of girls and skills training and financial incentives for entrepreneurs, while actively encouraging regional ICT integration and appointing consultants to help develop a program to enable better access to international banking and other financial services and integration of the region's capital and bond markets. The League is mandated to discuss with the World Bank the benefits of unilateral tariff reduction models. Citizens are increasingly involved in national governance and exchanges of best practice experience, characterize efforts to reorient the bureaucracy from control to economic facilitation.

Global Scenarios 2015

PARMENIDES
FOUNDATION

Global Drivers

- China's growth and conduct as it assumes a more significant role in the global economy, Japan's response to this and Russia's management of its hydrocarbon resources as it seeks to recover its superpower status are three key factors that will influence the security threat profile and global financial system over the next decade.

- The United States' inheritance in Iraq and in the Islamic world may cause a contraction of its global role, with China and Japan potentially filling any space it leaves in East Asia. In the period under review, Washington may refocus on U.S. national interests and pursue these through well-crafted alliance relationships, focus more narrowly on the 'war against terror', or withdraw temporarily from a fractious world whose fortunes it is unable to mould to its purposes.

- Europe's role will be shaped largely by factors beyond its control – in the Middle East and East Asia – and its response to these and its interaction with the United States will determine both its configuration and its influence.

- The three most contested areas of the globe are likely to be the Middle East, Central Asia and the Caspian region and the East China Sea.

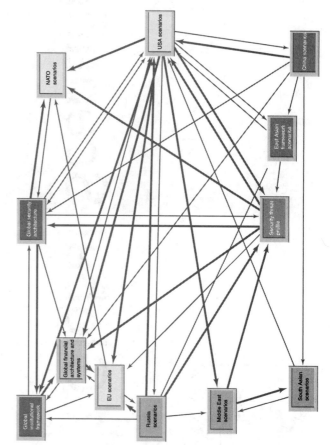

Faces of the Globe

PARMENIDES
FOUNDATION

Global scenarios for 2015

Realpolitik reborn

If only ....

Nasty prospect

Tense restructuring

-Four of 5,760,000 scenarios

PARMENIDES
FOUNDATION

Global scenarios: 2015

PARMENIDES FOUNDATION

FACTORS →

Global scenarios - 2015

ALTERNATIVE SCENARIOS →

Global Context	Security Threat Profiles	Global Financial Architecture & System	USA Scenarios	EU Scenarios	NATO scenarios	China Scenarios	East Asian Framework	Russia Scenarios	Broader Middle East Scenarios	Israel-Palestine scenarios
Inclusive Globalization	Islamism spreads – others constant	BWI marginally strengthened	Neo-conservative Wilsonian approach	Giscardian style constitutional model	NATO eff symbol of trans-Atlantic alliance	'Peaceful (modest) ascendancy'	US maintains trilateral balance	Autonomous regional power Caspian focus	Inclusive mutually reinforcing stability	Two-state solution
Pernicious Globalization	Rising clash of Islamist/western civilizations	Prolonged instability	Conservative neo-realism	Inner and outer cores - variable geometry	NATO atrophies – EDF is EU instrument	Taiwan provokes over reach	US withdrawal -PRC/Japan/Korean balance	Reorientation to Common European home	Islamic threatens monarchs & secular repressentatives	Prolonged lowlevel debilitating conflict
Regional Competition	Ethno-cultural particularism pervasive	Systemic crises	Narrow focus on 'war on terror'	Stalemate - then fracture & reorganization	Divergent EU agendas weaken Euro. defnc	Domestic political fracture from growth	Korean unification divides PRC/Japan	PRC alliance for super-power status	Shi'a-sunni clashes engulf region	Emergence of one (two) secular state(s)
Ideology-based System	Major regional security threat in East Asia	New G-20 paradigm	Global security and prosperity orientation	Confederal cooperative framework		High growth & destabilizing resource demand	N. Korean crisis prompts regional tensions	Trans-Caucasian fracture - orthoox/Islamic		Widening conflict-opportunistic alliances
Post-polar World	All potential threats subcritical		Reversionary isolationism				Resources competition triggers trilateral clash			

Global scenarios for 2015

PARMENIDES
FOUNDATION

Framework

To provide a framework for consideration of the possible evolution of the world until 2015, we have considered the interactions between different global contextual frameworks (drawing on earlier work by the US National Intelligence Council) and security threat profiles, the character of the global financial architecture and system; and scenarios for the USA, EU, NATO, China and Russia; interactions in East Asia, and scenarios for Israel-Palestine and the broader Middle East. These parameters were derived from the global drivers earlier defined.

The interactions, which are indicative, but by no means exhaustive, allow us to derive the scenarios. Four relatively high consistency scenarios are illustrated here. None of these constitute predictions. The full scenario set comprises 5,760,000 permutations.

Tense restructuring	Nasty prospect
If only...	Realpolitik reborn

Tense restructuring

Tense restructuring

FACTORS →

Global scenarios - 2015

ALTERNATIVE SCENARIOS →

Global Context	Security Threat Profiles	Global Financial Architecture & System	USA Scenarios	EU Scenarios	NATO scenarios	China Scenarios	East Asian Framework	Russia Scenarios	Broader Middle East Scenarios	Israel-Palestine scenarios
Inclusive Globalization	Islamism spreads – others constant	BWI marginally strengthened	Neo-conservative Wilsonian approach	Giscardian style constitutional model	NATO eff symbol of trans-Atlantic alliance	'Peaceful (modest) ascendancy'	US maintains trilateral balance	Autonomous regional power Caspian focus	Inclusive mutually reinforcing stability	Two-state solution
Pernicious Globalization	Rsing clash of Islamist/western civilizations	Prolonged instability	Conservative neo-realism	Inner and outer cores - variable geometry	NATO atrophies – EDF is EU instrument	Taiwan provokes over reach	US withdrawal -PRC/Japan/ Korean balance	Reorientation to Common European home	Islamic threatens monarchs & secular representatives	Prolonged low-level debilitating conflict
Regional Competition	Ethno-cultural particularism pervasive	Systemic crises	Narrow focus on 'war on terror'	Stalemate - then fracture & reorganization	Divergent EU agendas weaken Euro. defnc	Domestic political fracture from growth	Korean unification divides PRC/Japan	PRC alliance for super-power status	Shia-sunni clashes engulf region	Emergence of one (two) secular state(s)
Ideology-based System	Major regional security threat in East Asia	New G-20 paradigm	Global security and prosperity orientation	Confederal cooperative framework		High growth & destabilizing resource demand	N. Korean crisis prompts regional tensions	Trans-Caucasian fracture orthoox/Islamic		Widening conflict-opportunistic alliances
Post-polar World	All potential threats subcritical		Reversionary isolationism				Resources competition triggers trilateral clash			

Tense restructuring
On a post-polar world…

Tense restructuring

PARMENIDES FOUNDATION

PARMENIDES
FOUNDATION

Tense restructuring

Tense restructuring

In a post-polar world in which the US economy has slowed and Washington, wounded by its misadventures in Iraq, has withdrawn most US troops not only from the Gulf, but from Korea, Japan and Europe as well, the United States is no longer the dominant global power. NATO has ceased to function. Paralyzed domestically by structural tensions and unable to agree on its role in the festering Israel-Palestine conflict or the broader Middle East, Europe was no longer able to sustain unity in defense or foreign policy, and fractured politically in 2011. Russia's strength in the Caspian and its leverage of its oil and gas reserves, however, jolted European leaders, already shocked by continuing clashes between sunni and shi'a Muslims from the Gulf to Lebanon and in European cities, and forced a new vision and European compact among 22 countries in 2014. Concerned at signs of emerging US retrenchment and worried by the threat to oil security from violent clashes in the Gulf, China and Japan brought the Six Party Talks on Korea to a successful conclusion in 2008. With the reduction of US military forces in East Asia, Beijing and Tokyo brokered Korea's reunification in 2010. Sectarian violence in the Gulf had, however, disrupted oil supplies and China and Japan engaged in naked competition for gas in the East China Sea and African oil, with China competing with Russia in the Caspian also. Japan's decision to conduct a nuclear weapons test simulation in 2011 was intended to caution Beijing, but heightened tensions further, and the period closed with a dangerous stalemate.

Tense restructuring

Nasty prospect

Nasty prospect

PARMENIDES
FOUNDATION

FACTORS →

ALTERNATIVE SCENARIOS →

Global scenarios - 2015

Global Context	Security Threat Profiles	Global Financial Architecture & System	USA Scenarios	EU Scenarios	NATO scenarios	China Scenarios	East Asian Framework	Russia Scenarios	Broader Middle East Scenarios	Israel-Palestine scenarios
Inclusive Globalization	Islamism spreads - others constant	BWI marginally strengthened	Neo-conservative Wilsonian approach	Giscardian style constitutional model	NATO eff symbol of trans-Atlantic alliance	'Peaceful (modest) ascendancy'	US maintains trilateral balance	Autonomous regional power Caspian focus	Inclusive mutually reinforcing stability	Two-state solution
Pernicious Globalization	Rising clash of Islamist/western civilizations	Prolonged instability	Conservative neo-realism	Inner and outer cores - variable geometry	NATO atrophies – EDF is EU instrument	Taiwan provokes over reach	US withdrawal -PRC/Japan/ Korean balance	Reorientation to Common European home	Islamic threatens monarchs & secular representatives	Prolonged lowlevel debilitating conflict
Regional Competition	Ethno-cultural particularism pervasive	Systemic crises	Narrow focus on 'war on terror'	Stalemate - then fracture & reorganization	Divergent EU agendas weaken Euro. defnc	Domestic political fracture from growth	Korean unification divides PRC/Japan	PRC alliance for super-power status	Shi'a-sunni clashes engulf region	Emergence of one (two) secular state(s)
Ideology-based System	Major regional security threat in East Asia	New G-20 paradigm	Global security and prosperity orientation	Confederal cooperative framework		High growth & destabilizing resource demand	N. Korean crisis prompts regional tensions	Trans-Caucasian fracture - orthoox/Islamic		Widening conflict-opportunistic alliances
Post-polar World	All potential threats subcritical		Reversionary isolationism				Resources competition triggers trilateral clash			

Nasty prospect
The U.S. economy slowed ...

Nasty prospect

Nasty prospect

Nasty prospect

The US economy slowed after sustained falls in the US dollar. Washington, confronted with widening terror attacks from Islamist groups across the globe has been forced to maintain a narrow focus on the 'war against terrorism'. It proved impossible to reduce US troops in Iraq in 2007 due to the weakness of the government, and the rising threat to Gulf monarchies from Islamist groups resulted in further small deployments in other Arab countries. The Israel-Palestine conflict proved incapable of resolution as the Palestinians could not unify behind a negotiating position and the Israelis saw no solution that would bring improved security. Weakened by structural tensions and preoccupied by terrorism, Europe was unable to sustain unity on foreign policy or subsidies. An inner core of 15 Eurozone countries emerged as the heart of the new Europe with 12 others loosely associated. Russia's leverage of its oil and gas reserves hardened divisions in Europe, with some eastern European states balancing their relations with Moscow and the Euro-zone carefully, and putting paid to a pan-European constitution. The U.S. worked with China and Japan to bring the Six Party Talks on Korea to a successful conclusion in 2009, but sectarian violence in the Gulf, which disrupted oil supplies, and the continuation of the Israel-Palestine conflict, led China, whose growth rate remained above 8 percent, and Japan, to engage in fierce competition for African oil and commodities and to jostle for control of gas resources in the East China sea. The United States was hard pressed to hold the ring in the Pacific.

Nasty prospect

If only....

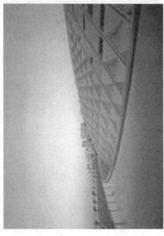

PARMENIDES
FOUNDATION

PARMENIDES FOUNDATION

If only...

FACTORS →

Global scenarios - 2015

ALTERNATIVE SCENARIOS →

Global Context	Security Threat Profiles	Global Financial Architecture & System	USA Scenarios	EU Scenarios	NATO scenarios	China Scenarios	East Asian Framework	Russia Scenarios	Broader Middle East Scenarios	Israel-Palestine scenarios
Inclusive Globalization	Islamism spreads – others constant	BWI marginally strengthened	Neo-conservative Wilsonian approach	Giscardian style constitutional model	NATO eff symbol of trans-Atlantic alliance	'Peaceful (modest) ascendancy'	US maintains trilateral balance	Autonomous regional power Caspian focus	Inclusive mutually reeinforcing stability	Two-state solution
Pernicious Globalization	Rising clash of Islamist/western civilizations	Prolonged instability	Conservative neo-realism	Inner and outer cores - variable geometry	NATO atrophies – EDF is EU instrument	Taiwan provokes over reach	US withdrawal -PRC/Japan/ Korean balance	Reorientation to Common European home	Islamic threatens monarchs & secular represenentatives	Prolonged lowlevel debilitating conflict
Regional Competition	Ethno-cultural particularism pervasive	Systemic crises	Narrow focus on 'war on terror'	Stalemate - then fracture & reorganization	Divergent EU agendas weaken Euro. defnc	Domestic political fracture from growth	Korean unification divides PRC/Japan	PRC alliance for super-power status	Shi'a-sunni clashes engulf region	Emergence of one (two) secular state(s)
Ideology-based System	Major regional security threat in East Asia	New G-20 paradigm	Global security and prosperity orientation	Confederal cooperative framework		High growth & destabilizing resource demand	N. Korean crisis prompts regional tensions	Trans-Caucasian fracture - orthoox/Islamic		Widening conflict-opportunistic alliances
Post-polar World	All potential threats subcritical		Reversionary isolationism				Resources competition triggers trilateral clash			

If only ...
All key challenges have been ...

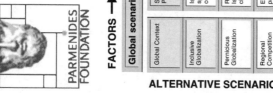

If only ...

If only…

PARMENIDES
FOUNDATION

If only …

All key challenges have been temporarily resolved: a virtuous circle between governance, growth and technology has reduced hydrocarbon dependency, and enabled a better distribution of resources and a balance between growth and security. In the aftermath of the Iraq debacle, an inclusive accommodation was crafted between Israel and its Arab neighbors, based on the Taba agreements and the Arab League Peace Plan of 2002, reducing the jihadist threat and allowing leading Arab states to engage Syria and persuade Iran to play a constructive role. China's ascendancy is being managed without threatening Washington, Tokyo or Moscow, and the G20 have reached agreement on a more equitable financial and developmental architecture. The European vision proves viable in this better balanced world and Moscow, seeing a lesser threat south of the Caucuses and benefits from closer association with a more confident Europe, becomes more accommodating, reaching long-term gas supply agreements and entering into petrochemical, industrial and mining joint ventures. The United States still the largest national economy, with the world's largest armed forces, has promoted regional security and development pacts in East and southeast Asia, enabling Korea's reunification with help from China and Japan, and a stable four-party agreement including Russia, within APEC. The UN and Bretton Woods institutions have been re-empowered and equipped to intervene to avert and assist in recovery from disaster and prevent and manage conflict where needed.

If only …

Realpolitik reborn

PARMENIDES
FOUNDATION

Realpolitik reborn

PARMENIDES FOUNDATION

FACTORS →

Global scenarios - 2015

ALTERNATIVE SCENARIOS →

Global Context	Security Threat Profiles	Global Financial Architecture & System	USA Scenarios	EU Scenarios	NATO scenarios	China Scenarios	East Asian Framework	Russia Scenarios	Broader Middle East Scenarios	Israel-Palestine scenarios
Inclusive Globalization	Islamism spreads – others constant	BWI marginally strengthened	Neo-conservative Wilsonian approach	Giscardian style constitutional model	NATO eff symbol of trans-Atlantic alliance	Peaceful (modest) ascendancy'	US maintains trilateral balance	Autonomous regional power Caspian focus	Inclusive mutually reinforcing stability	Two-state solution
Pernicious Globalization	Rising clash of Islamist/western civilizations	Prolonged instability	Conservative neo-realism	Inner and outer cores - variable geometry	NATO atrophies – EDF is EU instrument	Taiwan provokes over reach	US withdrawal -PRC/Japan/ Korean balance	Reorientation to Common European home	Islamic threatens monarchs & secular representatives	Prolonged lowlevel debilitating conflict
Regional Competition	Ethno-cultural particularism pervasive	Systemic crises	Narrow focus on war on terror'	Stalemate - then fracture & reorganization	Divergent EU agendas weaken Euro. defnc	Domestic political fracture from growth	Korean unification divides PRC/Japan	PRC alliance for super-power status	Shi'a-sunni clashes engulf region	Emergence of one (two) secular state(s)
Ideology-based System	Major regional security threat in East Asia	New G-20 paradigm	Global security and prosperity orientation	Confederal cooperative framework		High growth & destabilizing resource demand	N. Korean crisis prompts regional tensions	Trans-Caucasian fracture - orthoox/Islamic		Widening conflict- opportunistic alliances
Post-polar World	All potential threats subcritical		Reversionary isolationsism				Resources competition triggers trilateral clash			

Realpolitik reborn
The US economy slowed ...

Realpolitik reborn

PARMENIDES
FOUNDATION

Realpolitik reborn

Realpolitik reborn

The US economy slowed and Washington, wounded by its Iraq misadventure, reverted to a prudent neorealist strategy focused on US national interests and alliance diplomacy, leading to the restructuring of NATO around an Anglo-American alliance in 2010, after Europe, having decided that rapid expansion had been over-ambitious, split into an inner core of 14 countries and an outer group of 13. Awakened by the civil war in Iraq, clashes between sunni and shi'a Muslims spread across the region from the Gulf to Lebanon. No solution to the Israel-Palestine conflict emerged, but Israel concluded military and security alliances with several Arab states. Russia's ability to control its near-abroad fractured in 2011 when violent Islamist uprisings in Central Asia threatened control of Caspian resources. Russia and the United States found common cause in counterinsurgency operations. Concerned by the threat to the security of oil supplies from the Middle East, China and Japan competed for African oil and control of gas resources in the East China sea. China also exploited Russia's weaknesses in the Caspian and concluded petrochemical joint ventures with Iran, Kazakhstan, Qatar and Bahrain in 2013. Outflanked by China and needing to secure Moscow's agreement to deliver gas along a new pipeline from Angarsk to Nakhodka, Tokyo agreed to cede sovereignty of the Kurile Islands to Russia. Japan has demonstrated its nuclear-weapons capability in 2012 to caution Beijing, but tensions flared and the forces of the three nuclear powers in East Asia were put on alert in 2014.

Realpolitik reborn

Notes

Acknowledgments

1. The original is attributed to John Bradford (1510?–55), who on seeing criminals being led to execution, observed: 'But for the grace of God, there goes John Bradford.' J.M. and M.J. Cohen, *The Penguin Dictionary of Quotations*, Penguin Books, Harmondsworth, 1960, pp. 11, 64.

Introduction

1. Walter W. Skeat, *An Etymological Dictionary of the English Language* (4th ed. 1910), Clarendon Press, Oxford, 1978 impression.
2. Skeat, (1910), p. 102.
3. Peter L. Bernstein, *Against the Gods: The Remarkable Story of Risk*, Wiley, 1996, p. 1.
4. Often said to be the ideogram for *crisis*; the two concepts are, of course, closely related.
5. This is the definition in Webster's dictionary.
6. As we shall see later, *risk* is technically distinct from *uncertainty* and there are many consequences of this distinction, but it is, in the first instance, the uncertainty of the future that causes us to perceive the existence of risk.
7. Literally, *good father of the family*, the archetype of the 'reasonable man' at Roman law.
8. Paul Ormerod, *Why Most Things Fail: Evolution, Extinction and Economics*, Faber and Faber, 2005, p. 180.
9. Patterns of employment have, of course, changed, and jobs for life are no longer available in almost all environments.
10. Ludwig Von Mises, *Human Action*, 1949. See *http://www.mises.org/humanaction.asp*.
11. As we shall see in chapter 3, often inaccurately as well.
12. Martin Wolf, *Why Globalization Works*, Yale University Press, 2004, p. 43.

13. William Baumol, *The Free-Market Innovation Machine: Analyzing the Growth Miracle of Capitalism*, Princeton University Press, 2002.
14. Ormerod, *Why Most Things Fail.*
15. Bernstein (1996), p. 197.
16. More references can be found in the Global Risk Report published annually by the World Economic Forum in collaboration with some of its strategic partners. Please consult: http://www.weforum.org/pdf/CSI/Global_Risk_Report.pdf

Chapter 1 Today's risks are different: The impact of global risks

1. These instruments bring their own risks in the hands of inexperienced managers, and even their effective deployment depends on good judgment.
2. We use the term 'systemic' to denote risks that are inherent in a system and derive their character from *the workings of the system*. Systemic risks arise from close connections between several (or many) different elements in complex systems. They are characterized by strong feedback loops and indirect links that may not be easily discernible.
3. For reasons of convenience, issues that give rise to concern are often called 'risks,' but this description is not strictly accurate. A risk, as we shall see, is a specific, uncertain but foreseeable event, to the emergence of which we are able to assign an estimate of the probability of its occurring, and one of the severity of its impact if it eventuates. Terrorism, for example, is an issue about which we are properly concerned, but it is too general a concept to constitute a risk. Security agencies, however, could assess the probability of a terrorist incident affecting the transport system in London or New York in the next three months, encourage heightened public awareness and step up intelligence gathering and security precautions.
4. The notion of a 'flat and shrinking world' is developed by Thomas Friedman in *The World is Flat – A Brief History of the Twenty-First Century*, Farrar, Strauss and Giroux, New York, 2005. Friedman argues that globalization is no longer being driven exclusively by Western companies and individuals, and more and more by non-Western groups, particularly from India and China.
5. Risks arising outside the market environment in which the firm conducts its transactions, and beyond the control of the firm.
6. Paul Laudicina, then managing director of the Global Business Policy Council at A.T. Kearney, at the annual meeting of the World Economic Forum, Davos, January 28, 2005.

7. 'What Global Executives Think about Growth and Risk,' *The McKinsey Quarterly*, 2005, no. 2.

8. The same cannot be said of the global atmospheric environment, because industrial advancement translated directly into much higher carbon emissions.

9. See in particular the account offered in Peter Schwartz and Blair Gibb, *When Good Companies Do Bad Things: Responsibility and Risk in an Age of Globalization*, Wiley, 1999, pp. 51–5.

10. Karl von Clausewitz, *On War*, 1918. Quoted in Morgan Witzel: 'When best-laid plans meet flawed reality,' *Financial Times*, May 15, 2005.

11. Group of 10, Summary Report on Consolidation in the Financial Sector, January 2001, www.bis.org

12. Geoffrey Heal, Michael Kearns, Paul Kleindorfer and Howard Kenreuther, 'Interdependent Security in Interconnected networks,' in: 'Seeds of Disaster, Roots of Response – How Private Action Can Reduce Public Vulnerability,' Cambridge University Press, 2006, p. 258.

13. Moises Naim, 'Megaplayers Vs. Micropowers,' Foreign Policy, July/August 2006.

14. Social norms that favor sons, plus China's one-child policy, have led to higher female child mortality rates. Some estimates indicate that there are 60–100 million fewer women alive today than there would be in the absence of gender discrimination. Elizabeth M King, Andrew D Mason, 'Engendering Development – Through Gender Equality in Rights, Resources, and Voice,' *Policy Research Report*, World Bank, 2001.

15. Both are growing rapidly in reach and significance. There were 26,000 NGOs with operations in more than one country at the end of 1999, up from 6,000 in 1990. India has more than a million grassroots groups; and more than 100,000 such groups sprang up in Eastern Europe between 1988 and 1995. The not-for-profit sector is now a $1.1 trillion industry. (See *Global Civil Society: Dimensions of the Nonprofit Sector*, The Johns Hopkins Center for Civil Society Studies, Baltimore, 1999; and *The Yearbook of International Organization*, 2000, The Union of International Associations, 2000; both quoted in David Grayson and Adrian Hodges, *Everybody's Business – Managing Risks and Opportunities in Today's Global Society*, Dorling Kindersley, 2001). One of the most telling recent examples of the power of NGOs and social activists was the election of Ukrainian President Viktor Yushenko in January 2005. His victory (after the election of Yanukovitch was invalidated) was engineered by NGOs and social activists.

16. These and more are documented in *Business Week*, European edition, May 23, 2005.

17. The point of 'volatility in comparative advantage among nations' is made by Jagdish Bhagwati in *In Defense of Globalization*, Oxford University Press, 2004.

18. All these figures are given by Moises Naim in the same article: 'Mega-players Vs. Micropowers.'

19. Moore's law was formulated in 1965 by Gordon Moore, cofounder of Intel. Moore observed that the number of transistors per square inch on integrated circuits had doubled every year since they had been invented. He predicted that this trend would continue for the foreseeable future. The pace has slowed but data density has doubled every 18 months, and this is the current definition of the law, accepted by Moore. Most experts, including Moore himself, expect Moore's Law to hold for at least another two decades.

20. Both examples are quoted in 'What is Accelerating Technological Change?' *Accelerating Change 2005*, September 16–18, Stanford University. See *www.accelerating.org/ac2005*.

21. Del Jones, 'E-mail avalanche even buries CEOs,' *USA Today*, April 1, 2004.

22. Microsoft Annual CEO Summit, Redmond, May 2005.

23. Cognitive psychologists have shown that 'technostress' (having more information available to us than we can readily assimilate) results in reduced intellectual performance and poor judgment.

24. Hurricane Katrina was the eleventh named tropical storm and the fourth hurricane of the 2005 Atlantic hurricane season. It was the third most powerful storm of the season, behind Hurricane Wilma and Hurricane Rita, and the sixth-strongest storm recorded in the Atlantic basin.

25. As well as those watching BBC, Deutsche Welle and hundreds of national and local TV stations.

26. On August 31, the US Coast Guard reported that some 20 oil rigs were missing. By September 6, three refineries on the Gulf coast were back in operation, with four more expected to return to service in days. Six refineries in Alabama, Louisiana and Mississippi were still closed, with six others operating with fuel provided by the Strategic Petroleum Reserve. Almost 70 percent of daily crude production and 54 percent of natural gas were still offline. Release by the Department of Energy.

27. According to an estimate by Swiss Re, the world's second-largest reinsurer, on September 12, 2005.

28. New York Times News Service, 'Katrina's Economic Test,' *Gulf News*, September 6, 2005.

29. Dr Rajeev Dhawan, Director, Economic Forecasting Center, Georgia State University, interviewed on September 5, 2005.

30. 'After the Flood,' *The Economist*, September 3–9, 2005, p. 45.

Chapter 2 The idiosyncrasies of risk perception: Why your risk is different from mine

1. Paul Ormerod, 'Shun the rational agent to rebuild economics', Financial Times, Monday November 6, 2006.
2. Sendil Mullainathan, a behavioral economist, quoted in Craig Lambert, 'The marketplace of perceptions', Harvard Magazine, March–April 2006, See article at: http://www.harvardmagazine.com/on-line/ 0306000.html
3. See 'The Logic of Irrational Fear', *The Economist*, October 17, 2002.
4. The main findings of Prospect Theory are presented in the classic book *Judgement Under Uncertainty: Heuristics and Biases*, Tversky Kahnemann and Paul Slovic (ed.), New York: Cambridge University Press, 1982.
5. Wikipedia lists 74 different cognitive biases: http://en.wikipedia.org/wiki/ List_of_cognitive_biases
6. Matthias M. Bekker, Anna J. Bogardus, Timothy Oldham, *Mastering Revenue Growth in M&A*, McKinsey on Finance, Summer 2001. The authors cite studies by McKinsey and Company 2000, Ernst & Young 1999, A.T. Kearney 1998, Mercer 1996, Coopers & Lybrand 1996, Mitchell Maddison 1996, in support of the proposition that 'Study after study has shown that up to 80 percent of M&A deals completed during the 1990s failed to justify the equity that funded them.'
7. See also Hersh Shefrin, *Beyond Greed and Fear*, Harvard Business School Press, 2002.
8. The work on risk homeostasis was pioneered by Gerald Wilde, a psychologist at Queen University in Ontario, in 1994. A summary of his book 'Target Risk 2 – A New Psychology of Safety and Health' can be found at: http://psyc.queensu.ca/target/index.html
9. Brain imaging uses electro-encephalographs (EEG), positron emission topography (PET) and now, particularly, functional magnetic resonance imaging (FMRI), as well as single neuron measurement and electrical brain stimulation. Transcranial magnetic stimulation (TMS) is also used to disrupt brain function temporarily in particular regions, using pulsed magnetic fields; and diffusion tensor imaging (DTI) is used to observe water flows through sheathed neural axons. All these techniques provide clues into which regions control which neural functions, and ultimately enable an understanding of the circuits and how the brain solves different types of problems.
10. 'Neuroeconomics: Why economics needs brains', Colin Camerer, George Loewenstein and Drazen Prelec, *Scandinavian Journal of Economics*, vol. 106, no. 3, pp. 555–79, September 2004.

11. The theory is often entitled 'constrained utility maximization' and assumes that decisions are made in a state of deliberative equilibrium, where preferences, information and constraints would shape the decision if time and computational ability were unlimited. Cf. Colin Camerer, George Loewenstein and Drazan Prelec, 'Neuroeconomics: How Neuroscience can inform economics', monograph, August 2, 2004.

12. Camerer and Loewenstein quoted in *Newsweek Technology* – MSNBC, Mind Reading. (www.msnbc.com/id/5304846/site/newsweek).

13. Colin Camerer, George Loewenstein, and Drazen Prelec, *Neuroeconomics: Why economics needs brains*, Scandinavian Journal of Economics, vol. 106, no. 3, pp. 555–79, September 2004.

14. Zajonc (1980), (1984), (1998), LeDoux et al. (1996), cited in Camerer et al. (2004).

15. We are indebted to Albrecht von Müller for the triad of error categories.

16. Language always comes with 'frames'. Every word is defined relative to a conceptual framework. See Luca Celati, *The Dark Side of Risk Management: How People Frame Decisions in Financial Markets*, FT Prentice Hall, Harlow, 2004.

17. Celati (2004) summarizes these as (i) symmetry between risk and return, (ii) law of one price (no arbitrage condition), (iii) rationality and risk adversity of investors and (iv) complete markets, p. 44.

18. Celati (2004) cites Janis (1972, 1982, 1983, 1985, 1989), Janis and Mann (1977), Longley and Pruitt (1980) and Wheeler and Janis (1980), p. 89.

Chapter 3 The management of risk

1. Commission of Sponsoring Organizations for the Treadway Commission, addressing the internal control environment – environment, risk assessment, control activities, monitoring, information and communication.

2. This act requires CEOs to certify the accuracy of their financial statements under pain of criminal penalty, disclose off-balance sheet transactions and confirm that risk controls are in place and fully documented.

3. The core report on corporate governance in the United Kingdom, produced by a commission chaired by Sir Peter Cadbury.

4. Similar to the COSA (US).

5. A report by the leading British auditor, Nigel Turnbull, that requires listed companies to report annually on their risk assessment and management processes.

6. Legislated as AktG, par. 91, sect. 2, May 1, 1998. The legislation requires boards of listed companies in Germany to introduce measures to enable early identification of risks that can threaten corporate survival.

7. The Criteria of Control Board extends COSO in defining 20 control criteria under four groupings – purpose, commitment, capability, monitoring and learning.

8. Peter Bernstein, 1996, *Against the Gods: The Remarkable Story of Risk*, Wiley, p. 197.

9. Richard A Clarke, *Against All Enemies: Inside America's War on Terror*, Simon and Schuster UK Ltd, London, 2004.

10. National Commission on Terrorist Attacks Upon the United States, public report released on July 22, 2004; *http://www.9-11commission.gov.*

11. Andrew Holmes, 2004, *Smart Risk*, Capstone Publishing, McGraw Hill, p. 144.

12. Adapted from Holmes (2004), p. 144.

Chapter 4 Defining and assessing risk

1. Andrew Holmes, *Smart Risk*, Capstone Publishing, Chichester, 2004, pp. 45–6.

2. Derivatives are, however, inherently risk instruments themselves, as the Long-Term Capital Management saga discussed in appendix 1 shows all too clearly. Birmingham's Centre for Corporate Governance Research has suggested that companies' exposure to such instruments is a risk that needs to be assessed.

3. We defined global risks in the Introduction as events that have the potential to affect many different industries in several countries or regions, and which may inflict major economic and social damage in some or all of these. Their scope extends well beyond the universe of the firm although their impacts are felt by many firms and people. Because of their reach, no single entity can address them in isolation: cooperative responses are needed to avert them or mitigate their impacts.

4. Kevin Buehler and Gunnar Pritsch, 'Running with risk – It's good to take risks – if you manage them well,' *The McKinsey Quarterly*, 10 February, 2005.

5. Although there can be other impacts – on reputation or brand, for example – these are almost without exception capable of being expressed in financial terms. Given that shareholders are investors seeking a return on their investments, financial impact seems to be the best way of expressing this measure.

6. Paul Ormerod, *Why Most Things Fail*, p. 113.

7. Sarbanes-Oxley Act of 2002 (Public Law 107–204), signed into law on July 30, 2002.

8. In terms of section 302 of the act.

9. The Organization for Economic Cooperation and Development – an association of 30 member countries who 'share a commitment to democracy and a market economy' – Australia, Austria, Belgium, Canada, Czech Republic, Denmark, Finland, France, Germany, Greece, Hungary, Iceland, Ireland, Italy, Japan, Korea, Luxembourg, Mexico, Netherlands, New Zealand, Norway, Poland, Portugal, Slovak Republic, Spain, Sweden, Switzerland, Turkey, the United Kingdom and the United States.

10. Examples include the OECD Country Risk Classifications (prepared exclusively for the purpose of setting minimum premium rates for export credit arrangement transactions), the Dun & Bradstreet International Risk & Payment Reviews, Country Reports and Country RiskLine Reports, the Deutsche Bank Eurasia Group Stability Index, the PRS Group's International Country Risk Guide and the World Markets Research Centre's Advanced Country Analysis and Forecast Service. This last service offers daily interactive country risk ratings and sovereign credit ratings, as well as economic forecasts up to the year 2025, based on up to 150 indicators in 196 countries and historic data back to 1970.

11. D&B Country Report, Country Risk Indicator Definition; see *http://dbuk. dnb.com/english/RiskMan/Country_Report.pdf.*

12. See *http://www/eiu.com.*

13. The Deutsche Bank Eurasia Group Stability Index (DESIX) is a good example; see Ian Bremmer, 'Managing Risk in an Unstable World,' *Harvard Business Review*, June 2005, pp. 51–60.

14. DESIX, India, March 2005, *Harvard Business Review*, June 2005, p. 53.

15. The World Markets Research Centre promises to 'track issues and trends in more than 200 countries worldwide with WMRC's unique Same-day Analysis.'

16. Though related business intelligence services like the Economist Intelligence Unit's Country Reports, Country Profiles and Country Forecasts are no less useful in this respect.

17. DESIX, India, March 2005, *Harvard Business Review*, June 2005, p. 53.

18. Tarun Khanna, Krishna G. Palepu and Jayant Sinha, 'Strategies that Fit Emerging Markets,' *Harvard Business Review*, June 2005, pp. 63–76; see p. 65.

19. See *http://www.globalsecurity.org/military/world/war/congo.htm.*

20. Security risks are considered either under political risks, if this is the proper reference frame; or under social risks, if they derive from crime and other forms of social disorder.

21. Net Present Values – a means of calculating the value of an investment, following a discounted cash flow analysis, to determine if the opportunity justifies investing shareholders' funds.

22. London Inter Bank Offering Rate (LIBOR) is an average of the interest rate on dollar-denominated deposits, or Eurodollars, traded between banks in London. The LIBOR is an international index which reflects world economic conditions. It allows international investors to match their cost of lending to their cost of funds. The LIBOR compares closely to the US 1 year CMT index.

23. Kees Van Der Heijden, *Scenarios – The Art of Strategic Conversation*, Wiley, 1997, p. 84.

24. See Accenture's scenarios – Business in a Fragile World: *http://www.accenture.com/xd/xd.asp?it=enWeb&xd=ideas\wef\wef_scenarios.xml.*

25. *http://www.cia.gov/nic/NIC_globaltrend2020_es.html.*

26. *http://www.shell.com/home/Framework?siteId=royal-en&FC3=/royal-en/html/iwgen/our_strategy/scenarios/dir_scenarios_28022005.html&FC2=/royal-en/html/iwgen/leftnavs/zzz_lhn5_4_0.html.*

27. Initiated by Pieter Le Roux and Vincent Maphai, then at the University of the Western Cape, and facilitated by Adam Kahane of the Center for Generative Leadership in Boston and a member of the Global Business Network.

28. http://www.gbn.com/

29. *http://www.parmenides-foundation.org/content.phtml*

30. The Monte Carlo method was invented by Stanislaw Ulam, a Polish-born mathematician who worked for John von Neumann on the United States' Manhattan Project in World War II and with Edward Teller in designing the hydrogen bomb in 1951. He invented the Monte Carlo method in 1946 while considering the probabilities of winning at *solitaire.*

31. Unlike the trapezoidal rule or Simpson's method of numerical integration.

32. The standard error decreases with the square root of the sample size. Quadrupling the sample size halves the standard error.

33. Martha Amram and Nalin Kulatilaka, 'Real Options: Managing Strategic Investment in an Uncertain World, 1996,' and 'Disciplined Decisions: Aligning Strategy with the Financial Markets,' *Harvard Business Review*, January–February, 1999.

34. Michael Mauboissin, Get Real – 'Using Real Options in Security Analysis,' Credit Suisse First Boston Corporation, June 23, 1999.

35. Timothy Luehrman, 'Investment Opportunities as Real Options,' *Harvard Business Review*, July–August 1998.

36. Benoit Mandelbrot, Sterling Professor of Mathematical Sciences at Yale University and Fellow Emeritus at IBM's Thomas J Watson Laboratory. He is the inventor of fractal geometry, whose most famous example is the Mandelbrot Set. He has received the Wolf prize in physics, the Japan prize in science and technology, and awards from the US National Academy of Sciences and numerous universities.

37. Benoit Mandelbrot and Richard L Hudson, *The (Mis)Behavior Of Markets: A Fractal View of Risk, Ruin, and Reward*, Basic Books, 2004.
38. Benoit Mandelbrot, 'Do you see a pattern here?,' *Wired*, 08/2004, pp. 89–90.

Chapter 5 Mitigating risk

1. Joel Baum, 'The value of a failing grade,' *FT Mastering Risk, Financial Times*, September 9, 2005.
2. For a comprehensive analysis of the anomalies in terms of insurance decision-making, see Howard Kunreuther and Mark Pauly, 'Insurance decision-making and market behavior,' *Foundations and Trends in Microeconomics*, vol.1, issue 2, 2005.
3. To recall, global risks are potential events that have the potential to affect many different industries in several countries or regions, and which may inflict major economic and social damage in some or all of these. Their scope extends well beyond the universe of the firm although their impacts are felt by many firms and people. Because of their reach, no single entity can address them in isolation: cooperative responses are needed to avert them or mitigate their impacts.
4. See Howard Kunreuther, 'Risk analysis and risk management in an uncertain world,' *Risk Analysis*, vol. 22, no.4, 2002.
5. Patricia Born and W. Kip Viscusi, 'The catastrophic effects of natural disasters on insurance markets,' *Journal of Risk and Uncertainty*, vol. 33, nos 1–2, September, 2006.
6. Colin F. Camerer and Howard Kunreuther, 'Decision processes for low probability events: Policy implications,' *Journal of Policy analysis and Management*, vol. 8, no. 4, 565–92, 1989.
7. G. Lecomte and K. Gagahan, 'Hurricane insurance protection in Florida,' in H. Kunreuther and R. Roth Sr (eds), *Paying the price: The status and role of insurance in natural disasters in the United States*, Joseph Henry Press, Washington DC, 1998.
8. R. Roth Jr, 'Earthquake insurance protection in California,' in H. Kunreuther and R. Roth Sr (eds) *Paying the price: The status and role of insurance in natural disasters in the United States*, Joseph Henry Press, Washington DC, 1998.
9. Howard Hunreuther, 'Risk analysis and risk management in an uncertain world,' *Risk Analysis*, vol. 22, no. 4, 2002, p.662.
10. For a comprehensive analysis of the anomalies in terms of insurance decision making, see Howard Kunreuther and Mark Pauly, 'Insurance decision making and market behavior,' *Foundations and Trends in Microeconomics*, vol. 1, issue 2, 2005.

11. Insured losses from Hurricane Katrina are estimated at $45 billion, the highest insured loss ever. Since 1970, there has been an upward trend in worldwide insured losses from catastrophes, raising the question of what constitutes an insurable risk. See Howard Kunreuther and Erwann Michel-Kerjan, 'Climate change, insurability of large-scale disasters and the emerging liability challenge,' Paper prepared for University of Pennsylvania Law Review, Conference on climate change, Philadelphia, November 16–17, 2006.

12. Future contracts for copper and wheat were traded on the Chicago Board of Trade back in 1865, and put and call options were being traded in the United States as early as in the 1790s. See Bernstein (1996), pp. 304–9.

13. Ironically, Robert Merton and Myron Scholes were among the founders of the LCTM hedge fund, whose investment strategies were based on the mathematical models they had developed to price options. LTCM collapsed in 1998 and almost brought down the entire financial system.

14. Cat Bonds and Sidecars are analyzed in detail in Erwann Michel-Kerjan, 'Growing capacity provided by alternative risk transfer instruments,' Working paper, December 2006.

15. See Howard Kunreuther and Erwann Michel-Kerjan, 'Challenges for terrorism insurance in the United States,' *Journal of Economic Perspectives*, vol. 18 (4), Fall 2004, pp. 201–14.

16. Ormerod (2005), p. 180.

17. See Randy Starr, Jim Newfrock and Michael Delurey, 'Enterprise resilience: Managing risk in the networked economy,' in *Enterprise Resilience: Risk and Security in the Networked World*, (A *Strategy+ Business* Reader), Booz Allen Hamilton, 2003, p. 58.

18. Two useful discussions of these and related issues can be found in Mark Buchanan, *Nexus: Small Worlds and the Groundbreaking Science of Networks*, WW Norton and Co, New York/London, 2002; Duncan J Watts, *Six Degrees: The Science of a Connected Age*, William Heinemann, London, 2003.

19. Common era – a secular description of the date equivalent to the equally familiar, though purely Christian AD (Anno Domini – 'in the year of [Our] Lord'). As the young man was the (Islamic) Prophet Mohammed, the neutral CE is preferable. The dates used in Islamic tradition are calculated from 622 CE, the year of Hijrah, Mohammed's flight, after discovery of an assassination plot, from Mecca, with some 70 families, to Yathrib, which became known as *medinat-un-nabi*, 'the prophet's town,' or Medina. In the Arab world, the months are lunar months and the year is thus shorter, which accounts for the difference in dates in these jurisdictions and in Iran, which also uses a solar calendar, commencing in 622 CE.

20. Alfred North Whitehead, *Process and Reality*, Macmillan, 1929, p. 515; quoted in 'The rise of enterprise risk management and governance,' *Executive report*, vol. 1, n. 1, The Cutter Consortium, 2005.

21. See a discussion of the case at Mallenbaker.net, 'Companies in crisis: What to do when it all goes wrong,' Johnson & Johnson and Tylenol, *http://www.mallenbaker.net/csr/CSRfiles/crisis02.html*.

22. Stanford Graduate School of Business, 'Supply chains adapt to disruptions when there is no time for a huddle,' June 2005, *http://www.gsb. stanford.edu/news/headlines/scforum.shtml*.

23. Jared Diamond, professor of physiology at UCLA Medical School, Pulitzer Prize-winning author of *Guns, Germs and Steel*, T*he Third Chimpanzee, Why is Sex Fun* and over 200 articles in *Discover, Natural History, Nature*, and *Geo* magazines.

24. Jared Diamond, *Guns, Germs and Steel: The Fate of Human Societies*, Norton & Company, 1996.

25. Jared Diamond, *Collapse: How Societies Choose to Fail or Survive*, Allen Lane, 2005.

26. A detailed account of the response can be found in John Delly and David Stark, 'Crisis, recovery, innovation: Responsive organization after September 11,' *Environment and Planning*, 2002, vol. 34, pp. 1523–33.

27. Paz Estrella Tolentino, 'Hierarchical pyramids and heterarchical networks: Organisational strategies and structures of multinational corporations and its impact on world development,' *Contributions to Political Economy*, 2002, vol. 21, issue 1, pp. 69–89.

28. Interestingly, our brains function in much the same way. Among the most important characteristics of brain function are well-defined topology and modularity with extensive lateral interconnectivity, exceptional plasticity, redundancy and compensation and a combination of local circuits and distributed activities. There is no 'headquarters' in the cerebral cortex.

29. The concept is usually associated with patterns of molecular activity in phase migrations, as when a solid liquefies, or a liquid gasifies. The pattern of molecular activity observed in the transition between the two states is not identifiably that of a solid, a liquid or a gas. Only when the transition is complete, does a recognizable pattern reemerge. We experienced turbulence in financial markets during both the Asian financial crisis of 1997 and the following emerging markets crisis in 1998; and in the crisis that followed 9/11 and led to the collapse of the Argentinean economy.

30. We all operate individually on two levels at the same time. We process percepts in the cerebral cortex through a complex process of comparison and categorization and reach decisions on appropriate courses of action (subject, of course, to the affective elements we discussed in chapter 3). These decisions are processed through our central nervous systems and

result in premeditated acts. Simultaneously, our 'old' mammalian brains process opportunities and threats on an *instinctual* level, resulting in *reflex actions* processed through our autonomous nervous systems. As these ensure survival, they are generally appropriate, the exceptions being when new circumstances prevent proper comparisons. The challenge is to teach organizations to develop and apply similar skills.

31. An easily accessible account of the role of TPS in Toyota's success is available in Alex Taylor III, 'How Toyota defies gravity,' *Fortune*, December 8, 1997.

32. See for example, Dominic Basulto, 'The $1.4 trillion Mistake,' *http://www.techcentralstation.com/060705B.html,* but this estimate has been challenged by others.

33. Carl Bialk, 'How much is it really costing to comply with Sarbanes-Oxley?,' *Wall Street Journal*, June 16, 2005.

Chapter 6 Communicating risk

1. *Risk Communication – A Guide to Regulatory Practice*, Inter-Departmental Liaison Group on Risk Assessment, A guide produced for managers and staff in government departments and their agencies, United Kingdom, 1998, p. 1.

2. Sarbanes-Oxley, Turnbull, King, KonTRAG, etc., discussed in chapter 4.

3. The case is documented in Christopher Bowe, 'Risk reassessment: Changing attitudes to safety challenge the drugs industry,' *Financial Times*, August 1, 2005, p. 9.

4. Bowe, *Financial Times*, op. cit.

5. Following a jury decision of 10–2 that the arrhythmia that caused the death of triathlete Robert G. Ernst, was probably brought on by a clot and heart attack. Merck may well see the award to Ernst's widow reduced on appeal, and may even have the judgment reversed, but some analysts have speculated that Merck's liability could rise to $50 billion if more cases come to trial, if it appears that patients who have stopped medication are still at risk and if charges of criminal wrongdoing are lodged against the company. See 'The pain is just beginning: Why the Vioxx debacle will hobble Merck for years to come,' *Business Week*, September 5/12, 2005.

6. Kerry Capell, Michael Arndt and John Carey, 'Drugs Get Smart,' *Business Report*, September 5–12, 2005, pp. 38–45.

7. Bowe, *Financial Times*, op. cit.

8. The cognitive dissonance that can result when one fails to do this is well illustrated by an AP-Ipsos poll on President George W. Bush released on

August 5, 2005: Almost two-thirds of those polled described Bush as strong and likable, but 56 percent saw the president's confidence as arrogance. Approval of Bush's handling of Iraq had fallen to 38 percent. Approval of the way he was running the country was at 42 percent, with 55 percent disapproving, while 48 percent said he was honest and 50 percent said he was not.

9. From Covello, McCallum and Pavlova (eds), *Effective Risk Communication*, New York, Plenum Press, 1989. See also 'Seven cardinal rules of risk communication,' pamphlet drafted by Vincent Covello and Frederick Allen, US Environmental Protection Agency, Washington DC, April 1988, OPA-87-020.

10. There is no more fervent believer in this than Warren Buffett. Robert Miles, author of *Warren Buffett CEO: Secrets from the Berkshire Hathaway Managers* and *101 Reasons to Own the World's Greatest Investment: Warren Buffett's Berkshire Hathaway*, notes: 'Each year Mr. Buffett writes a letter to the chief executive officers of companies owned by Berkshire. He tells them, "We can afford to lose money. We can afford to lose a lot of money, but we can't afford to lose our reputation." He tells them not to do anything in the business that cannot be reported on the front page of the local newspaper ....'

11. See P Bennett, 'Understanding responses to risk: Some basic findings,' in *Risk Communication and Public Health*, P Bennett and K Calman (eds), New York, Oxford University Press, 1999, pp. 3–19.

12. This formula was coined in 1985 by Peter Sandman, one of the most famous risk communication specialists. See *http://www.psandman. com*; and for a list of the main outrage factors, see 'Bird flu: Communicating,' by Peter Sandman and Jody Lanard, *Perspective in Health*, vol. 10, n. 2, 2005. The principles of high hazard/low outrage – low hazard/high outrage are explained in Steven Levitt and Stephen Dubner, *Freakonomics: A Rogue Economist Explores the Hidden Side of Everything*, William Morrow, 2005, pp. 150–3.

13. *http://www.arrivealive.co.za/pages.asp?mc=info&nc=statspart2*

14. Thierry Vareilles, *Encyclopédie du terrorisme international*, L'Harmattan, November 2003.

15. *http://www.rense.com/general54/eeter.htm*

16. The more sophisticated consultancies have moved on to *Reputation Management*, a sensible concept that recognizes firstly, that reputation (which includes 'brand') is often the most valuable asset a company has, and cannot afford to lose; and secondly, that consistent, effective management of reputation is the best way of building and preserving it. In this sense, reputation management is a facet and an important element of risk management.

17. Apologies contribute to the reduction of outrage. There is evidence that when doctors say they are sorry after a medical procedure has gone awry, patients are less likely to sue, although if they do sue, it's more difficult for the doctor to defend the suit. See also 'Peter Sandman on corporate misbehaviour and public outrage,' Gillian Kendall, *The Sun*, Issue 336, December 2003, pp. 4–13.

18. After the September 11, 2001, attacks on the World Trade Center, Giuliani was widely hailed for his calm and effective leadership in the crisis. For this, he was named TIME magazine's Person of the Year for 2001 and was given an honorary knighthood by Queen Elizabeth II of the United Kingdom.

19. Rudolph W. Giuliani, *Leadership*, Hyperion, New York, 2002.

20. *www.psandman.com/ col/crisis.htm*. He also has a DVD on crisis communication available.

21. See Agence France Presse, Singapore, October 27, 2004.

Chapter 7 Managing global risks – Four examples

1. World Economic Forum, Global Risk Report, Geneva 2007.

2. Ayman Al Zawahiri was born to a prominent, though impoverished, family in Cairo in 1951 and graduated as a medical doctor in 1974, having become an Islamist in the tradition of Seyed Qutb. He was imprisoned and tortured after the assassination of Egyptian President Anwar Sadat in October 1981. While in prison, he initiated the *Islamic Jihad* faction of the Muslim Brotherhood, which soon came to compete for membership and influence with the *Al-Gamaa al-Islamiyya* (Islamic societies) faction led by the blind Sheikh Abdel Oman Rahman, whose rise to fame had occurred after his return from Saudi Arabia, when he began to preach against Sadat's signature at Camp David of the peace treaty with Israel. After his release from prison – there is nothing to suggest that he was involved with Sadat's assassination – Al Zawahiri traveled widely in the Islamic world and established an Islamic Jihad presence in Khartoum in the early 1990s, before Osama bin Laden arrived there. Many, who know the two men, suggest that it had proved an alliance of great convenience, with each contributing what the other lacked.

3. In 2001, Al Zawahiri identified the United Nations, 'the friendly rulers of the Muslim peoples, the multinational corporations, the international communications and data exchange systems, the international news agencies and satellite media channels and the international relief agencies, as 'tools' used by the United States and the West to attack Islam. See *Knights under the Banner of the Prophet*, publications in Al-Sharq al-Awsat, December 20, 2001; cited in Jason Burke, *Al-Qaeda: The True Story of Radical Islam*, Penguin Books, 2004.

4. These messages are widely disseminated on Islamist websites.

5. Hassan al-Banna was a Sufi, though he is said to have been influenced by the teachings of Al Wahhab. He is widely regarded as the father of modern Islamist ideology.

6. Sayyid Abdul a'la Maududi, born in 1903 in Hyderabad, is often cited as another prime source of modern 'political Islam.' He founded Jamaat Islami (Islamic society), in 1941 to serve as the vanguard of the Islamic revolution, Maududi first used the term *jahilyya* – which had always been used to describe the anarchic, barbarous condition of pre-Islamic Arabia – to describe the modern world and justify *jihad* to transform it.

7. The word derives from *salaf-as-salih* (righteous predecessors) and refers to the inhabitants of the city of the Prophet (Medina) in the years following his death who lived in accordance with the Qur'an and the sunnah of the Prophet – his way as validated by his companions.

8. The Saudi Arabia Information Resource, http://saudinf.com/main/c3.htm

9. A 19th century Islamic revivalist movement in India intended to enable Indian Muslims to retain their religious identity by maintaining the orthopraxis prescribed by the *Qur'an* and *sunna*. They were seen by the Saudis to be similar in orientation to the Wahhabists and worthy of financial support.

10. Religious schools characterized by rote learning, chiefly of religious texts.

11. 'The Brotherhood,' an abbreviation of *al-ikhwan al-muslimun*.

12. Traditions relating to the sayings and actions of the Prophet.

13. Qutb, who was also a literary critic, is credited with having brought Egyptian Nobel Prize-winning novelist Naguib Mahfouz to wide attention.

14. *Ma'alim fi-l-Tariq*, http://youngmuslims.ca/online_library/books/milestones/hold/index_2.asp; see also *Fi zilal al-Qur'an* (In the shades of the Qu'ran), and *Al-'adala al-Ijtima'iyya fi-l-Islam* (Social Justice in Islam).

15. Hassan al-Banna was killed by the Egyptian secret police in 1949 apparently in retaliation.

16. Jason Burke, *Al-Qaeda: The true story of radical Islam*, Penguin Books, 2004.

17. Jason Burke, (2004), p. 73.

18. His eldest son, Abdullah, was then about 11 years old, according to Burke.

19. See Burke (2004), chap. 7.

20. Islamic law.

21. Including the previously highly respected Maulvi Mohammed Nabi Mohammedi, a learned man who had led many of those present in the uprising against the Soviets. The charge against him was that he had sowed division among the people after the war.

22. Member of the ulema.
23. Sheikh Osama bin-Muhammad bin-Ladin; Ayman al-Zawahiri, Abu-Yasir Rifa'i Ahmad Taha, Shaykh Mir Hamzah, Fazlur Rahman (February 23, 1998). World Islamic Front for Jihad Against Jews and Crusaders: Initial fatwa statement, al-Quds al-Arabi.
24. On September 16, 2001, bin Laden denied involvement with the attacks in a statement broadcast by Al Jazeeral: 'I stress that I have not carried out this act, which appears to have been carried out by individuals with their own motivation.' This denial was broadcast worldwide in November 2001; US forces recovered a videotape from a house in Jalalabad, in which bin Laden is seen talking to Khaled al-Harbi. In the tape, which was broadcast on December 13, 2001, bin Laden admits foreknowledge of the attacks. On December 27, 2001, a second video was released in which bin Laden observes: 'Terrorism against America should be praised because it was a response to injustice, aimed at forcing America to stop its support for Israel, which kills our people.' Shortly before the US presidential election in 2004, bin Laden acknowledged al-Qaeda's involvement in a video, aired on Al Jazeera on October 30, 2004. He stated that he had personally directed the 19 hijackers. Another video obtained by Al Jazeera in September 2006 shows bin Laden with Ramzi Binalshibh and two hijackers, Hamza al-Ghamdi and Wail al-Shehri, as they make preparations for the attacks.
25. Jerry Markon and Karen DeYoung, 'Bin Laden: Moussaoui played no role in 9/11,' *Washington Post*, May 24, 2006.
26. The UN Security Council had passed Resolution 1333 on December 19, 2000, following the destruction of the US embassies in Nairobi and Dar-es-Salaam, requiring the Taliban to deliver bin Laden to the United States or a third country, for trial; and close terrorist training camps in Afghanistan.
27. See Seán Cleary, 'Managing the future threat,' South African Institute of International Affairs, 2002.
28. Robert S Leiken, 'Europe's angry Muslims,' *Foreign Affairs*, New York, July–August 2005, p. 130.
29. Former German Foreign Minister Joschka Fischer refered to the 'new totalitarianism' of militant Islamism in the context of such terrorist incidents. See *Die Rückkehr der Geschichte: Die Welt nach dem 11. September und die Erneuerung des Westens*, Kiepenheuer & Witsch, 2005, reviewed by Bernard Benoit in the *Financial Times*, August 20–1, 2005.
30. In Terrorism – The Protean Enemy, Stern suggests that 'act[ing] constructively in Islamic states' and 'working on alienated youth in the West' are two important components of success.
31. Robert S Leiken, 'Europe's angry Muslims,' p. 132.
32. Robert S Leiken, op.cit., p. 135.

33. UNDP, 2002; UNDP, 2003.
34. World Economic Forum, Arab Competitiveness Reports 2002, 2004.
35. The 22 member states of the Arab League.
36. Arab Business Council, unpublished research project, 2003–4, building on Arab World Competitiveness Report and Arab Human Development Reports, 2002, 2003.
37. Adopting policies that are calculated to advance Arab/Islamic competitiveness and success in a global environment is not capitulation to Western, secular norms. It is a proper response to the challenges of the age, and consistent with the approach taken by the Umayyad, Abbasid, Fatimid and Buyid dynasties to knowledge-accumulation, knowledge-utilization and knowledge-dissemination.
38. See M Shafik Gabr and Khalid Abdulla-Janahi, Chairman and Vice-Chairman, Arab Business Council, 'Partnership for global integration and an Arab renaissance: The role of the Arab business council,' Arab Competitiveness Report 2004, World Economic Forum, Geneva.
39. Christopher Dickey, 'Jihad Express: For Islamic militants in Europe, Iraq far outshines Afghanistan as an urban-terrorism training ground,' Newsweek, March 21, 2006, http://www.msnbc.msn.com/id/7169294/site/newsweek/
40. Richard Engel, 'Lebanon now a top terrorist breeding ground,' NBC News, December 5, 2006; http://www.msnbc.msn.com/id/16061160/
41. For a full discussion see Wharton Risk Management and Decision Processes Center, TRIA and Beyond, Howard Kunreuther et al., Wharton Business School, University of Pennsylvania, August 2005.
42. The distinction between 'domestic' and 'foreign' terrorism, the former not covered under TRIA, is tricky. The report asks how the bombings in London on July 7 would have been treated if they had occurred in the United States. The first series were executed by British-born men whose parents were immigrants, and who may have had foreign support. They were motivated by foreign events. It is unclear whether or not TRIA would have applied if the bombings had taken place in New York.
43. For a summary review of the recommendations see Richard Beales and Gillian Tett, 'Wall Street bankers warn of risks to derivatives industry, and policy forum stresses need for "time-honoured basics,"' Financial Times, July 29, 2005.
44. See Gretchen Morgenson and Jenny Anderson, 'A hedge fund's loss rattles nerves,' New York Times, September 19, 2006 http://www.nytimes.com/2006/09/19/business/19hedge.html?ex=1316318400&en=2732df67691f17e9&ei=5088&partner=rssnyt&emc=rss
45. Sebastian Mallaby, 'Capitalists We Don't Trust,' Washington Post, December 18, 2006.

46. Sebastian Mallaby, 'Hands off hedge funds,' Foreign Affairs, January–February 2007.

47. There are many subtypes of type A influenza viruses, which differ because of the proteins (hemagglutinin [HA] and neuraminidase [NA]) on the surface of the virus. There are 16 different HA subtypes and 9 different NA subtypes of influenza A viruses and many different combinations can occur. All known subtypes can be found in birds, but 'avian flu' viruses are subtypes chiefly found in birds which do not usually, although they can, infect humans. 'Human flu viruses' – subtypes H1N1, H1N2, and H3N2 – occur widely in humans. Some genetic parts of these viruses probably originally came from birds. (Extracted from *Key Facts About Avian Influenza (Bird Flu) and Avian Influenza A (H5N1) Virus*, Centers for Disease Control and Prevention, US Department of Health and Human Services, October 2005).

48. Which has now been identified as a strain of avian flu that infected and spread rapidly among humans.

49. The four essays on the risk of a pandemic by Garrett (on H5N1 and HIV/AIDS), Michael T. Osterholm, William B. Karesh and Robert A, Cook are well worth reading. They can be found in *Foreign Affairs*, New York, July–August 2005.

50. World Heath Organisation, Epidemic and pandemic alert and response, http://www.who.int/csr/disease/avian_influenza/country/cases_table_2006_11_29/en/index.html

51. The H5N1 virus that has caused human deaths is resistant to *amantadine* and *rimantadine*; the US Centers for Disease Control believe that *oseltamavir* and *zanamavir*, will probably work, but additional studies are needed. No vaccine to protect humans against the virus is commercially available as we write, but development efforts are underway. Research on a vaccine to protect humans began in April 2005 in the United States and clinical trials have started.

52. Director at the Center for Infectious Disease Research and Policy, Associate Director of the Department of homeland Security's National Center for Food Protection and Defense and Professor at the Schools of Public Heath at the University of Minnesota.

53. Australia, Canada, France, Germany, Italy, Japan, the Netherlands, the United Kingdom and the United States.

54. Manufactured by Roche at a single plant in Switzerland, though it has opened a second facility in the United States in 2005.

55. Michael T. Osterholm, 'Preparing for the next pandemic,' *Foreign Affairs*, July–August 2005, p. 36.

56. Osterholm, op. cit., p. 37.

57. World Economic Forum, Global Risk Report, Geneva 2007.

58. Lawrie Garrett, 'The lessons of HIV/AIDS,' *Foreign Affairs*, July–August, 2005, p. 52.

59. Global Summary of the AIDS epidemic, December 2006, http://data.unaids.prg/pub/EpiReport/2006/02-Global _Summary_2006_EpiUpdate_eng.pdf

60. Garrett, op. cit., p.53.

61. *http://www.assa.org.za/default.asp?id= 1000000095.*

62. *http://www.gatesfoundation.org/.*

63. Fred Pearce, 'The flaw in the thaw,' *New Scientist*, August 27, 2005, p. 30.

64. See Steve Connor, 'Global warming is "past the point of no return,"' *Sunday Independent*, Johannesburg, September 18, 2005: The article cites the conviction of scientists that 'the northern hemisphere may have crossed a critical threshold beyond which the climate may never recover … [and that] … the Arctic has now entered an irreversible phase of warming that will accelerate the loss of the polar sea ice that has helped to keep the climate stable for thousands of years.' This might cause 'continual loss of sea ice and with it the massive land glaciers of Greenland, which will raise sea levels dramatically.'

65. Professor Raymond Pierrehumbert, University of Chicago, cited in New Scientist, August 21, 2005, p. 28.

66. Fred Pearce, 'The flaw in the thaw,' op. cit., p. 27.

67. Pearce, op. cit., p. 29.

68. Pearce, op. cit., p. 30.

69. Steve Connor, 'Global warming is "past the point of no return,"' *Sunday Independent*, Johannesburg, September 18, 2005.

70. Pearce, op. cit., p. 30.

71. Hans Oerlemans, 'Extracting a climate signal from 169 glacier records,' Science 2005, vol. 308, pp. 67577; see also Pearce, op. cit., p. 29.

72. Pearce, op. cit., p. 29.

73. Statement from the board, *Millennium Ecosystem Assessment*, 'Living beyond our means: Natural assets and human well-being,' March 2005.

74. Address to Fellows of LEAD Cohort 10, Imperial College, Wye, 2004.

75. Statement from the Board, *Millennium Ecosystem Assessment*, March 2005, p. 12.

76. *Millennium Ecosystem Assessment*, op. cit., p.12.

77. Steve Connor, 'CO2 soil emissions may force re-think of Kyoto,' *Sunday Independent*, Johannesburg, September 18, 2005.

78. op. cit., p. 13.

79. *Millennium Ecosystem Assessment*, op. cit., p. 15.

80. Such as the ability of forests to absorb carbon dioxide and provide opportunities for recreation.

81. See *http://www.un.org/esa/sustdev/documents/agenda21/*.
82. Ben Crystal, *New Scientist*, Special Report, 'The big clean-up,' September 3, 2005, pp. 30–1.
83. Crystal, op. cit.
84. Crystal, op. cit.
85. Stephen Pacala and Robert Socolow, 'Stabilization wedges: Solving the climate Problem for the Next 50 Years with Current Technologies,' *Science*, 2004 305, pp. 968–72; see also Crystal, op. cit.
86. Often referred to as *carbon sequestration*.
87. Emma Young, *New Scientist*, Special Report, 'Going underground,' September 3, 2005, p. 35.
88. The Economics of Climate Change, The Stern Review, Nicholas Stern, Cabinet Office – HM Treasury, Cambridge University Press, 2006.
89. Gerry Lemcle et al., 'Hurricane season 2004: Unusual but not unexpected,' *Focus Report*, Swiss Re, 2004.
90. Lemcle et al., op. cit, 'Conclusions,' p. 11.
91. Swiss Re, 'Risk management,' *Investors Day*, 23.11.2004.
92. All the world's a stage,
    And all the men and women merely players:
    They have their exits and their entrances;
    And one man in his time plays many parts ....
    (*As You Like It*, II, 7)

Chapter 8 Pulling it together: Key success factors (and reasons for failure ...)

1. See *From Risk Management to Risk Strategy*, The Conference Board, 2005.
2. At the moment the balance seems to be tilting in favor of too much control. In 2004, Thierry Van Santen, the president of FERMA (Federation of European Risk Management Associations) remarked that 'the biggest risk to European corporations today is that they become so risk-averse [that] they wither away (...). Tightening rules on corporate governance, directors and officers' liability, and product safety, combined with an increasingly litigious environment, are squeezing the entrepreneurial flair that is essential to corporate success' (quoted in the *Financial Times*, *Business Report*, 'Risk Management,' October 27, 2004). This is also true for non-European companies: when asked at the annual meeting of the World Economic Forum in January 2004 what was the greatest risk for him, Jeffrey Greenberg, the chairman and CEO of Marsh & McLennan

Companies, said: 'Risk aversion is the biggest problem, a mindset that could lead to economic stagnation' (quoted in the session: 'Setting the 2004 Agenda: Risk,' WEF Annual Meeting, 2004).

3. Eddie Niestat, from PA Consulting Group, quoted in the *Financial Times*, *Business Report*, 'Risk Management,' August 3, 2005.

4. World Economic Forum, Global Risks 2007, A Global Risk Network report in collaboration with Citigroup, Marsh & McLennan Companies (MMC), Swiss Re and the Risk Management and Decision Processes Center of the Wharton School.

5. Refer to Howard Kunreuther, 'Risk analysis and risk management in an uncertain world,' *Risk Analysis*, vol. 22, n. 4, 2002, pp. 655–64.

6. Howard Kunreuther, 'Risk analysis and risk management in an uncertain world,' *Risk Analysis*, vol. 22, no. 4, 2002, p. 661.

7. Session on 'Managing new risks' at the WEF Annual Meeting, 2004.

8. These are now generally known as problems of interdependent security or IDS and are characterized by discrete payoffs (nonadditive damage), externalities (the risk is dependent on the actions of others) and stochastic uncertainty (an element of chance is always present).

9. Geoffrey Heal and Howard Kunreuther, You can only die once: Managing discrete interdependent risks, Working Paper 9885, National Bureau of Economic Research, July 2003 http://www.nber.org/papers/w9885.pdf.

10. See 'Risk governance. Towards an integrative approach, White paper no. 1, International Risk Governance Council, Geneva, September 2005.

11. The report is available at www.swissre.com.

12. Global Risks 2006 at http://www.weforum.org/pdf/CSI/Global_Risk_Report.pdf. Examples of other private–private partnerships led by the World Economic Forum are at http://www.weforum.org/en/initiatives/index.htm.

13. The importance of 'improving insight' and 'enhancing the flow of information' is stressed in the work of the Global Risk Network of the World Economic Forum. See: http://www.weforum.org/pdf/CSI/Davosrisk.pdf.

14. Jean-François Rischard, *High Noon. 20 global problems. 20 years to solve them*. Basic Books, 2002.

15. Diversity is key to the success of a network, which will otherwise be plagued by group thinking and silo-based approaches. As Lawrence Wilkinson, the founder of the Global Business Network (GBN) once put it: 'Poverty of curiosity is the evil opposite of the celebration of diversity.' For an elaboration of the argument, see James Surowiecki, *The Wisdom of Crowds*, Random House, 2005. Diversity prevents groups from succumbing to the problems that plague in-house teams: group think, peer pressure, homogeneity of thought. Whenever a management team feels that 'it is right and knows the answer,' it should seek a second – possibly contrarian – opinion.

16. Complexity here refers to the phenomenon of order emerging from the many interactions among the components of a system influenced by one or more simple guiding principles or behaviors which are not governed by natural laws.

17. Quoted in Charles Roxburgh, 'Hidden flaws in strategy – Can insights from behavioural economics explain why good executives back bad strategies?,' The McKinsey Quarterly, 2003, no. 2.

18. Jack and Suzy Welch, 'Ideas the Welch Way,' Business Week, August 7, 2006.

19. Quoted in 'How hubris and haste snarled Airbus A380,' International Herald Tribune, Tuesday, December 12, 2006.

20. Private reception hosted in honor of Rudolph Giuliani, Annual Meeting of the World Economic Forum, New York, January 30, 2002.

21. Private conversation with David Rothkopf, New York, October 2005.

22. Hurricane Katrina produced at least two similar examples of corporate resilience enabled by effective preparation. Fortune reports that Home Depot had mobilized four days before the storm struck the coast, battening down stores in the hurricane's path and moving electrical generators and support staff into locations along both sides of it. Two-thirds of its 33 stores in the impact zone reopened just one day after the storm hit, and five of nine stores in New Orleans itself were open a week later. Wal-Mart mobilized six days before the storm, sending armored cars to remove cash from its stores in the target zone – though it left behind guns that looters later stole. A hundred and twenty-six Wal-Mart stores in the Gulf Coast area were shut down by the storm, but by September 16, 18 days later, 113 were serving customers again. Wal-Mart had relocated 97 percent of its employees affected by the closures, trucked $3 million of supplies into the area, and contributed $17 million to relief programs. Fortune quotes Philip Capitano, of Kenner, Louisiana, as saying 'The Red Cross and FEMA (the Federal Emergency Management Agency) need to take a master class in logistics and mobilization from Wal-Mart. Justin Fox and Devin Leonard, 'After Katrina' Fortune, vol. 152, no. 6, 2005.

23. The example of Nokia vs Ericcson is analyzed in detail in Yossi Sheffi, The Resilient Enterprise – Overcoming Vulnerability for Competitive Advantage, The MIT Press, 2005. Many examples of built-in redundancies and reduction of vulnerabilities are also to be found in this book.

24. Jim Collins, Good to Great: Why Some Companies Make the Leap and Others Don't, HarperCollins, 2001.

25. The failure of Wal-Mart in Germany is documented and analyzed in Andreas Knorr and Andreas Arndt, 'Why did Wal-Mart fail in Germany (so far)?,' Monograph, University of Bremen, 2003.

26. 'Wal-Mart's German Flop – Retailer Bows Out Of German Market After Eight-Year Struggle,' CBS News, August 2, 2006.

27. 'Ten Trends to Watch in 2006, Nearly All Are Global–related,' McKinsey Quarterly reproduced in: http://borderbuster.blogspot.com/2006_02_01_borderbuster_archive.html, February 25, 2006.

Conclusion: Leadership and resilience

1. Eamonn Kelly and Steve Weber, 'A delicate balance between risk and reward,' *FT Mastering Risk, Financial Times*, September 9, 2005.

2. In a session 'Leading the great company' at the WEF Annual Meeting 2005. The originator of the phrase was the great American boxer, Muhammed Ali.

3. T. Jaap, *Enabling Leadership*, 1986.

4. Robert R. Blake and Anne Adams McCanse, *The Leadership Grid; Leadership Dilemmas – Grid Solutions*, 1991.

5. Cited in J. P. Kotter, *The Leadership Factor*.

6. Manfred Kets de Vries, *The Leader on the Couch: A Clinical Approach to Changing People and Organizations*, Jossey-Bass, 2006.

Appendix 1 The modern history of risk

1. Although we have used other sources as well, we have drawn liberally from Peter Bernstein's excellent book *Against the Gods: The Remarkable Story of Risk*, Wiley, 1998, in this appendix (appendix 1).

2. Although rudimentary concepts of nonmathematical probability find expression in the writings of both Plato and Aristotle.

3. Bernstein (1996, p. xxxiii) cites the English philosopher, Alfred North Whitehead as noting that zero is of no use in everyday life. '[It's] use,' Whitehead notes, 'is only forced on us by the needs of the cultivated modes of thought.'

4. Bernstein (1996), p. xxxiv.

5. *Blaise Pascal* (1623–62), French mathematician and philosopher.

6. Bernstein (1996), p. 43.

7. Baron Gottfried Wilhelm von Leibniz (1646–1716), German mathematician and philosopher.

8. Luca Pacioli, *Summa de arithmetic, geometria et proportionalità*, 1494.

9. Pierre de Fermat (1601–65), French lawyer, mathematician (who specialized in the theory of numbers) and true polymath.

10. The Persian polymath, Omar Khayyám (c. 1050–c. 1130) had developed the mathematics; the Chinese mathematician Chu Shih-chieh referred to it in 1303, as an existing device, naming it the *Precious Mirror of the Four Elements* (see Bernstein [1996], p. 64).
11. Jacob Bernoulli (1654–1705), Swiss mathematician and astronomer.
12. The difference between the observed value of a sample and its true value will diminish as the number of observations increases. An alternative expression of the principle is that if an experiment is repeated a large number of times then the relative frequency with which an event occurs equals the probability of the event. Bernoulli's discovery was triggered by Leibniz's observation that 'Nature has established patterns originating in the return of events, but only for the most part' (see Bernstein [1996], p. 4).
13. Abraham de Moivre (1667–1754), French mathematician.
14. In a normal distribution, 68.26% of all observations fall within one standard deviation from the mean and 95.46% within two standard deviations.
15. Daniel Bernoulli (1700–82),Swiss mathematician, nephew of Jacob Bernoulli.
16. Thomas Bayes (1702–61), English mathematician and nonconformist minister.
17. Carl Friedrich Gauss (1777–1865), German mathematician, astronomer and physicist.
18. Pierre Simon Laplace (1749–1827), French mathematician and astronomer.
19. Adrien-Marie Legendre (1752–1833), French mathematician.
20. Francis Galton (1822–1911), English polymath – geographer, meteorologist, explorer and eugenicist.
21. Adolphe Quetelet (1796–1874), Belgian mathematician and astronomer, whose index of obesity is the international norm even today. His enthusiasm for normal distribution led him to overstate its application in his researches.
22. Werner DeBondt and Richard H Thaler, 'Does the Stock Market Overreact?,' *Journal of Finance,* 1986, vol. XL, no.3, pp. 793–807.
23. Morningstar Mutual Funds, April 1, 1994, cited in Bernstein (1996), p. 176.
24. William Reichenstein and Dovalee Dorsett, *Time Diversification Revisited*, Research Foundation of the Institute of Chartered Financial Analysts, Virginia, 1995.
25. William J Baumol, 'Productivity Growth, Convergence, and Welfare: What the Long-run Data Show,' *American Economic Review*, American Economic Association, vol. 76 (5), 1986.
26. The ratio narrowed from 8:1 to 2:1 – cited in Bernstein (1996), p. 180.

27. Bradford J DeLong, 'Productivity Growth, Convergence and Welfare: A Comment,' *American Economic Review*, American Economic Association vol. 78 (5), 1988, pp. 1138–54.
28. John Maynard Keynes (1883–1946), English economist.
29. Jeremy Bentham (1748–1832), English social philosopher.
30. John Stuart Mill (1806–73), *Utilitarianism*, Everyman's Library, London, 1962, p. 6.
31. William Stanley Jevons (1835–82), English economist and logician.
32. In *The Theory of the Political Economy*, 1871.
33. Though he suggests, in a most Victorian tone, that 'the more refined and intellectual our needs become, the less they are capable of satiety.'
34. Louis Bachelier (1870–1946), French mathematician regarded as the father of financial mathematics.
35. Bachelier, 'Théorie de la Spéculation,' *Annales de l'École normale supérieure*, 1900.
36. Apparently without knowledge of Bachelier's work.
37. Henri Poincaré (1854–1912), French mathematician, dubbed the 'last universalist' – a man at ease in all branches of mathematics.
38. Bernstein (1996), p. 200.
39. James Gleick has written an elegant popular account of chaos theory: *Chaos: The Amazing Science of the Unpredictable*, Vintage, 1998.
40. Frank Knight (1885–1972), US economist who cofounded the Chicago School of economics with Jacob Viner. His dissertation, *Risk, Uncertainty and Profit* (1916, published in 1921) incorporated his famous distinction between 'risk' (randomness with knowable probabilities) and 'uncertainty' (randomness with unknowable probabilities).
41. The citation is from Bernstein (1996), p. 216.
42. Cf. Poincaré.
43. John Maynard Keynes, *The General Theory of Employment, Interest and Money*, Harcourt Brace, New York, 1936.
44. Bernstein (1996), p. 217.
45. Notably in *A Treatise on Probability*, Macmillan, London, 1921.
46. John Maynard Keynes, 'The General Theory,' *Quarterly Journal of Economics*, vol. LI, February, pp. 209–23, cited in Bernstein (1996), p. 229.
47. Kenneth J Arrow (1921–), US economist and Nobel Prize winner. His research focused on information as an economic variable and he can be said to be the 'father' of modern risk management.
48. Kenneth J Arrow, 'I know a Hawk from a Handsaw,' in M Szenberg, ed., *Eminent Economists: Their Life and Philosophies*, Cambridge University Press, Cambridge, 1992, pp. 42–50.
49. Frank H Hahn (1925–), English economist of the neo-Walrasian school.

50. Kenneth J Arrow and Frank H Hahn, *General Competitive Analysis*, Holden-Day, San Francisco, 1971, cited in Bernstein (1996), p. 205.

51. Arrow's emphasis on uncertainty and his choice of metaphor ('clouds of vagueness') is due to his experience as a Weather Officer in the US Army Air Corps and that month-long weather forecasts were no more accurate than random picks.

52. The United Nations and the Bretton Woods institutions (the International Monetary Fund and the International Bank for Reconstruction and Development [later the World Bank group]) were created immediately after the War; the General Agreement on Tariffs and Trade (GATT) – much later transformed into the World Trade Organization (WTO) rounded out the architecture in the 1950s.

53. The network of security alliances created to contain the risk of Soviet expansionism – NATO, SEATO and ANZUS primary among them.

54. János (John) von Neumann (1903–57), Hungarian mathematician who also studied chemistry and made exceptional contributions in theoretical physics. He was at Princeton University from 1930 and joined the famous Institute for Advanced Study at Princeton in 1933.

55. Bernstein (1996), p. 233.

56. Oskar Morgenstern (1902–76), German economist. He later worked on the accuracy of economic observations.

57. John von Neumann and Oskar Morgenstern, *Theory of Games and Economic Behavior*, Princeton University Press, Princeton 1944 (1953).

58. Alan Blinder (1945–), US economist, former Vice Chairman of the US Federal Reserve and member of the President's Council of Economic Advisers.

59. Alan S Blinder, 'Issues in the Coordination of Monetary and Fiscal Policies,' NBER Working Papers 0982.

60. John F Nash Jr (1928–), US mathematician and Nobel Prize winner for economics with John C Harsanyi and Reinhard Selten in 1994. Von Neumann and Morgenstern had only managed to solve noncooperative games in the case of 'pure rivalries.' Nash addressed rivalries with mutual gain, using best-response functions and Kakutani's fixed-point theorem. The Nash Equilibrium and another solution for two-person cooperative games, the Nash Bargaining Solution, were published in 1950.

61. The model was designed by Professor Paul Milgrom of Stanford University.

62. The winner's curse is a Pyrrhic victory. In this case, the spectrum, in principle, has a similar value for all bidders. Each player estimates the value before and during bidding. The winner is the highest bidder. If the bidders are estimating accurately on average, however, the highest bidder has overestimated the value and overpaid. The winner's curse is also greater

the larger the number of bidders, as the more bidders there are, the more likely it is that some have greatly overestimated.

63. Merrill Flood and Melvin Dresher developed what became known as the 'prisoner's dilemma' in 1950, as part of the Rand Corporation's investigations into applications of game theory to global nuclear strategy. The title and the version with prison sentences as payoffs are due to Albert Tucker.

64. This account is taken from Paul Ormerod, *Why Most Things Fail*, Faber and Faber, London, 2005.

65. See Jacob K. Goeree and Charles A. Holt, 'Ten Little Treasures of Game Theory and Ten Intuitive Corrections,' *American Economic Review,* December 2001, 91, 1402–22.

66. For a sharply critical review, see Philip Morowski, 'When Games Grow Deadly Serious: The Military Influence on the Evolution of Game Theory,' *History of Political Economy*, 1991, vol. 23, pp. 227–60; and 'What were von Neumann and Morgenstern trying to Accomplish?,' *History of Political Economy*, 1992, vol. 24, pp. 113–47.

67. In an effort to make complex mathematical solutions easily comprehensible, we have drawn in part on explanations provided at *http://www.risk-glossary.com*

68. Harry Markowitz (1927–), US Nobel Prize-winning economist. He shared the 1990 Nobel Prize for economics with Merton Miller and William Sharpe.

69. William F. Sharpe (1934–), US Nobel Prize-winning economist. He shared the 1990 Nobel Prize for economics with Harry Markowitz and Merton Miller.

70. Merton H. Miller (1923–2000), US Nobel Prize-winning economist. He shared the 1990 Nobel Prize for economics with Harry Markowitz and William Sharpe. He is best known for a paper in 1958 with Franco Modigliani on 'The Cost of Capital, Corporate Finance and the Theory of Investment,' which concluded that the ratio of debt to equity on a company's balance sheet was irrelevant in determining the cost of capital, so companies should seek to minimize tax liability and maximize net corporate wealth without reference to the debt ratio.

71. In an article published in 1952, entitled 'Portfolio Selection,' *Journal of Finance*, vol. VII, no. 1 (March), pp. 77–91, expanded into a book in 1959.

72. Using single-period returns for securities as random variables, one assigns expected values, standard deviations and correlations and determines the expected return and volatility of any portfolio. Portfolios that optimally balance risk and reward comprise an *efficient frontier* of portfolios, from which an investor should select one.

73. Mathematically, the return on a diversified portfolio will be the average of the rates of return on its individual components. The portfolio's volatility, however, is less than the mean of the volatility of the individual instruments.

74. James Tobin, 'Liquidity preference as behavior towards risk,' *The Review of Economic Studies*, vol. 25, 1958, pp. 65–86.

75. This occurs where the *capital market line*, drawn from the *risk-free rate of return* tangentially touches the *efficient frontier*.

76. There is no certain answer to the question, but concerns about volatility have played the determinant role in shaping the ubiquitous risk-hedging instruments known as *derivatives*.

77. *Value-at-risk* refers to a group of risk measures that describe the market risk of a trading portfolio in terms of probability.

78. *Prospect Theory* integrates economics and cognitive science to explain seemingly irrational risk management behavior in humans.

79. A field of finance that proposes hypotheses based on psychology to explain stock market anomalies. It assumes that the information structure and the behavioral characteristics of market actors influence individuals' investment decisions and thus market outcomes.

80. Daniel Kahneman (1934–), Israeli-born pioneer (with Amos Tversky) of behavioral finance, and Nobel Prize winner in economics, with economist Vernon L. Smith in 2002.

81. Amos Tversky (1937–96), Israeli cognitive psychologist and pioneer of behavioral finance, who died before the Nobel Prize was awarded to his collaborator, Daniel Kahneman and economist Vernon L. Smith in 2002.

82. Amos Tversky and Daniel Kahneman, 'Advances in Prospect Theory: Cumulative Representation of Uncertainty,' *Journal of Risk and Uncertainty*, 1992, vol. 5, no. 4, pp. 297–323.

83. Richard H Thaler (1945–), US economist and Business School professor, cited by Daniel Kahneman as having made a major contribution to behavioral finance in Kahneman's Nobel Prize acceptance speech.

84. With Werner DeBondt.

85. Werner DeBondt and Richard H Thaler, 'Does the Stock Market Overreact?,' *Journal of Finance*, 1986, vol. XL, no. 3, pp. 793–807.

86. Josef Lakonishok, Robert W Vishny, Andrei Shleifer, 'Contrarian Investment, Extrapolation and Risk,' NBER Working Paper no. 4360, May 1993.

87. Bernstein (1996), p. 293.

88. Fischer Black (1938–95), US mathematician and economist; codeveloper of the Black–Scholes equation and the Black-Derman-Toy option-valuation model.

89. Myron S. Scholes (1941–) Canadian-born economist; codeveloper of the Black–Scholes equation; Scholes (with Robert Merton) received the 1997 Nobel Prize in economics. (Black was ineligible, as he had died in 1995).

90. The Black–Scholes model is a model of the varying price over time of financial instruments, and in particular stocks. Black–Scholes is a mathematical formula developed by Fisher Black and Myron Scholes and published in 1973, for the theoretical value of European put and call stock options derived from the assumptions of the model. Black and Scholes built on earlier work by Paul Samuelson and Robert Merton. The fundamental insight is that the call option is implicitly priced if the stock is traded.

Appendix 2 Global risk in historical and future perspective

1. Walter W. Skeat, *An Etymological Dictionary of the English Language* (4th ed., 1910), Clarendon Press, Oxford, 1978 impression.

2. Ceuta is an enclave in mainland Morocco, covering an area of 19.7 sqkm, administered by the Cádiz Province of Spain to this day. It is one of two remaining fragments of long-established Spanish presence in North Africa.

3. Ships that sailed along the African coast risked running aground and those that set out into open water could be blown out to sea.

4. The first to succeed was Gill Eannes in 1434. Eannes sailed out into the Atlantic before turning back to the African coast. When he saw land again, Cape Bojador was behind him.

5. Under the patronage of King Manoel I, Da Gama sailed from Lisbon on July 8, 1497, heading for the Indies. Many believed the voyage would fail as it was thought that the Indian Ocean was not connected to any other sea. Da Gama rounded the Cape of Good Hope on November 22 and reached Calicut on May 20, 1498.

6. In 1415 Ceuta had approximately 24,000 commercial establishments – some no more than market stalls – dealing in precious metals, silks, spices and weapons.

7. Lord Kitchener of Khartoum (1850–1916): Governor of the British Red Sea territories in 1886 and Commander in Chief of the Egyptian army in 1892. In 1898 he crushed the Sudanese forces of al-Mahdi and occupied Khartoum.

8. Founded by Protestant evangelists in 1795 with the aim of spreading 'the knowledge of Christ among heathen and other unenlightened nations,' it was renamed the *London Missionary Society* in 1818. Although broadly interdenominational, it was Congregationalist in outlook and membership.

9. Cecil John Rhodes (1853–1902), the sickly son of an English vicar, was sent to Natal to join his brother on a cotton farm in 1870. They moved to Kimberley in 1871, where he persisted with his dream of wealth despite harsh conditions and bad luck, until he achieved success and great wealth as a financier and politician.

10. See The European Voyages of Discovery, *http://www.ucalgary.ca/applied_history/tutor/eurvoya/henry2.html.*

11. Prophet Mohammed (570–632 CE).

12. After Mohammed's death in 632 CE, his successors aspired to become a world power and a universal religion. The weakness of the Byzantine Empire, the rivalry between the Greek and Latin churches, the schisms of Nestorius and Eutyches, the failing power of the Sassanian court in Iran, the power of the sword and of religious belief, the hope of plunder and the love of conquest, combined with the genius of the Caliphs to effect the conquest of Palestine, Syria, Mesopotamia, Egypt, North Africa and southern Spain.

13. The Abbasid dynasty were descended from Abbas, the uncle of the Prophet, and ruled from 750–1258 CE from Baghdad, which the second Abbasid Caliph had founded in 762 and from Samara in the 9th century.

14. When the caliphs lost power, precipitating the Ottoman takeover.

15. The practices of the Prophet – the way he lived his life.

16. Descriptions of the way the Prophet lived and behaved.

17. The Fatimids were an Ismaili Shi'i dynasty which ruled parts of the Islamic world between 909–1171 CE. Toward the end of the 10th century, they made Egypt their center, and controlled the holy cities of Mecca and Medina.

18. According to the historian al-Maqrizi. See 'From Cuneiform' to Topkapi, *Saudi Aramco World*, March–April, 1987.

19. Caliph al-Hakam II al-Mustansir (961–976 CE).

20. Muhammad ibn Muhammad ibn al-Hasan al-Tusi (1201–1274 CE).

21. Ibn al-Shatir (or Ibn ash-Shatir) (1304–1375 CE) an astronomer of Damascus who worked as timekeeper in the Umayyad mosque and constructed a magnificent sundial for its minaret in 1371–2. He proposed a system that was only approximately geocentric, rather than exactly so, having demonstrated trigonometrically that the earth was not the exact center of the universe. Copernicus at one point used the same model as al-Shatir, though it is unclear if he was directly influenced by al-Shatir's work.

22. Shihab al Ahmed bin Majid al Najdi (c.1500 CE) wrote a masterpiece entitled *The Book of Profitable Things Concerning the First Principles and Rules of Navigation*, which featured highly detailed and reliable astronomical observations.

23. Perhaps the most famous work is by Hassan al Rammah, a 13th century Syrian researcher, who introduced the military rocket and clarified the purification of potassium nitrate and the proper proportions of gunpowder well before Huo Lung Ching in 1412. Islamic armies made widespread use of cannon in the 13th and 14th centuries.

24. Paper manufacture commenced after the Battle of Talas, the only time that Arab and Chinese armies clashed, when the Chinese were driven out of Central Asia. The battle was the crucial link in the westward transmission of Chinese papermaking as some Chinese prisoners of war were artisans with this skill. Paper was soon manufactured widely in Samarkand, passed into general use and became an important export commodity. By 794 CE there was a paper mill in Baghdad, and similar factories were soon found in every Muslim country. The advent of paper lowered the price of books and libraries were soon common throughout the Islamic world, raising the literacy rate. Christian Europe's tardiness in acquiring this technology explains why even the most important monastic libraries possessed only hundreds of books while the great Muslim libraries had tens or hundreds of thousands.

25. From the 7th century, Islamic societies inherited the technological knowledge of Roman glass manufacturers. Syrian glassworkers made small vessels to contain kohl, perfumes or oils in the 7th–8th centuries. In the 8th century, Egyptian artisans started decorating glass with copper and silver stains to create a palette from yellow to amber. Such glassware was soon also made in Iraq and Syria.

26. Ismael ibn al Razzaz al Jazari (12th century).

27. Medieval Muslim scientists focused on hydraulic engineering as water was precious. Various kinds of water-raising machines, some powered by animals others by rivers, were developed. The waterwheels along the Orontes River in Syria were used for irrigation until modern times. Watermills were used to grind grain, and in Iran water power was supplemented or replaced by wind.

28. Bridges and dams were built to channel water. In addition to beam, cantilever and arch bridges, bridges of boats also spanned rivers. Dams were used to divert rivers into irrigation canals and *qanats* – subterranean aqueducts that carried water for hundreds of miles. Cisterns and underground ice houses were used for storage. Instruments were used to measure water flow and the Nilometer, built in 861–2, still stands on Rawda Island in Cairo.

29. Seljuks A. Turcic, central Asian people who established themselves in Iran (Great Seljuks 1037–1157) and Anatolia (Seljuks of Rum 1077–1300), destroyed the Buyids and occupied Baghdad in 1055, taking the Abbasid caliph under their protection.

30. The Fatimids – see note 19 – were displaced by the Ayyubid dynasty, of Kurdish origins, who ruled Egypt, Syria and northern Iraq from about 1171 to 1250. The Ayyubids fell to the Mongols in Syria in 1260.

31. Buyids (932–1055), an Iranian Shi'ite dynasty from southern Iran, occupied Baghdad in 945 and turned the caliph into a puppet. The spiritual-secular unity of Islam was eliminated at the highest level. Although the Buyids were Shi'ite, they paid lip service to the caliph and allowed him to remain in office.

32. The Mongols pushed into Central Asia and Persia early in the 13th century under Genghis Khan. Bukhara and Samarkand fell in 1220 and by 1221 the Iranian cities of Merv, Nishapur and Balkh were also captured. Isfahan fell in 1237, and the Mongols moved on Baghdad. The decision to attack the Abbasid capital was made in 1251.

33. By the middle of the 13th century, all that was left of Muslim Spain was the Kingdom of Granada on the southern coast. The Christians had reconquered Cordoba in 1236 and Seville in 1248. In the late 15th century the marriage of Ferdinand of Aragon and Isabella of Castile and León, united Spain and strengthened the Christian forces. In 1492, the Christians defeated the Muslims permanently. Ferdinand of Spain then used the Inquisition to eliminate the Jewish and Muslim religions in his domains.

34. The Ottoman Empire (1281–1924) was eventually dismantled, with its arch enemy, the Austro-Hungarian Empire, in 1919 in the aftermath of World War I.

35. Sinan (1489–1588 CE), born of Greek Christian parents in Anatolia, he was drafted as a soldier into the Ottoman royal house in 1512 and advanced to construction officer in which role he built bridges and fortifications. He subsequently built mosques, palaces, harems, chapels, tombs, schools, almshouses, madrassahs, caravanserais, granaries, fountains, aqueducts and hospitals. Generally considered the greatest Ottoman architect, his great mosques are the archetypal image of Turkish Ottoman architecture.

36. Safavids, (1501–1732 CE) an Iranian dynasty based in Isfahan and responsible for encouraging some of the most remarkable Islamic architecture and faïence.

37. The Mogul Empire (1526–1827) ruled most of India and Pakistan in the 16th and 17th centuries and was eventually displaced by British rule in the 19th century. It consolidated Islam in South Asia and spread Muslim (particularly Persian) arts and culture.

38. The meaning of the word Islam is 'subjugation' or 'submission' and a Muslim is one who thus subjects himself to God's will.

39. The Shi'ite orthopraxis is slightly more extensive: Salāh (Namaaz in Persian) – performing the five daily prayers; Sawm – fasting during

Ramadan; Haj – performing the pilgrimage to Mecca; Zakāt – paying money to the poor; Khums – paying the tax of 20 percent, levied on untaxed, annual profit; and Jihād – struggling to please God. (The greater or internal jihad is the struggle against the evil within one's own soul. The lesser, or external jihad is the struggle against the evil of one's environment in every aspect of life).

40. Sharia (Islamic law) is subject to interpretation and to the changing needs of society. Its principles were devised to protect both the individual and society, and it was not a set of fixed rules. To address the changing needs of Muslim societies, learned scholars (*mujtahid*) relied on *ijtihad* (carefully reasoned efforts to arrive at a correct legal ruling). This process is based not only on the primary sources of the *Qur'an* and *sunna*, but also on reason, deduction, and prioritization of interests. (For a far more extensive discussion of *ijtihad* see *http://www.troid.org/articles/ibaadah/ knowledge/taqleedandmadhaahib/ijtihaadandtaqleed.htm*).

41. Learned legal scholars, entitled to clarify the application of the *Qur'an* and *sunna*, and the quality of *ahadith*.

42. Scholasticism consists of the conviction that reason is to be used in the elucidation of spiritual truth and in defense of the dogmas of faith. Although leading Scholastics like Thomas Aquinas, set limits to the power of reason to prove spiritual truth and maintained that the mysteries of faith cannot be proved by unaided reason, they applied dialectical reasoning to the study of nature, humanity and supernatural truth. They admitted the force of human authority when it had been validly applied.

43. Thomas Aquinas (1225–74), son of the south Italian Count Landulf and the Norman Countess Theodora of Theate; Dominican priest and the most prominent of the Scholastics; author of many liturgical, dogmatic and philosophical works, the most famous being the *Summa Theologica*;

44. Robert Grosseteste (1168–1253), educated at Oxford University where he was Chancellor from 1215–21. After filling several church posts, he was consecrated Bishop of Lincoln in 1235. He worked on geometry, optics and astronomy and believed that experimentation was needed to verify a theory. Grosseteste translated many Greek and Arabic scientific writings into Latin.

45. The Italian Renaissance (1330–1550) followed the rapid urbanization in Italy in the 12th and especially the 13th centuries. Trading cities like Venice, the hub of European trade with the Arab and Byzantine empires, accumulated great wealth. Some of these wealthy cities became the earliest banking centers in Europe; church doctrine had earlier prohibited the lending of money at interest as it was a sin, but principle bent before

opportunity. The growth of wealth led to the emergence of city-states whose rulers sought to glorify their wealth and power by subsidizing literature, philosophy, science, architecture and the arts.

46. Desiderius Erasmus (1466–1536), Dutch humanist, born at Rotterdam as Gerrit Gerritszoon. He entered an Augustinian monastery near Gouda and his experience of the ways of the monks made him their relentless enemy.

47. Martin Luther (1483–1546), initially sought to return the Catholic Church to its roots. He became an Augustinian monk in 1505, earned a doctorate in theology from the University of Wittenberg and protested the misuse of indulgences in his *95 Theses* in 1517. He was charged in 1518 to defend his arguments before Cardinal Cajetan and refused to recant. He was excommunicated in 1521, leading to the split in the Christian church that led to decades of religious wars in Christian Europe. Luther's concept of *Freiheit* (freedom or liberty) later gave rise to the notion of individual freedom and political freedom, and presaged the European Enlightenment.

48. John Calvin (1509–64), Swiss lawyer and champion of Northern Renaissance humanism. After the citizens of Geneva overthrew the House of Savoy, Calvin was invited to build a new church. He focused on church governance and social organization, modeling the latter on biblical principles; and developed a catechism which imposed a strict moral code on the citizens. By the mid-1550s, Geneva was the Protestant center of Europe, attracting Protestants expelled from France, England, Scotland and the Netherlands. Calvinism became the dominant branch of Protestantism from the seventeenth century onward.

49. The origins of the 18th century enlightenment lie in the rediscovery of Aristotelian logic by Thomas Aquinas, through Latin translations of the writings of our old acquaintance Ibn Rushd. Aquinas used the logic of Aristotle to codify Christian dogma and his scholastic successors continued the tradition. The Humanists advanced the cause of reason by celebrating God's greatest creation – man. This paved the way for early European rationalists like Montaigne and Descartes to challenge dogma and establish that scientific knowledge of the material world is possible.

50. Under the pseudonym Christopher North, John Wilson composed social commentaries for *Blackwood's* Magazine from 1822–35. In one article, he referred to 'His Majesty's dominions, on which the sun never sets.' In the form, 'the sun never sets on the British Empire,' the phrase came to describe the extent of Britain's colonial holdings from the Imperial Age until after World War II. At its height in the 1930s, the empire spanned

nearly a third of the world's surface, including possessions in Asia, Latin America, the Middle East, Australia and Africa.

51. It is worth distinguishing between three concepts that are often confused: data (which are simply facts and figures); information (which is data in context); and knowledge (which is systemically integrated information that enables intelligent action). The central importance of knowledge in assessing and managing risk is thus self-evident.

52. The word means *love of wisdom.*

53. John W Burton, *Resolving Deep-Rooted Conflict: A Handbook*, University Press of America, Lanham, New York, London, 1987; see also *Conflict and Communication*, Macmillan, London, 1986.

54. Intelligence and security services.

55. Michael Scheuer, *Imperial Hubris: Why the West is Losing theWar on Terror*, Potomac Books, 2004.

56. Robert S Leiken, 'Europe's Angry Muslims', *Foreign Affairs*, New York, July–August 2005.

57. A forceful sexual epithet.

58. The word 'Islamist' here delineates certain radical Muslims who evidence these characteristics, and expressly excludes the millions of devout Muslims, as well as persons of secular inclination in Muslim societies, who do not share these perspectives.

59. An early and insightful exploration of these elements is available in Bassam Tibi, 'Human Rights, Universal Morality and International Relations', *HR Quarterly*, 16 (1994) Johns Hopkins University Press.

60. Terrorism is defined as the use of violence against civilians for ideological ends, the purpose being to inspire terror. Attacks by insurgents against security forces are more correctly described as guerilla warfare or insurgency.

61. See for example, George Soros, 'The Crisis of Global Capitalism: Open Society Endangered', BBS Public Affairs, 1998 and Seán Cleary, 'Discontinuous Change at the End of the 20th century: An Opening Salvo', South African Institute of International Affairs, Johannesburg, 2000.

62. Indeed all four scenarios developed by the US National Intelligence Agency in 1999–2000 for the world in 2015, anticipated poor performance from these regions. See *Global Trends 2015, A Dialogue about the Future with Non-governmental Experts*, National Intelligence Council, 2000.

63. See Arab Competitiveness Reports, 2002 and 2004, World Economic Forum, Geneva.

64. Bahrain and the UAE have made significant progress in reducing their dependence on oil earnings as their reserves are falling fast; Saudi Arabia

and Libya have the highest dependency. Until the policy reforms in 2004, Egypt's economy was exceptionally closed; between 1980 and 2000, exports grew by only 2 percent per annum, substantially below growth in real output.

65. Bassam Tibi, 'Post-Bipolar Order in Crisis: The Challenge of Politicised Islam', *Millennium: Journal of International Studies*, 2000, vol. 29, no. 3, p. 848; citing Munir M Najib, *al-Harakat al-Qawmiyya al-Haditha fi Mizan al-Islam*, Jordan, Maktabat al-Manar, 1983.

66. Between Catholic and Protestant states.

67. This established the principle of *cuius region, eius religio* – 'each state, its own religion,' that of the reigning prince, of course.

68. *Mustafa Kemal Atatürk* (1881–1938), founder of the Turkish Republic and its first President, emerged as a military hero at the Dardanelles in 1915, and became the leader of the Turkish national liberation struggle in 1919. He put an end to the Ottoman dynasty and led Turkey to independence in 1923. As president for 15 years until his death in 1938, Atatürk introduced sweeping reforms in the political, social, legal, economic and cultural spheres, making Turkey a secular state. Its subsequent history has seen the military act as a bulwark of secularism, though religious forces remain strong.

69. Reza Shah Pahlavi (1878–1944) Shah-en-shah (emperor) of Iran 1925–41. In 1941, the British and Russians, concerned by Iran's neutrality in the war, and his sympathy with Germany, forced him to step down in favor of his son, Mohammed Reza Shah Pahlavi. Mohammed Reza was overthrown in 1979, and the Islamic Republic of Iran was instituted with the Ayatollah Ruhollah Khomeini (1902–89) as the Supreme Leader.

70. The Declaration of Independence of the United States, drafted by Thomas Jefferson in 1776, begins: 'We hold these truths to be self-evident, that all men are created equal, that they are endowed by their Creator with certain unalienable Rights, that among these are Life, Liberty and the pursuit of Happiness.'

71. The Declaration of Independence continues: 'That to secure these rights, Governments are instituted among Men, deriving their just powers from the consent of the governed, That whenever any Form of Government becomes destructive of these ends, it is the Right of the People to alter or to abolish it, and to institute new Government, laying its foundation on such principles and organising its powers in such form, as to them shall seem most likely to effect their Safety and Happiness.'

72. The paper we now know as the US Declaration of Independence was originally a paper, titled 'Instructions to the Delegates', by Jefferson, was

printed as *A Summary View of the Rights of British America.* It offered the first rational argument for the refutation of royal sovereignty.

73. Recall the definition of a Muslim – one who submits (subjects himself) to Allah.

74. These are indeed universal principles which one also finds in Confucian, Hindu and Hellenistic traditions.

75. Matthew 22:13; Mark 12:31, Luke 10:27, Romans 13:8–9; Galatians 5:14; see also Leviticus 19:18, 19:34.

76. Luke 6:31, Matthew 7:12, see Talmud Shabbath, Hillel (fl. 30 BC–10 CE): 'What is hateful to you, do not do to your neighbor: this is the whole Torah. The rest is commentary.' K'ung Fu Tzu (Confucius) was asked 'Is there one word which may serve as a rule of practice for all one's life?' He replied, 'Is not reciprocity such a word? What you do not want done to yourself, do not do to others.' Meng-zi (Mencius) (371–289 BC), taught that trying to treat others as one wishes to be treated is the shortest path to goodness and peace. Socrates (469–399 BC) *Advice to Nicocles:* 'What stirs your anger when done to you by others, that do not to others.'

77. Examples would include severance of hands for theft, stoning for adultery and the veiling of women.

78. Clifford Geertz, *The Interpretation of Cultures*, New York, 1993.

79. First called for in 1997 by former Iranian President Hojjat ol-Eslam Seyyed Mohammad Khatami (1943–)

80. And indeed many others: there are parallels with the concept of African *renaissance,* where the search for African authenticity and the demand for African leadership in rebuilding the continent is elegantly balanced by a sober and inspiring commitment to 'democratic regimes … committed to the protection of human rights, people-centered development and market-oriented economies.' See Thabo Mbeki, Address to the Joint Sitting of the National Assembly and the National Council of Provinces, October 31, 2001.

81. Hedley Bull, *The Anarchial Society: A Study of Order in World Politics*, New York, Columbia University Press, 1997.

82. Toyota is Japan's biggest car company and the second largest in the world, the largest being General Motors. It is estimated to produce about 8 million vehicles this year, not much smaller anymore than the 9 million produced by GM. The company is immensely profitable, and its massive cash reserves dwarf those of many countries: See *http:// en.wikipedia.org/wiki/ Toyota#Performance.*

83. If Wal-Mart were its own economy, it would rank 33rd in the world, with a GDP between Ukraine and Colombia. It is the largest private employer in the United States, Mexico and Canada. It holds an 8.9 percent retail store

market share – $8.90 out of every $100 spent in US retail stores is spent at Wal-Mart. See *http://en.wikipedia.org/wiki/Wal-mart.*

84. Out of a total world population of about 6.5 billion at present, only 1.2 billion live in the developed world. If current UN population projections are correct, the number living in these countries will remain constant over the next 45 years, while 7.8 billion people will inhabit the currently 'developing' countries in 2050. Almost half of the roughly 76 million people added to the world every year will be born in six countries – India (22%), China (11%), Pakistan (4%), Nigeria (4%), Indonesia (4%) and Bangladesh (3%). See *http://www.theglobalist.com/StoryId. aspx?StoryId=4629.*

85. A recent study on Japanese and Korean management practices concluded that: ' ... collectivism is deeply rooted in the culture of both countries and building and cultivating relationships through the social constructs of *wa* (Japan) and *inwha* (Korea) is important to management practices in both systems. See *http://blake.montclair.edu/~cibconf/conference/DATA/ Theme4/Australia6.pdf.*

86. A person is a person through other people, *motho ke motho ka batho ba bangwe.*

87. The report of the South African Truth and Reconciliation Commission quotes Constitutional Court Judge Pius Langa: 'During violent conflicts and times when violent crime is rife, distraught members of society decry the loss of ubuntu. Thus, heinous crimes are the antithesis of ubuntu. Treatment that is cruel, inhuman or degrading is bereft of ubuntu' (TRC 1, 127).

88. Y. Mokgoro, 'Ubuntu and the Law in South Africa' – *http://www.puk. ac.za/lawper/1998-1/mokgoro-2.html.*

89. High sales of Sports Utility Vehicles (SUVs) at a time when high petrol prices reflect the fear of global oil shortages is a good example. SUVs continue to gain in popularity in the United States, despite safety concerns and poor fuel economy.

90. S. P. Huntington, *The Clash of Civilizations and the Remaking of World Order,* Simon and Schuster, 1996.

91. Henry Kissinger, *Diplomacy,* Simon and Schuster, 1994.

92. Joseph S. Nye Jr., US Policy and Strategy after Iraq, Foreign Affairs. July–August 2003.

93. IMF World Economic Outlook. 2005.

94. Economist Intelligence Unit, Foresight 2020.

95. Zheng Bijian, China's 'Peaceful Rise' to Great Power Status, Foreign Affairs, September–October 2005.

96. Dmitri Trenin, Russia leaves the West, Foreign Affairs, July–August, 2006.

97. Evangelical Christianity is gaining ground in Latin America, accounting
for 10 percent of churchgoers in Chile in 2005, 25 percent in Guatemala
and advancing in China, where there are about two million Evangelical
converts a year. Established churches in Africa are losing members to the
charismatic sects. Fundamentalist Buddhist and Hindu strains are said to
be growing. The rise of religious radicalism seems to be linked to *uncertainty*. Belief in an omnipotent deity serves fearful men better than reason
and personal responsibility. Reversion to religious literalism may be an
understandable response to rapid change, incomprehensible complexity
and socioeconomic uncertainty.

Bibliography

Risk is a vast subject and can be approached from many different perspectives. In the list that follows, we have suggested a few titles which we have found useful. Many others, especially articles dealing with specific elements of the topic, are mentioned in Notes.

General – History and understanding of risk

Adams, John, 1995, *Risk*, UCL Press.

Arrow, Kenneth and Hahn, Frank, 1971, *General Competitive Analysis*, Holden-Day.

Bernstein, Peter, 1996, *Against the Gods: The Remarkable Story of Risk*, Wiley.

Buchanan, Mark, 2002, *Nexus: Small Worlds and the Groundbreaking Science of Networks*, WW Norton and Co.

Camerer, Colin, Loewenstein, George and Prelec, Drazen, 'Neuroeconomics: Why economics needs brains,' *Scandinavian Journal of Economics*, vol. 106, no. 3, pp. 555–79, September 2004.

Celati, Luca, 2004, *The Dark Side of Risk Management: How People Frame Decisions in Financial Markets*, FT Prentice Hall, Pearson Education, London.

Diamond, Jared, 2005, *How Societies Choose to Fail or Survive*, Allen Lane.

Gleick, James, 1998, *Chaos: The Amazing Science of the Unpredictable*, Vintage.

Kahneman, Daniel, Tversky, Amos and Slovic, Paul, eds, 1982, *Judgement Under Uncertainty: Heuristics and Biases*, Cambridge University Press.

Levitt, Steven and Dubner, Stephen, 2005, *Freakonomics: A Rogue Economist Explores the Hidden Side of Everything*, William Morrow.

Omerod, Paul, 2005, *Why Most Things Fail: Evolution, Extinction and Economics*, Faber and Faber.

Shefrin, Hersh, 2002, *Beyond Greed and Fear*, Harvard Business School Press.

Sherden, William, 1998, *The Fortune Sellers: The Big Business of Buying and Selling Predictions*, Wiley.

Von Neumann, John and Morgenstern, Oskar, 1944, *Theory of Games and Economic Behaviour*, Princeton University Press.

Watts, Duncan, 2003, *Six Degrees: The Science of a Connected Age*, William Heinemann.

Global risks – Risk in today's world

Apgar, David, 2006, *Risk Intelligence: Learning to Manage What We Don't Know*, Harvard Business School Press.

Auerswald, Philip, Branscomb, Lewis, La Porte, Todd and Michel-Kerjan, Erwann, 2006, *Seeds of Disaster, Roots of Response – How Private Action Can Reduce Public Vulnerability*, Cambridge University Press.

Bodansky, Yossef, 2001, *Bin Laden: The Man who Declared War on America*, Forum Books, Prima.

Burke, Jason, 2004, *Al-Qaeda: The True Story of Radical Islam*, Penguin.

Clarke, Richard, 2004, *Against All Enemies: Inside America's War on Terror*, Simon and Schuster.

Daniels, Ronald, Kettl, Donald and Kunreuther, Howard, 2006, *On Risk and Disaster – Lessons from Hurricane Katrina*, University of Pennsylvania Press.

Emerging Risks in the 21st Century: An Agenda for Action, 2003, OECD (Organisation for Economic Co-operation and Development).

Friedman, Thomas, 2005, *The World Is Flat – A Brief History of the Twenty-First Century*, Farrar, Straus and Giroux.

Huntington, Samuel, 1996, *The Clash of Civilizations and the Remaking of World Order*, Simon and Schuster.

Kissinger, Henry, 1994, *Diplomacy*, Simon and Schuster.

Laudicina, Paul, 2005, *World Out of Balance: Navigating Global Risks to Seize Competitive Advantage*, McGraw Hill.

Mapping the Global Future, 2004, Report of the National Intelligence Council's 2020 Project, National Intelligence Council.

McGuire, Bill, 2002, *A Guide to the End of the World: Everything You Never Wanted to Know*, Oxford University Press.

Millennium Ecosystem Assessment, *Living beyond our Means: Natural Assets and Human Well-Being*, March 2005.

Randall Rothenberg, ed., *Enterprise Resilience: Risk and Security in the Networked World*, 2003, Booz Allen Hamilton.

Rischard, Jean-François, 2002, *High Noon: 20 Global Problems, 20 Years to Solve Them*, Basic Books.

Rothchild, John, 1998, *The Bear Book: Survive and Profit in Ferocious Markets*, Wiley.

Scheuer, Michael, 2004, *Imperial Hubris: Why the West is Losing the War on Terror*, Potomac Books.

Schwartz, Peter, 2003, *Inevitable Surprises: Thinking Ahead in a Time of Turbulence*, Gotham Books.

Schwartz, Peter and Gibb, Blair, 1999, *When Good Companies Do Bad Things – Responsibility and Risk in an Age of Globalization*, Wiley.

Stiglitz, Joseph, 2002, *Globalization and its Discontents*, Norton.

Tibi, Bassam, 2002, *The Challenge of Fundamentalism: Political Islam and the New World Disorder*, University of California Press.

Vareilles, Thierry, 2003, *Encyclopédie du Terrorisme International*, L'Harmattan.

Wolf, Martin, 2004, *Why Globalization Works*, Yale University Press.

Risk assessment, management, mitigation and communication

Barton, Thomas, Shenkir, William and Walker, Paul, 2002, *Making Enterprise Risk Management Pay Off: How Leading Companies Implement Risk Management*, Financial Times – Prentice Hall.

Bennett, P and Calman, K, eds, 1999, *Risk Communication and Public Health*, Oxford University Press.

Covello, Vincent, McCallum, David and Pavlova, Maria, eds, 1989, *Effective Risk Communication: The Role and Responsibility of Government and Non-government Organizations*, Plenum Press.

Daniell, Mark, 2000, *World of Risk. Next Generation Strategy for a Volatile Era*, Wiley.

Dembo, Ron and Freeman, Andrew, 1998, *Seeing Tomorrow: Rewriting the Rules of Risk*, Wiley.

Doherty, Neil, 2000, *Integrated Risk Management: Techniques and Strategies for Reducing Risk*, McGraw Hill.

Grayson, David and Hodges, Adrian, 2001, *Everybody's Business: Managing Risk and Opportunities in Today's Global Society*, DK.

Holmes, Andrew, 2004, *Smart Risk*, Capstone Publishing, McGraw Hill.

Morgan, Granger, Fischhoff, Baruch, Bostrom, Ann and Atman, Cynthia, 2002, *Risk Communication: A Mental Models Approach*, Cambridge University Press.

Ropeik, David and Gray, George, 2002, *Risk: A Practical Guide for Deciding What's Really Safe and What's Really Dangerous in the World Around You*, Houghton Mifflin.

Sheffi, Yossi, 2005, *The Resilient Enterprise: Overcoming Vulnerability for Competitive Advantage*, MIT Press.

Shiller, Robert, 2003, *The New Financial Order. Risk in the 21st Century*, Princeton University Press.

Shirreff, David, 2004, *Dealing with Financial Risk*, The Economist.

TRIA and Beyond: Terrorism Financing in the U.S., 2005, A Report issued by the Wharton Risk Management and Decision Processes Center, The Wharton School, University of Pennsylvania.

Web sites

www.riskglossary.com: everything one should know about the definitions of all concepts associated with risk!

www.nonprofitrisk.org: provides assistance with risk assessment and management for nonprofiit organizations. Rich in articles and tutorials.

www.accelerating.org: on the acceleration of change in today's world.

www.weforum.org/en/initiatives/globalrisk/index.htm: presents some of the work of the Global Risk Network of the World Economic Forum.

Index